T0212426

Lecture Notes in Computer Science 11794

More information about this series at http://www.springer.com/series/7412

Hongen Liao · Simone Balocco ·
Guijin Wang et al. (Eds.)

Machine Learning and Medical Engineering for Cardiovascular Health and Intravascular Imaging and Computer Assisted Stenting

First International Workshop, MLMECH 2019
and 8th Joint International Workshop, CVII-STENT 2019
Held in Conjunction with MICCAI 2019
Shenzhen, China, October 13, 2019
Proceedings

 Springer

Editors
Hongen Liao
Tsinghua University
Beijing, China

Simone Balocco
University of Barcelona
Barcelona, Spain

Guijin Wang
Tsinghua University
Beijing, China

Additional Workshop Editors *see next page*

ISSN 0302-9743   ISSN 1611-3349 (electronic)
Lecture Notes in Computer Science
ISBN 978-3-030-33326-3   ISBN 978-3-030-33327-0 (eBook)
https://doi.org/10.1007/978-3-030-33327-0

LNCS Sublibrary: SL6 – Image Processing, Computer Vision, Pattern Recognition, and Graphics

This Springer imprint is published by the registered company Springer Nature Switzerland AG
The registered company address is: Gewerbestrasse 11, 6330 Cham, Switzerland

Additional Workshop Editors

First International Workshop on Machine Learning and Medical Engineering for Cardiovascular Healthcare, MLMECH-MICCAI 2019

Feng Zhang
Chinese Academy of Sciences
Beijing, China

Yongpan Liu
Tsinghua University
Beijing, China

Zijian Ding
Tsinghua University
Beijing, China

Joint MICCAI-Workshops on Computing and Visualization for Intravascular Imaging and Computer Assisted Stenting, CVII-STENT 2019

Luc Duong
École de Technologie Supérieure
Montreal, QC, Canada

Renzo Phellan
University of Calgary
Calgary, AB, Canada

Guillaume Zahnd
Technical University of Munich
Munich, Germany

Katharina Breininger
Friedrich-Alexander-University
Erlangen-Nürnberg
Erlangen, Germany

Shadi Albarqouni
Technical University of Munich
Munich, Germany

Stefano Moriconi
University College London
London, UK

Su-Lin Lee
Imperial College London
London, UK

Stefanie Demirci
Technical University of Munich
Munich, Germany

Satellite Events Chair

Kenji Suzuki
Tokyo Institute of Technology
Yokohama, Japan

Workshop Chair

Hayit Greenspan
Tel Aviv University
Tel Aviv, Israel

Challenge Chairs

Qian Wang
Shanghai Jiaotong University
Shanghai, China

Bram van Ginneken
Radboud University
Nijmegen, The Netherlands

Tutorial Chair

Luping Zhou
University of Sydney
Sydney, Australia

MLMECH-MICCAI 2019 Preface

MLMECH-MICCAI 2019 is the first International Workshop on Machine Learning and Medical Engineering for Cardiovascular Healthcare. This workshop aims to provide a forum leading to interdisciplinary collaborations among experts from cardiovascular physicians, information technicians, big data scientists, and machine learning scientists.

Machine learning techniques have achieved much progress to improve diagnosis accuracy for cardiovascular diseases. In January 2019, Nature Medicine published eight articles concerning on new digital technologies transforming medicine and healthcare, as well as the related regulatory challenges. Among these eight articles, two reported new advances and findings on how to apply convolution neural network to analyze ECG data. Hannun et al. used a 34-layer deep convolution neural network to predict 10 types of diseases along with "normal" and "noise". Tested on a dataset containing 328 single lead ECGs, this deep network outperforms 7 ECG technicians in almost every cardiovascular disease. Atti et al. reported that a deep convolution neural network can screen for cardiac contractile dysfunction only based on ECG data. In addition to these works based on ECG data, retinal fundus photographs have also been used to predict several cardiovascular risks via deep learning. Poplin et al. reported that age, gender, smoking status, systolic blood pressure, and major cardiac events can be predicted with rather high accuracies. These works contribute to the fact that machine learning can make a difference in facilitating the diagnostic efficiencies in clinics.

The MLMECH-MICCAI 2019 proceedings contain 16 high-quality papers selected through a rigorous peer-review process. For each submitted paper, we invited two to three reviewers for double-blind review. We ensured that each paper was handled by an expert who had no conflict of interest with the author. The final papers received were roughly divided into three types of topics. One is to use deep learning methods to automatically diagnose heart disease through ECG data or to predict the risk of heart disease based on the heart disease dataset. Secondly, the use of neural network models for medical image segmentation and anatomical structure detection. The third is the new tools to label and analyze the ECG data. In addition, the workshop also included several lectures by experts from universities and hospitals. We hope this event will bring together physicians, technicians, and machine learning scientists to discuss the latest progressions in cardiovascular healthcare.

August 2019

Guijin Wang
Feng Zhang
Yongpan Liu
Zijian Ding

Organization

Organizing Committee

Guijin Wang	Tsinghua University, China
Feng Zhang	Chinese Academy of Sciences, China
Yongpan Liu	Tsinghua University, China
Zijian Ding	Tsinghua University, China

Scientific Committee

Jinghao Xue	University College London, UK
Chengquan Li	Tsinghua University, China
Ping Zhang	Beijing Tsinghua Changgung Hospital, China
Haiyi Liu	Beijing Tsinghua Changgung Hospital, China
Dapeng Fu	Beijing Zhongguancun Hospital, China
Yuan He	Beijing Tongren Hospital, CMU, China
Fang Luo	Fuwai Hospital and National Center for Cardiovascular Diseases, China

Sponsors

DLAB

Joint MICCAI-Workshops on Computing and Visualization for Intravascular Imaging and Computer Assisted Stenting (MICCAI CVII-STENT 2019)

Preface

MICCAI 2019 again hosted the Joint MICCAI-Workshops on Computing and Visualization for Intravascular Imaging and Computer Assisted Stenting (MICCAI CVII-STENT). The MICCAI-CVII-STENT conference series focuses on the technological and scientific research concerning endovascular procedures. This series of workshops have become an important annual platform for the exchange of knowledge and ideas for medical experts and technological researchers in the field. Many of the authors have been involved with the workshop since its infancy and continue to be part of this research community.

We greatly appreciated this year's invited talks and presentations on the state of the art in imaging, treatment, and computer-assisted interventions in the field of endovascular interventions. We also extend our many thanks to the reviewers who helped to ensure a high quality of papers presented at CVII-STENT 2019.

July 2019

Simone Balocco
Stefano Moriconi
Luc Duong
Guillaume Zahnd
Katharina Breininger
Renzo Phellan
Shadi Albarqouni
Stefanie Demirci
Su-Lin Lee

Organization

Organizational Chairs

Simone Balocco	University of Barcelona, Spain
Stefano Moriconi	King's College London, UK
Luc Duong	École de technologie supérieure, Montreal, Canada
Guillaume Zahnd	Technical University of Munich, Germany
Katharina Breininger	Friedrich-Alexander-University Erlangen-Nürnberg, Germany
Renzo Phellan	University of Calgary, Canada
Shadi Albarqouni	Technical University of Munich, Germany
Stefanie Demirci	Technical University of Munich, Germany
Su-Lin Lee	Imperial College London, UK

Steering Committee

Petia Radeva	University of Barcelona, Spain
Markus Kowarschik	Siemens Healthcare, Germany
Amin Katouzian	IBM Almaden Research Center, USA
Gabor Janiga	Otto-von-Guericke Universität, Germany
Ernst Schwartz	Medical University Vienna, Austria
Marcus Pfister	Siemens Healthcare, Germany
Simon Lessard	Centre hospitalier de l'Université de Montréal (CHUM), Canada
Jouke Dijkstra	Leiden University Medical Center, The Netherlands

Industrial Committee

Ying Zhu	Siemens Corporate Research, USA
Regis Vaillant	General Electric, France
Amin Katouzian	IBM Almaden Research Center, USA
Heinz Kölble	Endoscout GmbH, Germany
Torsten Scheuermann	Admedes Schuessler GmbH, Germany
Frederik Bender	piur imaging GmbH, Germany

Medical Committee

Frode Manstad-Hulaas	St. Olavs Hospital, Norway
Hans-Henning Eckstein	Klinikum rechts der Isar, Germany
Reza Ghotbi	Kreisklinik Muenchen-Pasing, Germany
Christian Reeps	Klinikum rechts der Isar, Germany
Mojtaba Sadeghi	Klinikum Landkreis Erding, Germany

Contents

Proceedings of the Machine Learning and Medical Engineering for Cardiovascular Health

Arrhythmia Classification with Attention-Based Res-BiLSTM-Net

Chengbin Huang, Renjie Zhao, Weiting Chen[✉], and Huazheng Li

MOE Engineering Research Center for Hardware/Software Co-Design Technology and Application, Shanghai Key Laboratory of Trustworthy Computing, East China Normal University, Shanghai, China
wtchen@sei.ecnu.edu.cn

Abstract. In the modern clinical diagnosis, the 12-lead electrocardiogram (ECG) signal has proved effective in cardiac arrhythmias classification. However, the manual diagnosis for cardiac arrhythmias is tedious and error-prone through ECG signals. In this work, we propose an end-to-end deep neural network called attention-based Res-BiLSTM-Net for automatic diagnosis of cardiac arrhythmias. Our model is capable of classifying ECG signals with different lengths. The proposed network consists of two parts: the attention-based Resnet and the attention-based BiLSTM. At first, ECG signals are divided into several signal segments with the same length. Then multi-scale features are extracted by our attention-based Resnet through signal segments. Next, these multi-scale features from a same ECG signal are integrated in chronological order. In the end, our attention-based BiLSTM classifies cardiac arrhythmias according to combined features. Our method achieved a good result with an average F1score of 0.8757 on a multi-label arrhythmias classification problem in the First China ECG Intelligent Competition.

Keywords: Cardiac arrhythmias classification · Attention · Resnet · BiLSTM

1 Introduction

The cardiac arrhythmias become more and more popular due to the population aging, and these diseases have achieved more and more attentions [1]. Electrocardiogram (ECG) is commonly used for detecting rhythm/morphology abnormalities. However, manually analyzing ECG records is tedious and error-prone. Thus, many researchers have been devoted to developing some methods for automatic arrhythmia classification.

In early studies, researchers were dedicated themselves to extracting hand-crafted features for automatic arrhythmia classification. These features were captured by QRS detection [2] or obtained from time domain [3], frequency domain [4], and time-frequency domain [5]. Now, more and more deep learning approaches are developed for automatic diagnose of arrhythmias. For example, in [6], the authors proposed an ECGNet which consisted of a deep convolution neural network and a LSTM, and their model achieved good results on three different kinds of datasets.

In this paper, we proposed an attention-based Res-BiLSTM-Net for automatic diagnosis of cardiac arrhythmias. Our model divides a long ECG signals into several

© Springer Nature Switzerland AG 2019
H. Liao et al. (Eds.): MLMECH 2019/CVII-STENT 2019, LNCS 11794, pp. 3–10, 2019.
https://doi.org/10.1007/978-3-030-33327-0_1

short signal segments. Then multi-scale features are extracted from these signal segments. At last, multi-scale features are combined to determine which kinds of cardiac diseases the ECG signals contain. Our model achieved a high average F1score of 0.8757 in the First China ECG Intelligent Competition [7].

The rest of this article is organized as follows. In next section, our attention-based Res-BiLSTM-Net is described in detail. In Sect. 3, we show the results in the First China ECG Intelligent Competition. We conclude this paper in the last section.

2   Methods

In this section, we show details of our proposed attention-based Res-BiLSTM-Net model. The architecture of our model is shown in Fig. 1. Our model consists of two parts: the attention-based Resnet and the attention-based BiLSTM. At first, we divide a long ECG signal into several signal segments with the same length. Then signal segments from a long ECG signal are projected into attention-based Resnet to obtain multi-scale features. These multi-scale features are received by our attention-based BiLSTM in chronological order. Since an ECG signal may contain more than one abnormity, our attention-based BiLSTM will output which categories this long ECG signal belongs to.

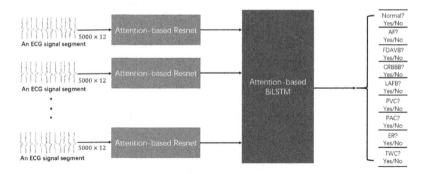

Fig. 1. Attention-based Res-BiLSTM-Net

2.1   Attention-Based Resnet

Details of our attention-based Resnet are presented in Fig. 2. The numbers in the figure are the input or the output shapes of each module. Our attention-based Resnet consists of five RN blocks, channel attention models, a time-distributed dense layer, and an average pooling. These five RN blocks share the same architecture. And channel attention models following the five RN blocks have the same processing steps. The operation of concatenation is to concatenate outputs from the 5 channel attention models on the channel dimension. In Fig. 2, the dense layer outside the green box is only used to pre-train our attention-based Resnet. The output shape of dense layer is 9 * 1, which is exactly corresponding to the number of classification categories. In detection process, we only use features from the average pooling, and these features will be integrated and sent to the attention-based BiLSTM.

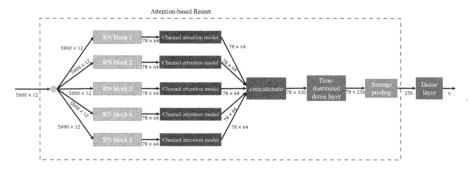

Fig. 2. The structure of attention-based Resnet (Color figure online)

RN Block. The structure of our RN block is shown in Fig. 3. Padding is used for each convolution layer. In Fig. 3, the network structure labeled with the red rectangle is repeated six times. In this way, we can obtain more abstract features.

During the period of training a deep network, we may usually come across the problems with gradient explosion and gradient vanishing. To prevent these occurrences, we adopt a residual connection [8], which is defined to be:

$$y = F(x) + x \tag{1}$$

$F(x)$ is the residual, and x is the input, while y is the output. With this residual connection, we can design a deep neural network.

After each convolution layer, we use leaky Relu [9] as an activation function with the definition of

$$f_{LeakyRelu} = \begin{cases} x & x > 0 \\ \alpha x & otherwise \end{cases} \tag{2}$$

Here, we let $\alpha = 0.3$.

The only difference of our five RN blocks is the kernel sizes of convolution layers. The kernel sizes in RN1, RN2, RN3, RN4, RN5 are 2, 4, 8, 16, 32 respectively. Our five RN blocks with different kernel sizes help our model capture more multi-scale features.

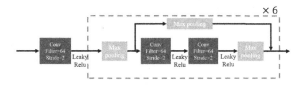

Fig. 3. The structure of RN block (Color figure online)

Channel Attention Model. In order to exploit the difference of channel-wise output from our RN blocks, we adopt the attention model of [10] for arrhythmia classification. The output of the channel attention model is computed by the following equations:

$$X = f_{reshape1}(X_{input}) \tag{3}$$

$$Y_{atten} = \sigma_g(X \cdot W_{atten} + b_{atten}) \tag{4}$$

$$Y_1 = f_{reshape2}(Y_{atten}) \tag{5}$$

$$Y_2 = f_{average}(Y_1) \tag{6}$$

$$Y_3 = f_{copy}(Y_2) \tag{7}$$

$$Y_{output} = X_{input} \odot Y_3 \tag{8}$$

Here, X_{input} denotes the output from the attention-based Resnet model with a shape of (n_S, n_T, n_C). Y_{output} is the output of the channel attention model. n_S, n_T, and n_C represent the number of samples, time steps and channels respectively. X, Y_{atten}, Y_1, Y_2, Y_3, and Y_{output} are the matrices of size $(n_S \times n_T, n_C)$, $(n_S \times n_T, n_C)$, (n_S, n_T, n_C), (n_S, n_C), (n_S, n_T, n_C), and (n_S, n_T, n_C) respectively. W_{atten} is the weight matrix and b_{atten} is the bias matrix. σ_g is a non-linear activation function. $f_{reshape1}$ and $f_{reshape2}$ are the reshaping operations. $f_{average}$ is to average the second axis of the matrix. f_{copy} is a copying operation to share the averages over all the time steps. $\odot$ denotes an element-wise multiplication between matrices.

Time-Distributed Dense Layer. The time-distributed dense layer can assign a dense layer with the same structure and parameters to each time step, which is packaged in keras [11].

Average Pooling Layer. Average pooling layer can average the features on temporal dimension.

2.2   Attention-Based BiLSTM

Our attention-based Resnet can extract features of each signal segment, and we need to combine these features for arrhythmia classification. In order to combine these features from a long signal, we propose the attention-based BiLSTM, whose architecture is illustrated in Fig. 4. At first, features from a long signal are projected into a two-layer bidirectional long short-term memory (BiLSTM) to capture temporal features. Then a time attention model is applied to obtain the importance of different time steps for arrhythmia classification. After that, global features are got by a time-distributed dense layer and an average pooling layer. In the end, a dense layer with an activation function of sigmoid outputs probabilities that a long signal belongs to each category. The long signal is classified as the category whose probability score is beyond 0.5. The time-distributed dense layer and average pooling layer in our attention-based BiLSTM are same with that in our attention-based Resnet.

Fig. 4. The architecture of the attention-based BiLSTM

BiLSTM. The BiLSTM concatenates the outputs of two separate hidden layers, which is to process forward and backward sequential data respectively [11]. The outputs of two layers are calculated by the standard LSTM computation steps, which can be described as the Eqs. (9)–(14) according to [12] and [13]:

$$f_t = \sigma_g(W_f x_t + U_f h_{t-1} + b_f) \tag{9}$$

$$i_t = \sigma_g(W_i x_t + U_i h_{t-1} + b_i) \tag{10}$$

$$o_t = \sigma_g(W_o x_t + U_o h_{t-1} + b_o) \tag{11}$$

$$\tilde{C}_t = tanh(W_C x_t + U_C h_{t-1} + b_C) \tag{12}$$

$$C_t = f_t \odot C_{t-1} + i_t \odot \tilde{C}_t \tag{13}$$

$$h_t = o_t \odot tanh(C_t) \tag{14}$$

Here W_f, W_i, W_O and W_C are the weight matrixes. The U_f, U_i, U_o and U_C are the recurrent matrixes, and b_f, b_i, b_o, b_C are the bias weights. The C_t and h_t are the layer outputs. σ_g is a activation function and *tanh* is the hyperbolic tangent function. $\odot$ is the element-wise multiplication.

Time Attention Model. Different time steps of the features from the two-layer BiLSTM have different importance for cardiac arrhythmias classification. In order to evaluate these importance, we propose a time attention model. The output of our time attention model is computed by the following equations:

$$X = f_{reshape1}(X_{input}) \tag{15}$$

$$Y_{atten} = \sigma_g(X \cdot W_{atten} + b_{atten}) \tag{16}$$

$$Y = f_{reshape2}(Y_{atten}) \tag{17}$$

$$Y_2 = f_{copy}(Y) \tag{18}$$

$$Y_{output} = X_{input} \odot Y \tag{19}$$

Where X_{input} is the output from the two-layer BiLSTM with a shape of (n_S, n_T, n_C). Y_{output} is the output of the channel attention model. n_S, n_T, and n_C represent the number of samples, time steps and channels respectively. X, Y_{atten}, Y, and Y_2 are the matrices of size $(n_S \times n_T, n_C)$, $(n_S \times n_T, 1)$, $(n_S, n_T, 1)$, and (n_S, n_T, n_C) respectively. W_{atten} is the weight matrix and b_{atten} is the bias matrix. σ_g is a non-linear activation function. $f_{reshape1}$ and $f_{reshape2}$ are the reshaping operations. f_{copy} is a copying operation to share the averages over all the channels. $\odot$ denotes an element-wise multiplication between matrices.

3   Experiment

3.1   Dataset Description

The dataset is from the First China ECG Competition [7]. The dataset of this competition contains a training set including 6500 MAT files with labels and a testing set without labels. Each MAT file includes a 12-lead ECG signal, the information about the gender and age of the patient. The ECG signals are recorded at 500 Hz and their lengths vary between 9 s to 99 s.

The competition is to solve a multi-label classification problem. Every ECG signal of this competition contains 9 labels, which are normal, atrial fibrillation (AF), first-degree atrioventricular heart block (FDAVB), complete right bundle branch block (CRBBB), left anterior fascicular block (LAFB), premature ventricular contraction (PVC), premature atrial contraction (PAC), early repolarization (ER), and T wave change (TWC).

3.2   Experiment Setup

Data Preprocessing. Different lengths of signal segments were tested when we divided long ECG signals. And we tended to choose the long ECG signals because the longer segments better represent the whole signals. A short signal length causes the model to capture less morphological feature. Moreover, in the dataset with labels, there are only two ECG signals with a length less than 10 s. And the ECG signals with a 10-second length occupy a large percentage in the dataset with labels. So we set the length to 10 s.

For ECG signals with a length less than 10 s, they are filled to 10 s. The padded data is copied from the last point of the original ECG signals. For ECG signals with a 10-second length, they remain the same. For ECG signals with a length greater than 10 s, they are divided into several segments with a length of 10 s. When splitting a long ECG signal, a sliding window with a length of 10 s and a time overlap of 1 s is applied to get signal segments. If the last time window doesn't contain a 10-second signal, the time window will scroll forward until it contains a 10-second signal.

Details of Training. When we trained our attention-based Resnet and attention-based BiLSTM, we used binary cross entropy as our loss function. In the training process of our attention-based Resnet, all the signal segments are labeled as the class label of their parents, the optimization algorithm is RMSProp, and the learning rate is 0.0002. In the training process of our attention-based BiLSTM, the optimization algorithm is also RMSProp, and the learning rate is 0.0008.

3.3 Evaluation Metrics

The First China ECG Intelligent Competition adopts an average F1score to evaluate the ability of our model on multi-label classification. The average F1scores are computed by the following equations:

$$Recall_i = \frac{TP_i}{TP_i + FN_i} \tag{20}$$

$$Precision_i = \frac{TP_i}{TN_i + FP_i} \tag{21}$$

$$F1score_i = \frac{2 \cdot Precision_i \cdot Recall_i}{Recall_i + Precision_i} \tag{22}$$

$$F1score = \frac{1}{9} \sum_{i=1}^{9} F1score_i \tag{23}$$

where TP_i, TN_i, FP_i, and FN_i represent the number of true positive samples, the number of true negative samples, the number of false positive samples, and the number of false negative samples respectively.

3.4 Model Performance on Test Dataset

In order to achieve the robust and accurate classification performance, we conducted an 8-fold cross experiment to obtain 8 best models. The final probability of each category is the average of the probability obtained by the 8 best models. If the final probabilities of some categories in some ECG signals are greater than 0.5, these signals are considered to belong to these categories; if not, otherwise.

Table 1 shows the F1scores of individual classes on the testing dataset. And our method achieved a high average F1score of 0.8757.

Table 1. F1scores of individual classes on the testing set

Class	Normal	AF	FDAVB	CRBBB	LAFB	PVC	PAC	ER	TWC
F1score	0.8960	0.9774	0.9179	0.9815	0.7220	0.9630	0.8986	0.7331	0.7916

4 Conclusion and Discussion

In this paper, we proposed an attention-based Res-BiLSTM-Net model for cardiac arrhythmias classification. The main advantages of our model are on three aspects: (1) Our designed model is capable of classifying ECG signals with different lengths. (2) Our attention-based Resnet can extract multi-scale features from ECG signal segments with a same length. (3) Our attention-based BiLSTM can combine rich features from a long ECG signal and output the classification result.

In the First China ECG Intelligent Competition, we achieved a good result with an average F1score of 0.8757 on the multi-label arrhythmias classification problem.

We have conducted a 10-fold cross-validation experiment to test the effect of our attention-based Resnet on the dataset with labels, and got an average F1score of 0.865. And our whole model, attention-based Res-BiLSTM-Net achieved an average F1score of nearly 0.880. It is obvious that our attention-based BiLSTM is efficient for integrating the features from attention-based Resnet.

Training attention-based Resnet and attention-based BiLSTM together may improve the performance of our whole model a lot. However, it is hard to train them together due to the large difference in signal length. During the training process, we must fix the input shape, and this operation lead to a huge memory usage. So at the maximum hardware support, we trained these two models separately.

Acknowledgment. This work was supported by the National Natural Science Foundation of China (Grant Nos. 61672231), Shanghai Natural Science Foundation (Grant No. 18ZR1411400), and Fundamental Research Funds for the Central Universities.

References

1. Chow, G.V., Marine, J.E., Fleg, J.L.: Epidemiology of arrhythmias and conduction disorders in older adults. Clin. Geriatr. Med. **28**(4), 539–553 (2012)
2. Pan, J., Tompkins, W.J.: A real-time QRS detection algorithm. IEEE Trans. Biomed. Eng. **32**(3), 230–236 (1985)
3. Mazomenos, E.B., Chen, T., Acharyya, A., et al.: A time-domain morphology and gradient based algorithm for ECG feature extraction. In: 2012 IEEE International Conference on Industrial Technology, pp. 117–122. IEEE (2012)
4. Lin, C.H.: Frequency-domain features for ECG beat discrimination using grey relational analysis-based classifier. Comput. Math. Appl. **55**(4), 680–690 (2008)
5. Christov, I., Gómez-Herrero, G., Krasteva, V., et al.: Comparative study of morphological and time-frequency ECG descriptors for heartbeat classification. Med. Eng. Phys. **28**(9), 876–887 (2006)
6. Murugesan, B., Ravichandran, V., Ram, K., et al.: ECGNet: deep network for arrhythmia classification. In: 2018 IEEE International Symposium on Medical Measurements and Applications (MeMeA), pp. 1–6. IEEE (2018)
7. The First China ECG Intelligent Competition. http://mdi.ids.tsinghua.edu.cn/#/
8. He, K., Zhang, X., Ren, S., et al.: Deep residual learning for image recognition. In: Proceedings of the IEEE Conference on Computer Vision and Pattern Recognition, pp. 770–778 (2016)
9. Xu, B., Wang, N., Chen, T., et al.: Empirical evaluation of rectified activations in convolutional network. arXiv preprint arXiv:1505.00853 (2015)
10. Yao, X., Li, X., Ye, Q., et al.: A robust deep learning approach for automatic seizure detection. arXiv preprint arXiv:1812.06562 (2018)
11. Graves, A., Schmidhuber, J.: Framewise phoneme classification with bidirectional LSTM and other neural network architectures. Neural Netw. **18**(5–6), 602–610 (2005)
12. Gers, F.A., Schmidhuber, J., Cummins, F.: Learning to forget: continual prediction with LSTM (1999)
13. Greff, K., Srivastava, R.K., Koutník, J., et al.: LSTM: A search space odyssey. IEEE Trans. Neural Netw. Learn. Syst. **28**(10), 2222–2232 (2016)

A Multi-label Learning Method to Detect Arrhythmia Based on 12-Lead ECGs

Jinjing Zhu[1], Kaifa Xin[1], Qingqing Zhao[2], and Yue Zhang[1(✉)]

[1] Division of Information Science and Technology, Tsinghua University,
Beijing, China
zhangyue@mails.tsinghua.edu.cn
[2] Renmin Hospital of Wuhan University, Wuhan University, Wuhan, China

Abstract. Cardiovascular disease (CVD) is one of the most serious diseases that harm human life and gives a huge burden to the health care system. Recent advances in deep learning have achieved great success in object detection, speech and image recognition. Although deep learning has been applied to the detection of arrhythmia, detection accuracy is limited because of three major issues: 1. Each ECG signal maybe contains more than one-label information; 2. It is hard to classify ECG with different lengths; 3. Data imbalance problem is severe for arrhythmia detection. In this paper, we present a multi-label learning algorithm to address the class imbalance and detection on ECGs with different durations. We utilize Deep Convolutional Generative Adversarial Networks (DCGANs) and Wasserstein GAN-Gradient Penalty (WGAN-GP) to generate new positive samples and use two losses to balance the importance between positive samples and negative samples. Moreover, we construct a Squeeze and Excitation-ResNet (SE-ResNet) module for normal rhythm and arrhythmia detection. In order to solve the multi-label classification problem, we train nine different binary classifiers for each category and determine which types of rhythm the ECG signals belong to. Experimental results on The ECG Intelligence Challenge 2019 dataset demonstrate that our multi-label learning method achieves competitive performance in multi-label ECGs classification.

Keywords: Arrhythmia · ECG · DCGANs · WGAN-GP · SE-ResNet · Multi-label learning

1 Introduction

Cardiovascular disease (CVD) is one of the most serious diseases that harm human life and gives a huge burden to the health care system [1]. Some statistics show that about 80% of sudden cardiac death is caused by arrhythmia [2]. Therefore, there is an important significance for the early diagnosis of various arrhythmia. Electrocardiogram (ECG) provides a powerful and convenient way to solve the problem of arrhythmia detection because of high security, non-invasive nature, and simplicity. Naturally, ECG has been widely applied for arrhythmia detection and has achieved excellent results. In previous work, a large number of researches based on machine learning are applied to arrhythmia detection. Such methods mainly include four steps: (1) ECG signal pre-processing; (2) segmentation; (3) feature extraction; and (4) classification. In the last

© Springer Nature Switzerland AG 2019
H. Liao et al. (Eds.): MLMECH 2019/CVII-STENT 2019, LNCS 11794, pp. 11–19, 2019.
https://doi.org/10.1007/978-3-030-33327-0_2

step, the most popular algorithms include: support vector machine [3], artificial neural network [4], linear discrimination [5], and Reservoir Computing with logistic Regression [6]. In recent years, deep learning has made great progress on object detection, speech and image recognition and also shows an exciting result in detecting arrhythmia. Hong et al. design ENCASE for ECG classification using a combination of expert features, center wave features, and deep features to train several gradient decision boosting tree classifiers [7]. Hannun.et al. develop a 34-layer deep neural network (DNN) in an end-to-end manner to classify 12 rhythm classes. The network is trained on a dataset of 91232 single-lead ECGs from 53549 patients. The result shows that an end-to-end deep learning approach can classify quantities of arrhythmia and get similar performance to cardiologists [8]. Zhang et al. introduce a novel method of transforming 1-D ECGs to 2-D images and then utilize a convolutional neural network to automatically extract features from ECG images [9].

However, for some complex diseases, the 1-lead ECG signal is difficult to accurately detect the diseases, so 12-lead ECGs with more effective information are used for diagnosis in this paper. On the other hand, each segment of the ECG signal contains more than one disease information, and more likely contains multiple disease information. Therefore, we propose a multi-label learning method to detect normal rhythm and the other eight arrhythmia using the ECG Intelligence Challenge 2019 training dataset. Based on the information and data distribution of the dataset and the knowledge of Multi-label learning [10], we design a SE-ResNet module to detect each label ECG signal separately for nine times. Moreover, due to the class imbalance of the dataset, we exploit two methods to augment positive examples and two losses to balance the importance of positive/negative examples.

2   Dataset and the Proposed Method

2.1   Database

The ECG Intelligence Challenge 2019 training dataset is constituted of 6500 12-lead ECG recordings (leads I, II, III, aVR, aVL, aVF, V1, V2, V3, V4, V5, and V6). The duration of ECG recordings lasts from 9 s to 91 s and each record is sampled with 500 Hz. The ECG recordings are classified into the nine following categories: normal rhythm (N), atrial fibrillation (AF), first-degree atrioventricular block (FDAVB), complete right bundle branch block (CRBBB), left anterior fascicular block (LAFB), premature ventricular contraction (PVC), atrial premature contraction (PAC), early repolarization (ER), and T-wave changes (TWC). The number of each category is shown in Table 1 and an example of normal and abnormal rhythm is reported in Fig. 1. In addition to normal recordings, each ECG recording may have one or more categories. Moreover, the hidden validation set contains 500 recordings and the length of recordings ranges from 10 s to 39 s.

Table 1. The number of recordings of each class in training dataset.

Classes	N	AF	FDAVB	CRBBB	LAFB	PVC	PAC	ER	TWC
Records	1953	504	534	826	180	654	672	224	2156

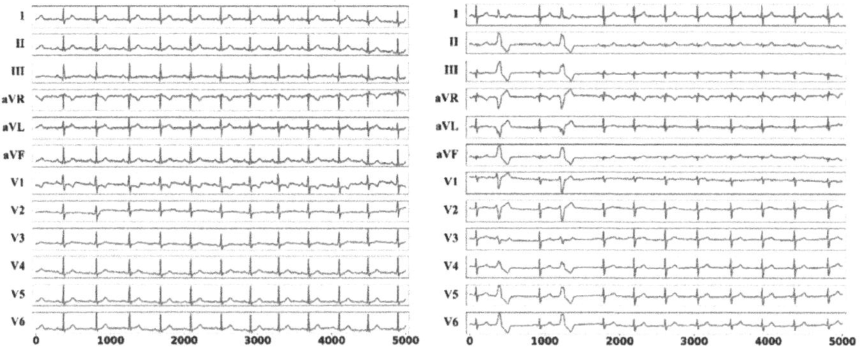

Fig. 1. 12-lead Normal and abnormal ECG signals of 10-second duration.

2.2 Data Preprocessing

First, we choose a 4-order Butterworth bandpass(1–40 Hz) filter applied to each ECG recording to eliminate baseline wander, muscle noise and power-line inference [11] which probably creates problems of detecting arrhythmia. Because the length of each ECG recording exceeds 4096*12 points, the different duration ECG signal is divided into segments for every 4096*12 points taken as input to train a classifier. Based on the distributed characteristic of each category example in the dataset, we choose to perform nine binary classifiers to detect the labels that each ECG belongs to. Moreover, due to the imbalance between the positive and negative samples of each label, such as LAFB (1:35 ratio of positive to negative examples) and ER (1:28 ratio of positive to negative examples), we utilize the following methods to augment positive samples of the imbalanced dataset to solve the problem:

(1) crop positive samples to obtain a 1:3 ratio of positive to negative examples
(2) generate new positive samples using DCGANs and WGAN-GP networks

Crop Positive Samples. To reserve the medical features of ECGs, we segment the positive samples at regular intervals based on the imbalance ratio until reach the 1:3 ratio.

Generate New Positive Samples. Generative Adversarial Networks (GANs) [12] which contain two networks: a generator produces synthetic data with a noise source and a discriminator discriminates between true and false data are a much effective class of generative models. It has been successful used in image super-resolution, object detection, and image-to-image translation. Because of stable architecture and good representation ability, we implement DCGANs [13] to generate new positive examples to augment the dataset.

On the other hand, in order to have strong modeling performance and stability, we choose the loss introduced by Gulrajani et al. [14]. And the loss is defined as:

$$L = \mathop{\mathbb{E}}_{\tilde{x} \sim \mathbb{P}_g} [D(\tilde{x})] - \mathop{\mathbb{E}}_{x \sim \mathbb{P}_r} [D(x)] + \lambda \mathop{\mathbb{E}}_{\hat{x} \sim \mathbb{P}_{\hat{x}}} \left[\left(\|\nabla_{\hat{x}} D(\hat{x})\|_2 - 1 \right)^2 \right] \tag{1}$$

Where $\mathbb{P}_g$ is the model distribution, $\mathbb{P}_r$ is the data distribution and $\mathbb{P}_{\hat{x}}$ is sampling distribution along straight lines between pairs of points from $\mathbb{P}_g$ and $\mathbb{P}_r$. In generating new positive examples, we use the default $\lambda = 10$. Then all the new data and raw data will be as inputs to the SE-ResNet module.

2.3   Two Losses

In addition to amplifying positive sample data, we also use two effective losses: Focal Loss and GHM (gradient harmonizing mechanism) Loss to adjust the weight of the training samples when using classifiers to confirm labels of ECG recordings.

Focal Loss. The Focal Loss is proposed to address the extreme imbalance between foreground and background classes during training in one-stage object detection scenario [15]. In this paper, we use the Focal Loss to solve the imbalance between positive and negative samples and the Focal Loss is defined as:

$$\text{FL}(p_t) = -\alpha_t (1 - p_t)^\gamma \log(p_t) \tag{2}$$

The p_t is defined:

$$p_t = \begin{cases} p & \text{if } y = 1 \\ 1 - p & \text{otherwise} \end{cases} \tag{3}$$

For notational convenience, the method of defining α_t is analogous with p_t. α_t balances the importance of positive/negative examples and $(1 - p_t)^\gamma$ is utilized to focus training on hard, misclassified negatives. After defining Focal Loss, we will find the optimal value of α_t and γ when training our SE-ResNet modules.

GHM Loss. Li et al. [16] point out the class imbalance can be summarized to the imbalance in gradient norm distribution and introduces a harmonizing approach with regard to gradient density. The gradient density harmonized form of the loss function is formulated as Eq. (4):

$$L_{ghm} = \sum_{i=1}^{N} \frac{L_{CE}(p_i, p_i^*)}{GD(g_i)} \tag{4}$$

$L_{CE}(p_i, p_i^*)$ is binary cross entropy loss and $GD(g_i)$ is the gradient density function defined in the Li et al. [16]. While training the SE-ResNet module, the GHM Loss will be utilized as a method to address class imbalance in this work.

2.4   SE-ResNet

After processing the dataset and obtaining 4192*12-sample inputs, we develop an 86-layer SE-ResNet to classify these inputs of each category into two classes. The ResNet [17] is designed to address the degradation problem in deeper neural networks by introducing a residual block. In this study, we firstly construct an 86-layer ResNet, the main residual module (Fig. 2a) consists of two convolutional layers and before each convolutional layer we both add batch-normalization layer and ReLU layer, moreover, we also add dropout layer between two convolutional layers. Finally, we insert MaxPooling as shortcut connections utilized to reduce the dimension of input future vector by half to match dimensions and make the network easier to optimize.

Based on the residual module, we add the SE (Squeeze and Excitation) module into residual module. The SE block [18] is designed to improve the representational capacity of a network by performing dynamic channel-wise feature recalibration and had high performance on image classification. In this part, we combine residual module with SE block to train models which can greatly improve classification accuracy. In the SE block, we use global average pooling to squeeze global spatial information into a channel descriptor and apply excitation operation mainly consisting of two fully connected layers and a ReLU layer to fully capture channel-wise dependencies. Finally, the SE-ResNet module (Fig. 2b) is designed to improve the accuracy of detection.

On the basis of the two modules, all 4192*12-samples inputs would be fed into the first convolutional layer, followed by a Batch-normalization layer, ReLU activation layer, and MaxPooling layer. Then there is SE-ResNet module after the activation layer. There are four stacks followed the SE-ResNet module and each stack is made up of four SE-ResNet blocks and a similar plain block in the residual block. These stacks were followed by four SE-ResNet modules. Finally, the network end with Batch-

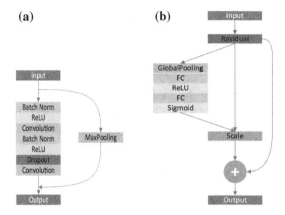

Fig. 2. Residual module (a) and SE-ResNet module (b).

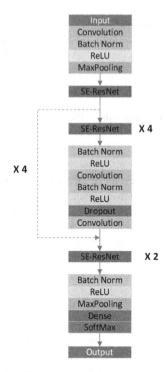

Fig. 3. The proposed network architecture.

normalization layer, ReLU activation layer, Maxpooling layer, and a fully-connected layer with Softmax to produce a distribution over the 2 output classes. The proposed SE-ResNet architecture is depicted in Fig. 3.

We utilize the weights as described by He et al. [17], and Adam optimization [19] with the default parameters $\beta\_1 = 0.9$ and $\beta\_2 = 0.999$. The minibatch size of the training is 64 which means 64 ECG signals would be employed as the input for each epoch. The learning rate is set to be 0.01 at the beginning and gradually decays as the epochs increase. The dropout probability is 0.2 in the residual module and the reduction ratio is defined as 16 in the SE-ResNet module.

2.5   Test Protocol

In the validation dataset, we use the methods of addressing the imbalance and SE-ResNet module to train the best module for each class separately. In detail, for each category detection, cropping the positives, generating new positives, Focal Loss and GHM Loss are utilized to train SE-ResNet respectively. After optimizing the tuning parameters by grid search, the best module for each label will be found and saved to test on the hidden test data.

3 Experimental Results

We evaluate nine models of detecting nine ECG rhythms respectively on the hidden validation set and hidden test set. The performance of classification is evaluated by mean F_1 score. The mean F_1 score is defined as:

$$F_1 = \frac{1}{9} \sum F_{1j} \tag{5}$$

In this paper, we need to detect nine types of ECG signals. Firstly, the following four variables are defined for the *jth* category, where $0 \le j \le 8$,

$$TP_j = \left| \left\{ x_i \middle| y_j \in Y_i, y_j \in f(x_i), 1 \le i \le N \right\} \right| \tag{6}$$

$$FP_j = \left| \left\{ x_i \middle| y_j \notin Y_i, y_j \in f(x_i), 1 \le i \le N \right\} \right| \tag{7}$$

$$TN_j = \left| \left\{ x_i \middle| y_j \notin Y_i, y_j \notin f(x_i), 1 \le i \le N \right\} \right| \tag{8}$$

$$FN_j = \left| \left\{ x_i \middle| y_j \in Y_i, y_j \notin f(x_i), 1 \le i \le N \right\} \right| \tag{9}$$

Then, the Precision, Recall and F_1 scores for each class can be calculated:

$$Precision_j = \frac{TP_j}{TP_j + FP_j} \tag{10}$$

$$Recall_j = \frac{TP_j}{TP_j + FN_j} \tag{11}$$

$$F_{1j} = \frac{2 \cdot Precision_j \cdot Recall_j}{Precision_j + Recall_j} \tag{12}$$

Table 2 lists the F_1 scores of each category rhythm and mean F_1 scores on hidden validation and test set. The F_1 score shows that our method has high performance in detecting multi-label ECGs.

Table 2. The F_1 scores for each type and mean F_1 scores on validation and test set

F_1 score	N	AF	FDAVB	CRBBB	LAFB	PVC	PAC	ER	TWC	Mean F_1
Val set	0.903	0.962	0.879	0.985	0.759	0.972	0.851	0.556	0.887	0.862
Test set	0.852	0.961	0.873	0.965	0.627	0.969	0.887	0.683	0.770	0.843

4   Conclusions

In this work, we construct some approaches to solve the class imbalance by GANs and two effective loss, and a multi-label learning algorithm based on SE-ResNet to detect normal rhythm and arrhythmia. Experiment results on the hidden dataset demonstrate the specificity and validity of the proposed method for ECG classification. Future work will improve classification performance and try to apply our method in routine clinical practice.

Acknowledgements. This work was supported by the National Natural Science Foundation of China (No.61571628).

References

1. Thomas, H., Diamond, J., Vieco, A., et al.: Global atlas of cardiovascular disease 2000–2016: the path to prevention and control. Glob. Heart **13**(3), 143 (2018)
2. Mehra, R.: Global public health problem of sudden cardiac death. J. Electrocardiol. **40**(6-supp-S1), S118–S122 (2007)
3. Ye, C., Kumar, B.V.K.V., Coimbra, M.T.: Combining general multi-class and specific two-class classifiers for improved customized ECG heartbeat classification. In: 2012 21st International Conference on Pattern Recognition (ICPR 2012). IEEE Computer Society (2012)
4. Mar, T., Zaunseder, S., Martínez, J.P., Llamedo, M., Poll, R.: Optimization of ECG classification by means of feature selection. IEEE Trans. Bio-Med. Eng. **58**(8), 2168–2177 (2011)
5. Chazal, P.D., O'Dwyer, M., Reilly, R.B.: Automatic classification of heartbeats using ECG morphology and heartbeat interval features. IEEE Trans. Biomed. Eng. **51**(7), 1196–1206 (2004)
6. Moran, M.E., Soriano, M.C., Fischer, I., et al.: Electrocardiogram classification using reservoir computing with logistic regression. IEEE J. Biomed. Health Inform. **19**(3) (2014)
7. Hong, S., Wu, M., et al.: ENCASE: an ensemble classifier for ECG classification using expert features and deep neural networks (2017)
8. Hannun, A.Y., Rajpurkar, P., Haghpanahi, M., et al.: Cardiologist-level arrhythmia detection and classification in ambulatory electrocardiograms using a deep neural network. Nat. Med. **25**, 65–69 (2019)
9. Zhang, Q., Zhou, D.: Deep Arm/Ear-ECG image learning for highly wearable biometric human identification. Ann. Biomed. Eng. **46**(1), 1–13 (2017)
10. Zhang, M.-L., Zhou, Z.-H.: A review on multi-label learning algorithms. IEEE Trans. Knowl. Data Eng. **26**(8), 1819–1837 (2014)
11. Poungponsri, S., Yu, X.H.: An adaptive filtering approach for electrocardiogram (ECG) signal noise reduction using neural networks. Neurocomputing **117**, 206–213 (2013)
12. Goodfellow, I.J., et al.: Generative adversarial nets. In: NIPS (2014)
13. Radford, A., Metz, L., Chintala, S.: Unsupervised representation learning with deep convolutional generative adversarial networks. arXiv preprint arXiv:1511.06434 (2015)
14. Gulrajani, I., Ahmed, F., Arjovsky, M., Dumoulin, V., Courville, A.C.: Improved training of wasserstein GANs. CoRR, abs/1704.00028 (2017)

15. Lin, T., Goyal, P., Girshick, R.B., He, K., Dollar, P.: Focal loss for dense object detection. In: IEEE ICCV (2017)
16. Li, B., Liu, Y., Wang, X.: Gradient harmonized single stage detector. In: AAAI Conference on Artificial Intelligence (2019)
17. He, K., Zhang, X., Ren, S., Sun, J.: Deep residual learning for image recognition. In: CVPR (2016)
18. Hu, J., Shen, L., Sun, G.: Squeeze-and-excitation networks. In: CVPR (2018)
19. Kingma, D.P., Ba, J.L.: Adam: a method for stochastic optimization. In: Proceedings of International Conference on Learning Representations, pp. 1–15 (2015)

An Ensemble Neural Network
for Multi-label Classification
of Electrocardiogram

Dongya Jia[✉], Wei Zhao, Zhenqi Li, Cong Yan, Hongmei Wang, Jing Hu,
and Jiansheng Fang

Central Research, Guangzhou Shiyuan Electronic Technology Company Limited,
No. 6 Yunpu 4th Road, Guangzhou, China
`jiadongya@cvte.com`

Abstract. An electrocardiogram (ECG) record potentially contains
multiple abnormalities concurrently, therefore multi-label classification
of ECG is significant in clinical scenarios. In this paper, we propose an
ensemble neural network to address the multi-label classification of 12-
lead ECG. The proposed network contains two modules, which treat
the multi-label task from two different perspectives. The first module
deals with the task in a sequence-generation manner by a novel encoder-
decoder structure. The second module treats the multi-label problem
as multiple binary classification tasks, by employing two convolutional
neural networks of different structure. Finally, the predictions of two
modules are integrated as the final result. Our method is trained and
evaluated on the dataset provided by the First China ECG Intelligent
Competition, and yields a Macro-F_1 of 0.872 on the test set.

Keywords: Deep learning · ECG · Multi-label · Classification

1 Introduction

The electrocardiogram (ECG), which measures electrical activity of heart, is an
important tool for clinical diagnosis of multiple cardiac diseases. Abnormal ECG
is often relevant to various heart abnormalities, however, manual interpretation
of ECG by cardiac experts is costly and challenging, due to variability between
individuals as well as multiple sources of noise, such as baseline drift and motion
artifacts. Additionally, a wide range of abnormalities possibly exist concurrently
in a single ECG record, detecting all of them is a difficult task. Thus, the development of algorithms, which is capable of recognizing multiple cardiac diseases
simultaneously from ECG, is of great significance.

In clinical practice, ECG is interpreted based on some measurable morphological features, such as the RR interval, length of PR segment or amplitude of T
wave. There are many automated ECG delineation algorithms [1–3] to measure

H. Liao et al. (Eds.): MLMECH 2019/CVII-STENT 2019, LNCS 11794, pp. 20–27, 2019.
https://doi.org/10.1007/978-3-030-33327-0_3

these clinical parameters. However, due to effect of artifacts and patient variability, the performance of existing algorithms is not accurate enough to support direct interpretation of ECG.

Some methods based on machine learning are developed to analyze and recognize ECG. In traditional workflow, the ECG record is pre-processed first. Then a variety of features are extracted via different techniques, such as Discrete Wavelet Transform (DWT) [4], Pan Tompkins algorithm [5] and some ECG delineation algorithms [6]. Finally, an appropriate classifier, such as Radial Basis Function Neural Network (RBFNNN) [5] or Support Vector Machine (SVM) [6], is employed for classification. The contributions of existing works mainly focus on pre-processing techniques, feature extraction and selection of classifier. However, these traditional methods rely heavily on hand-crafted features, which are often redundant and restricted by priori knowledge.

In recent years, deep learning methods are developed and introduced to extract high-level features from ECG in a learning-based manner, and yield better performance. In [7], a Convolutional Neural Networks (CNN) is proposed to classify the single-lead ECG into multiple kinds of rhythm, and achieved performance exceeding the average cardiologists. In [8], CNN is also utilized for detection of myocardial infraction from normal beat. These methods regard multiple cardiac abnormalities as mutually exclusive classes and view the problem as a multi-class or binary classification task. However, an ECG record is potentially indication of multiple kinds of abnormalities concurrently. The recognition of ECG should be addressed as a multi-label classification task in real scene.

In this paper, we propose a novel ensemble neural network to address multi-label classification of 12-lead ECG. From the perspective of label prediction way, our ensemble network mainly consists of two streams: sequence generation module and multi-task module. Each module is composed of one or two sub-networks with different architectures. In the end, voting ensemble is applied to the predictions of these sub-networks. Our method is trained and evaluated on the dataset provided by the rematch of the First China ECG Intelligent Competition [9]. Our method achieves a Macro-F_1 of 0.872 over nine classes on the test set.

2   Model Architecture

The architecture of our ensemble network is shown in Fig. 1. Our network consists of two modules to deal with multiple labels. In the first module, the multilabel task is viewed as a sequence generation task. A Long Short-term Memory (LSTM) acts as a decoder to generate labels one by one according to features extracted by a preceding encoder network. In the second module, the multi-label task is viewed as multiple binary classification tasks. Hard parameter mechanism is applied in this module by sharing the feature-extraction layers between all tasks, and each class is predicted via its label-specific classifier respectively.

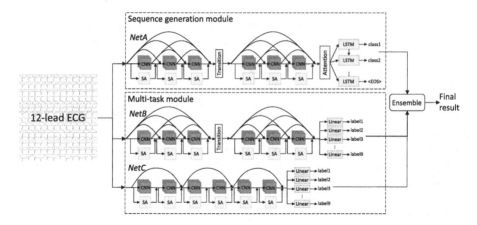

Fig. 1. Architecture of our ensemble neural network, which consists of two modules: sequence generation module and multi-task module. The predictions of these two modules are combined by voting ensemble strategy yielding the final result.

2.1   Sequence Generation Module

In this module, the goal is to find an optimal subset sequence y from label space $\{l_1, l_2, ..., l_c\}$, where c is the number of class. In our work, a sub-network (NetA) with the encoder-decoder structure is employed. The architecture of NetA is adapted from the Sequence Generation Model (SGM) [10], which is originally designed to solve multi-label classification in natural language processing. Different from SGM, the encoder in our method is composed of multiple CNNs with self-attention (SA) mechanism to model dependency between different positions in a sequence. The similarity lies in the decoder, which consists of a LSTM with global attention mechanism.

Encoder. As shown in Fig. 2, the architecture of encoder is motivated by Dense Convolutional Network (DenseNet) [11]. Different from DenseNet using two-dimensional operations, we utilize one-dimension (1-d) layers instead, including 1-d convolution layer, 1-d batch normalization (BN) and 1-d pooling layer. In our method, each dense block is composed of multiple bottleneck composite functions H_l [11], with structure of BN-ReLU-Conv-BN-ReLU-Conv. Within each dense block, for each H_l, the outputs of all preceding H_l are concatenated as its input so as to strengthen feature propagation.

Self Attention: To capture correlation between different locations far apart along a sequence, Scaled Dot-Product Attention [12] (yellow boxes in Fig. 2) is employed in parallel with all convolution layers, except those with a kernel size of 1. The outputs from each convolution layer and corresponding attention layer are concatenated. The attention function is described in Eq. (1) [12].

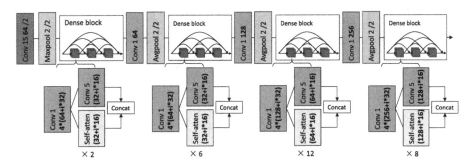

Fig. 2. The detailed architecture of feature-extraction CNN in NetA and NetB. Each convolution layer (light blue blocks) and self-attention unit is preceded by a combination of BN-ReLU. The bold number represents number of output channels. /2 means a stride of 2. (Color figure online)

$$\text{Attention}(\boldsymbol{Q}, \boldsymbol{K}, \boldsymbol{V}) = \text{softmax}(\frac{\boldsymbol{Q}\boldsymbol{K}^T}{\sqrt{d_k}})\boldsymbol{V} \tag{1}$$

where $\boldsymbol{Q}$ and $\boldsymbol{K}$ denote the queries and keys of dimensional d_k, and $\boldsymbol{V}$ denotes the values of dimensional d_v.

Decoder. The architecture of our decoder mainly consists of a Long Short-term Memory (LSTM) with the global attention mechanism [13].

Global Attention: For the feature map from encoder, each portion makes different contribution while decoding. Thus, we utilize the global attention mechanism to learn where to focus on when predicting different labels. For the i-th portion of feature map, the weight α_{ij} assigned to it when predicting j-th label is computed as follow:

$$e_{ij} = \boldsymbol{v}_a^T tanh(\boldsymbol{W}_a \boldsymbol{s}_j + \boldsymbol{U}_a \boldsymbol{h}_i) \tag{2}$$

$$\alpha_{ij} = \frac{exp(e_{ij})}{\sum_{t=1}^m exp(e_{tj})} \tag{3}$$

where $\boldsymbol{s}_j$ denotes the hidden state of LSTM at time-step j. $\boldsymbol{h}_i$ denotes the i-th portion of feature map. e_{ij} denotes measurement of correlation between $\boldsymbol{s}_j$ and $\boldsymbol{h}_i$. $\boldsymbol{W}_a$, $\boldsymbol{U}_a$, $\boldsymbol{v}_a$ denote weight parameters. m denotes the amount of feature map portion. And the weighted feature map $\boldsymbol{c}_j$ at time-step j is calculated as Eq. (4):

$$\boldsymbol{c}_j = \sum_{i=1}^m \alpha_{ij} \boldsymbol{h}_i \tag{4}$$

The predicted probability distribution $\boldsymbol{y}_j$ over all labels at time-step j is calculated as follow:

$$\boldsymbol{y}_j = \text{softmax}(\boldsymbol{W}_o tanh(\boldsymbol{W}_s \boldsymbol{s}_j + \boldsymbol{W}_c \boldsymbol{c}_j) + \boldsymbol{I}_j) \tag{5}$$

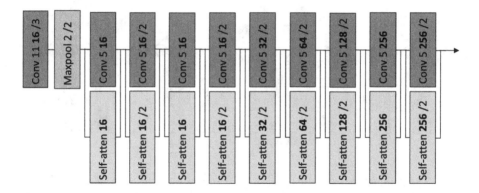

Fig. 3. The detailed architecture of feature-extraction CNN in NetC. The outputs from each convolution layer and corresponding self-attention layer are concatenated, and then processed by BN and ReLU.

where $\boldsymbol{W}_o$, $\boldsymbol{W}_s$, $\boldsymbol{W}_c$ are weights, $\boldsymbol{I}_j$ is a mask vector [10] to prevent generating repeating labels. $I_j^{(i)} = -\infty$ if label i is generated previously, otherwise $I_j^{(i)} = 0$. When decoding $\boldsymbol{y}_j$, a global embedding (GE) [10] is employed to embed $\boldsymbol{y}_{j-1}$, which is calculated as Eq. (6). The global embedding is composed of two embeddings $\boldsymbol{E}_1$ and $\boldsymbol{E}_2$, as shown in Eq. (7). $\boldsymbol{E}_1$ is the embedding of the probability distribution of $\boldsymbol{y}_{j-1}$, and $\boldsymbol{E}_2$ is the embedding of the label with highest probability in $\boldsymbol{y}_{j-1}$. A learning-based gate mechanism is utilized to combine result from these two embedding layers.

$$GE(\boldsymbol{y}_{j-1}) = (1 - \boldsymbol{H}) \odot \boldsymbol{E}_1 + \boldsymbol{H} \odot \boldsymbol{E}_2 \tag{6}$$

where $\boldsymbol{H}$ denotes the gate, which is calculated by $\boldsymbol{H} = \boldsymbol{W}_1 \boldsymbol{E}_1 + \boldsymbol{W}_2 \boldsymbol{E}_2$, where $\boldsymbol{W}_1$ and $\boldsymbol{W}_2$ are weight parameters.

$$\boldsymbol{E}_1 = \sum_{i=1}^{C} y_{j-1}^{(i)} \boldsymbol{e}_{1i} \text{ and } \boldsymbol{E}_2 = (\arg \max_{i \in C} y_{j-1}^{(i)}) \boldsymbol{e}_2 \tag{7}$$

where $y_{j-1}^{(i)}$ denotes predicted probability of i-th label at time-step $j - 1$. $\boldsymbol{e}_{1i}$ denotes the matrix that embeds predicted probability of ith label. And $\boldsymbol{e}_2$ denotes the matrix that embeds label with the highest probability. C denotes the number of labels.

2.2 Multi-task Module

In the multi-task module, the classification of each label is viewed as an individual task. Each label is predicted independently using corresponding classifier. This module comprises two sub-networks with different structures of CNN, their final prediction are integrated by voting ensemble.

The first sub-network (NetB) is composed of two parts, one for feature-extraction and the other for classification. The architecture of feature extraction part is identical to the encoder in NetA (see Fig. 2), and all tasks share the parameters of the encoder. For classification, each task possesses its own task-specific classifier, which is a fully-connected layer.

The second sub-network (NetC) is similar to NetB, consisting of shared feature-extraction part and independent classification part. Different from NetB, the shared part of NetC is a CNN with multiple shortcut connections [15], which is used to handle degradation problem in deep neural network, as shown in Fig. 3.

2.3 Implementation Details

The input of our neural network is 12-lead ECG. The high-frequency noise and baseline wandering noise are removed by a band-pass Butterworth filter, which is of range 0.5 Hz–48 Hz. At training stage, each ECG record is segmented nonoverlappingly into 18-second fragments with a sliding window. The label of a record is shared among all corresponding fragments. For those records shorter than 18 s, zero-padding are applied to the rear of them. Specifically, at inference stage of NetA, the ECG record is used as a whole without segmentation.

For NetA, the label sequence is sorted according to the frequency of appearance of labels in the training set, which is proved effective in [10]. And a weighted cross-entropy loss is adopted for training. For NetB and NetC, a weighted multi-label hinge loss is adopted for training.

3 Experiment

3.1 Dataset and Evaluation Metric

Dataset. The dataset is provided by the rematch of the First China ECG Intelligent Competition. In this dataset, each record contains 12 leads and the length ranges from 9 to 91 s. The sampling frequency is 500 Hz. For each record, nine classes are labeled, including normal, atrial fibrillation (AF), first-degree atrioventricular block (FDAVB), complete right bundle branch block (CRBBB), left anterior fascicular block (LAFB), premature ventricular contraction (PVC), premature atrial contraction (PAC), early repolarization (ER) and T wave change (TWC). The dataset is officially partitioned into three parts: training set (6500), validation set (500) and test set (6500). Labels of the validation set and test set are unpublished.

Evaluation Metric. We adopt Macro-F_1 as our evaluation metric. It is calculated by averaging the F_1 values over all classes, as shown in Eq. (8)

$$\text{Macro-}F_1 = \frac{1}{C} \sum_{i=1}^{C} F_{1i} \tag{8}$$

where C represents number of classes ($C = 9$ in our case), F_{1i} represents the F_1 score of class i.

Table 1. The Macro-F_1 and F_1 of each label on the test set. The result is yielded by integrating the predictions of three networks from 5-fold cross validation.

Macro-F_1	Normal	AF	FDAVB	CRBBB	LAFB	PVC	PAC	ER	TWC
0.872	0.873	0.983	0.930	0.983	0.733	0.959	0.908	0.730	0.750

3.2 Results

For each sub-network, we perform 5-fold cross-validation on training set. The models with the best performance on the hold-out set are selected. These models are evaluated on the test set and their predictions are integrated via the voting ensemble strategy.

The experimental result is shown in Table 1. The proposed method yields a Macro-F_1 of 0.872 on the test set. The F_1 scores of LAFB and ER are low relative to other classes, possibly due to lack of records in training set. The F_1 of TWC is also relatively low, indicating that our method is weak at capturing variation of the T wave.

4   Conclusion and Future Work

In this paper, we propose an ensemble neural network for multi-label classification of 12-lead ECG, which contains two modules from different perspectives to approach the multi-label problem. In the first module, the task is viewed as a sequence generation problem and the architecture resembles the sequence-to-sequence model. In the second module, the task is viewed as a multi-task problem. The predictions from two modules are integrated to yield the final result. From the experimental result, our method yields a Macro-F_1 of 0.872.

In our case, a ECG record possesses 9 labels at most, while in real scenario there will be far more labels. In the future, we plan to evaluate our method on ECG dataset with more labels. Additionally, more effective neural network architecture need to be developed.

References

1. Martinez, J.P., Almeida, R., Olmos, S., Rocha, A.P., Laguna, P.: A wavelet-based ECG delineator: evaluation on standard databases. IEEE Trans. Biomed. Eng. **51**(4), 570–581 (2004)
2. Gao, P., Zhao, J., Wang, G., Guo, H.: Real time ECG characteristic point detection with randomly selected signal pair difference (RSSPD) feature and random forest classifier. In: 38th Annual International Conference of the IEEE Engineering in Medicine and Biology Society, Orlando, USA, pp. 732–735. IEEE (2016)
3. Xia, Z., et al.: Real-time ECG delineation with randomly selected wavelet transform feature and random walk estimation. In: 40th Annual International Conference of the IEEE Engineering in Medicine and Biology Society, Hawaii, USA, pp. 2691–2694. IEEE (2018)

4. Vijayavanan, M., Rathikarani, V., Dhanalakshmi, P.: Automatic classification of ECG signal for heart disease diagnosis using morphological features. Int. J. Comput. Sci. Eng. Technol. (IJCSET) **5**(4), 449–555 (2014)
5. Korurek, M., Dogan, B.: ECG beat classification using particle swarm optimization and radial basis function neural network. Expert Syst. Appl. **37**(12), 7563–7569 (2010)
6. Park, K.S., et al.: Hierarchical support vector machine based heartbeat classification using higher order statistics and hermite basis function. In: Computers in Cardiology, Bologna, Italy, pp. 229–232. IEEE (2008)
7. Hannun, A.Y., et al.: Cardiologist-level arrhythmia detection and classification in ambulatory electrocardiograms using a deep neural network. Nat. Med. **25**, 65–69 (2019)
8. Acharya, U.R., Fujita, H., Oh, S.L., Hagiwara, Y., Tan, J.H., Adam, M.: Application of deep convolutional neural network for automated detection of myocardial infraction using ECG signals. Inf. Sci. **415–416**, 190–198 (2017)
9. The First China ECG Intelligent Competition. http://mdi.ids.tsinghua.edu.cn. Accessed 28 June 2019
10. Yang, P.C., Sun, X., Li, W., Ma, S.M., Wu, W., Wang, H.F.: SGM: sequence generation model for multi-label classification. In: Proceedings of the 27th International Conference on Computational Linguistics, pp. 3915–3926. Association for Computational Linguistics, New Mexico, USA (2018)
11. Huang, G., Liu, Z., Maaten, L., Weinberger, K.Q.: Densely connected convolutional networks. In: 2017 IEEE Conference on Computer Vision and Pattern Recognition (CVPR), Honolulu, Hl, USA, pp. 2261–2269. IEEE (2017)
12. Vaswani, A., et al.: Attention is all you need. In: 31st Conference on Neural Information Processing Systems (NIPS), Long Beach, CA, USA, pp. 2261–2269 (2017)
13. Luong, T., Pham, H., Manning, C.D.: Effective approaches to attention-based neural machine translation. In: Proceedings of the 2015 Conference on Empirical Methods in Natural Language Processing, Lisbon, Portugal, pp. 1412–1421. Association for Computational Linguistics (2015)
14. Wiseman, S., Rush, A.M.: Sequence-to-sequence learning as beam-search optimization. In: Proceedings of the 2015 Conference on Empirical Methods in Natural Language Processing, Austin, Texas, USA, pp. 1296–1306. Association for Computational Linguistics (2016)
15. He, K.M., Zhang, X.Y., Ren, S.Q., Sun, J.: Deep residual learning for image recognition. In: 2016 IEEE Conference on Computer Vision and Pattern Recognition (CVPR), Las Vegas, NV, USA, pp. 770–779. IEEE (2016)
16. Kingma, D.P., Ba, J.: Adam: a method for stochastic optimization. In: 2015 International Conference on Learning Representations (ICLR), San Diego, USA, pp. 770–779 (2015)
17. Srivastava, N., Hinton, G.E., Krizhevsky, A., Sutskever, I., Salakhutdinov, R.: Dropout: a simple way to prevent neural networks from overfitting. J. Mach. Learn. Res. **15**(1), 1929–1958 (2014)

Automatic Diagnosis with 12-Lead ECG Signals

Ke Wang, Xuan Zhang, Haoxi Zhong, and Ting Chen[✉]

Tsinghua University, Beijing, China
`tingchen@mail.tsinghua.edu.cn`

Abstract. Electrocardiogram (ECG) is strong evidence in the diagnosis of a wide range of heart-related diseases, and it is becoming increasingly important in the medical field recently. However, inferencing diseases with ECG signals is both time-consuming and error-prone even for licensed physicians, which arises the urgency of developing a fast and accurate automatic diagnosis algorithm. In this paper, we explore both deep learning models and well-designed feature engineering from ECG waveform. By combining the two methods, we propose an automatic diagnosis framework that can extract meaningful features both with and without human interventions. Experimental results on the ECG competition demonstrate that our framework can reach accurate results on heart-related diseases diagnosis.

Keywords: ECG · Deep learning · Feature engineering · Automatic diagnosis framework

1 Introduction

Electrocardiogram (ECG) is a measurement of the electrical activity of heartbeat. It is strong evidence in the diagnosis of several cardiovascular diseases, including arrhythmia, ventricular hypertrophy, myocardial infarction, etc. Since ECG test is noninvasive, painless and inexpensive, it has been widely put in clinical usage. However, analyzing ECG manually is very time-consuming, thus an accurate computer-aided method would greatly benefit cardiologists in the analysis of ECG.

There exist quantities of works focusing on automatic ECG diagnosis. The two main approaches are feature engineering approach and deep learning approach. For feature engineering approach, many knowledge-based features are extracted from raw ECG signals. Then, traditional machine learning techniques such as decision tree [11] and support vector machine [5] are applied to these features for final classification. It has been proved with several works that this approach performs well on ECG classification. However, since this approach relies on many handcraft-features, there are at least two disadvantages. One disadvantage is that this process is usually based on strong prior knowledge and does not consider the whole information of a heartbeat. The other disadvantage is that

© Springer Nature Switzerland AG 2019
H. Liao et al. (Eds.): MLMECH 2019/CVII-STENT 2019, LNCS 11794, pp. 28–35, 2019.
https://doi.org/10.1007/978-3-030-33327-0_4

extracted features such as PR interval, may not be accurate, which will influence the classification result.

For deep learning approach, various deep neural network models, e.g. convolutional neural network [2], long short-term memory network [3], deep residual network [7], are directly applied to the original ECG signal without manual feature extraction. Although deep learning approach overcomes those disadvantages in feature engineering approach, in general, deep learning technique requires a large quantity of annotated data, which is the key limitation for many researchers. Moreover, it is well known that deep learning model is lacking in interpretability, which is significant in medical application.

In this paper, we propose a framework that combines the two approaches together. Since deep learning is known as a powerful tool of representation learning, which means it can automatically learn a suitable feature mapping, one natural intuition is to integrate features represented by deep learning model with features based on human knowledge together. We have tried two different deep learning models: attention-based sequential model [13] and 1D Resnet. After comparison, we finally choose 1D Resnet since its performance is slightly better than that of attention-based sequential model. The 1D Resnet can automatically extract meaningful features from ECG signals. Besides, we also extract many features from ECG signals manually, including RR intervals, amplitudes of key points, time differences between key points and wavelet decomposition features. These features are highly correlated to ECG diagnosis [6]. Given these features, we use multi-layer perceptron as the classifier. The training is end-to-end and experiments show that the performance of this approach can exceed both pure feature engineering approach and pure deep learning approach.

We attended **the First China ECG Intelligent Competition** [1]. Our team ranks 10/308 in the preliminary session and 19/100 in the intermediary session. We applied the proposed method in the intermediary session. The overall F1 score on the test dataset is 85.50. Results show that our framework can reach accurate results on the diagnosis of heart-related diseases.

2   Dataset Description

The data is from **the First China ECG Intelligent Competition** [1]. The data includes 6, 500 pieces of 12-lead ECG signals with sampling rate at 500 Hz. The sequence length is not fixed, i.e. varies from 5, 000 to more than 40, 000 time points. Eight different diseases as well as normal condition are taken into account in this task, i.e. atrial fibrillation (AF), first degree A-V block(FDAVB), complete right bundle branch block (CRBBB), left anterior fascicular block (LAFB), premature ventricular contraction (PVC), premature atrial contraction (PAC), early repolarization (ER) and T-wave change (TWC). Since each patient may have multiple diseases, this is a multi-label classification task. From the provided dataset we can observe that the label distribution is extremely unbalanced among different labels, as is shown in Table 1.

Table 1. Sample number over nine categories.

Label	Normal	AF	FDAVB	CRBBB	LAFB	PVC	PAC	ER	TWC
Sample number	1953	504	534	826	180	654	672	224	2156

3   Methods

3.1   Data Pre-processing

In this section, we will introduce our method of data pre-processing, which in detail, includes data denoising and data augmentation.

Data Denoising. The ECG signals are recorded with electronic equipment, and as a result, noises are introduced in the recording process. In general, there are three types of noises in ECG signals: baseline drift, power frequency inference and electromyographical inference.

Baseline drift is generally caused by human respiration and its frequency is less than 5 Hz. The baseline drift can result in a 15% fluctuation of baseline, and can affect the localization of key points. To address the problem, we utilize median filter, and set the window width to be 500 points.

Power frequency inference is caused by power current and its frequency is 50 Hz. The electromyographical inference is caused by muscle vibration and its frequency can reach up to 2000 Hz. From the medical view, the main power of ECG is restricted in the range of 0 Hz to 35 Hz. To eradicate these two kinds of noises, we employ low-pass finite impulse response filter, and set the cut-off frequency to be 45 Hz.

The raw ECG signal and denoised ECG signal are shown in Fig. 1. It's clear that baseline drift is eliminated and high-frequency inference is reduced to a certain content.

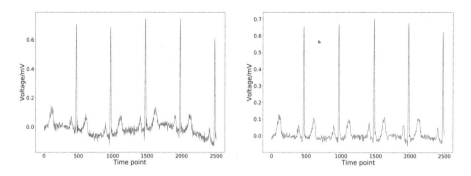

Fig. 1. The raw ECG signal and denoised ECG signal.

Data Augmentation. To address the problem of data insufficiency, we apply random start as a means of data augmentation. Suppose a piece of ECG signal as $\{t_1, t_2, \ldots, t_N\}$, where N is the length of ECG signal. Random start first randomly chooses a time point i as the new start, and concatenates $\{t_i, t_{i+1}, \ldots, t_N\}$ and $\{t_1, t_2, \ldots, t_{i-1}\}$ to form a new sequence.

Since the sequence length varies a lot in the dataset (i.e. from 5,000 to more than 40,000), we unify the sequence length to 40000. Specifically, for data with length less than 40000, we pad them by duplication; and for data with length more than 40000, we cut off the redundant part. We choose length of 40000 because it is a balance of computation efficiency and information retention.

3.2   Feature Engineering

As the size of the dataset is not large enough, traditional deep learning method tends to overfit the training set. To address this issue, we need to extract knowledge-based features to strengthen the generalization of our model.

ECG signals consist of a series of heartbeats and usually all heartbeats share a same pattern, i.e. a sequence of P wave, QRS complex and T wave. Therefore, we can try to describe the shape heartbeats by detecting several key points of the heartbeats. Based on years of research experience of doctors, there are several important points in a single heartbeat as shown in Fig. 2.

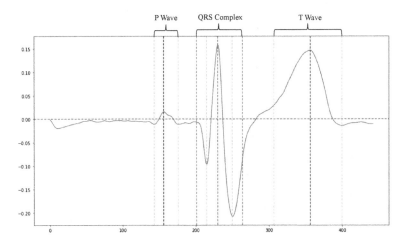

Fig. 2. The results of extracting key points from the signal of one single beat. (Color figure online)

– **Baseline.** For an ECG signal, there should be a baseline that the result of all measurements is the relative difference to it. As a result of median filtering, we simply use the horizontal zero line as the baseline in practice. (the green line in the Fig. 2)

- **QRS complex**. In Fig. 2, the part from the first light blue line to the second light blue line is called QRS complex, where R point is the highest point in the middle (the red line in the Fig. 2), while Q and S are the minimum points in the left and right parts of point R (the yellow line in the Fig. 2).
- **T wave** and **P wave**. Before the QRS complex, there is a small peak named P wave. Symmetrically, after the QRS complex, there is a higher peak named T wave. The maximum value, the width and other features of these two waves are also important for disease inference. In Fig. 2, the two yellow lines represent the begin and the end of these two waves, and the dark blue line represents the maximum point of these two waves.

After locating all key points in one single heartbeat, we can extract important features from the heartbeat. These features are summarized by experienced physicians, which are beneficial for automatic diagnosis. The selection of features follows the setting in [6], and the features include:

- **RR Interval**. The time difference between two adjacent R points, which is a direct representation of heart rate.
- **Amplitude of special points**. The amplitude of key points can directly reflex whether there exists abnormality in the signals. We calculate the amplitudes of R wave, S wave, T wave, the starting and ending position of T wave as the features of amplitudes. Moreover, the ratio of amplitude of R wave and S wave is also included in the features.
- **Time difference between special points**. The time difference between different points are also crucial for automatic diagnosis. Some illness like tachycardia and bradycardia can be directly detected by these features. As a result, we calculate the distance between several pairs of points as our features. (QS, RS, QR, RT, etc.)
- **Wavelet Decomposition Features**. We also apply wavelet decomposition to the signals of one beat to extract features at different frequencies.

After extracting these features, we should notice that the number of heartbeats in a ECG record varies a lot in the dataset. Consequently, there will be different number of features for different piece of data, which is hard for deep learning methods to handle. To address this issue, we calculate the minimum, maximum, average and variance of each feature, and as a result, we will generate a feature vector with dimension 356 for one lead ECG signal, and a feature vector with dimension $4,272$ for one piece of 12-lead ECG record.

3.3   Deep Learning Models

Deep learning models are utilized in our framework to extract features without human intervention. In this part, we will introduce two different deep learning models that we have explored in detail.

Attention-Based Sequential Model. Since ECG is essentially sequential signal, it is straightforward that we can use sequential models like Recurrent Neural Network (RNN) [10], Gated Recurrent Unit (GRU) [4] or Long Short Term Memory (LSTM) [8]. However, different from traditional sequential tasks in NLP, we only have 12 amplitudes for each time step which are not enough for sequential models to learn useful information from the data. To address this issue, we propose a two-stage sequential model. In the first stage, we divide the sequence to beat-level segments, and use Convolutional Neural Network (CNN) to extract features for each beat segment. The CNN in this stage is used as a beat encoder. In the second stage, we use LSTM on the encoded data at the previous stage to get the sequential features. As mentioned before, the data can be quite long so it's very hard to locate the most important part of the encoded results. To address this issue, we apply a self-attention module [13] to target the most important parts in the encoded results, and then use linear layer to predict the results.

1D Resnet. In computer vision field, Resnet is a widely used model and it has reached state-of-the- art in many computer vision tasks. However, Resnet is used in 2D images and cannot directly apply to our task. To address this issue, we propose a 1D Resnet for automatic diagnosis for ECG signals. The reason that we choose 1D Resnet is its bottleneck architecture, which allows the gradients to backpropagate freely in deep convolutional networks.

Specifically, the main changes we do is that we modify the 2D convolutional layers and the 2D pooling layers into 1D layers. However, in the origin settings of Resnet, it will encode the image with size 224×224 to a small feature map with size 7×7. This cannot be directly used in our task as the length of the signals may be longer than $10,000$ and it will result in the situation that the size of final feature vector is greater than 200. To solve this problem, we add several max pooling layers in the model to conduct repetitive down-sampling on the data, and finally apply an adaptive average pooling layer to feature vector and get the deep learning features from the ECG signals.

3.4 Overall Framework

From above, we can extract both human-designed features and deep-learning based features from ECG signals, and here we use a fully connected layer to integrate these two features and inference final diagnosis. The illustration figure of the overall framework is shown in Fig. 3.

It's noticeable that in Fig. 3, we use 1D Resnet instead of attention-based sequential model because we find that 1D Resnet performs slightly better than the other one.

To address the problem of label imbalance, we use different weight for each label in the loss function. The empirical value for each weight we adopt is half the value of the reciprocal of label proportion.

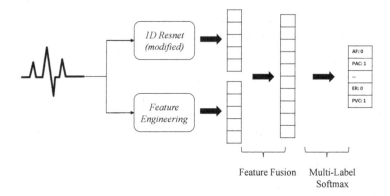

Fig. 3. Illustration figure of the overall framework.

3.5 Training

We adopt multi-label cross entropy as loss function, with optimizer to be Adam [9] and learning rate at 0.001. To prevent overfitting, we adopt dropout [12] and L2-regularization as well.

4 Competition Results

For now, the competition has finished the preliminary session and intermediary session.

In the intermediary session, we rank 19th among all 100 teams, and successfully enter the final stage to be held in August. The overall grade and detailed grade for each category is shown in Table 2.

Table 2. Intermediary results for intermediary session.

Label	Normal	AF	FDAVB	CRBBB	LAFB	PVC	PAC	ER	TWC	Overall
F1	84.79	96.96	90.33	98.08	68.22	96.79	86.12	72.58	75.67	85.50

5 Conclusion

In this paper, we propose an accurate automatic diagnosis framework. In this framework, features from both human-designed feature engineering and deep learning models are integrated together to inference final results, which means comprehensive features can be utilized in our framework. Competition results demonstrate that our method can reach accurate results in heart-related diseases inference.

In the future, we will focus on improving the interpretability of our automatic diagnosis framework.

Acknowledgements. The work was supported by the National Natural science Foundation of China (NSFC) Projects (Nos. 61673241, 61721003, 61872218), Beijing National Research Center for Information Science and Technology, Tsinghua-Fuzhou Institute research program, and Tsinghua Institute of Data Sciences.

References

1. The first China ECG intelligent competition. http://mdi.ids.tsinghua.edu.cn/#/. Accessed 25 June 2019
2. Acharya, U.R., et al.: A deep convolutional neural network model to classify heartbeats. Comput. Biol. Med. **89**, 389–396 (2017)
3. Chauhan, S., Vig, L.: Anomaly detection in ECG time signals via deep long short-term memory networks, pp. 1–7 (2015)
4. Cho, K., et al.: Learning phrase representations using RNN encoder-decoder for statistical machine translation. arXiv preprint arXiv:1406.1078 (2014)
5. Daamouche, A., Hamami, L., Alajlan, N., Melgani, F.: A wavelet optimization approach for ECG signal classification. Biomed. Signal Process. Control **7**(4), 342–349 (2012)
6. Feng, Y., Chen, W., Cai, G.: Feature extraction and identification of biometric information from ECG. Comput. Digit. Eng. **46**(6), 1099–1103 (2018)
7. Hannun, A., et al.: Cardiologist-level arrhythmia detection and classification in ambulatory electrocardiograms using a deep neural network. Nat. Med. **25**(1), 65–69 (2019)
8. Hochreiter, S., Schmidhuber, J.: Long short-term memory. Neural Comput. **9**(8), 1735–1780 (1997)
9. Kingma, D.P., Ba, J.: Adam: a method for stochastic optimization. In: Proceedings of the Third International Conference on Learning Representations (2015)
10. Mikolov, T., Karafiát, M., Burget, L., Černocký, J., Khudanpur, S.: Recurrent neural network based language model. In: Eleventh Annual Conference of the International Speech Communication Association (2010)
11. Pan, G., Xin, Z., Shi, S., Jin, D.: Arrhythmia classification based on wavelet transformation and random forests. Multimedia Tools Appl. **77**(17), 21905–21922 (2018)
12. Srivastava, N., Hinton, G., Krizhevsky, A., Sutskever, I., Salakhutdinov, R.: Dropout: a simple way to prevent neural networks from overfitting. J. Mach. Learn. Res. **15**(1), 1929–1958 (2014)
13. Vaswani, A., et al.: Attention is all you need. In: Advances in Neural Information Processing Systems, pp. 5998–6008 (2017)

Diagnosing Cardiac Abnormalities from 12-Lead Electrocardiograms Using Enhanced Deep Convolutional Neural Networks

Binhang Yuan[1] and Wenhui Xing[2(✉)]

[1] Rice University, Houston, TX, USA
by8@rice.edu
[2] Prudence Medical Technologies Ltd., Shanghai, China
wenhui@prudencemed.com

Abstract. We train an enhanced deep convolutional neural network in order to identify eight cardiac abnormalities from the standard 12-lead electrocardiograms (ECGs) using the dataset of 14000 ECGs. Instead of straightforwardly applying an end-to-end deep learning approach, we find that deep convolutional neural networks enhanced with sophisticated hand crafted features show advantages in reducing generalization errors. Additionally, data preprocessing and augmentation are essential since the distribution of eight cardiac abnormalities are highly biased in the given dataset. Our approach achieves promising generalization performance in the First China ECG Intelligent Competition; an empirical evaluation is also provided to validate the efficacy of our design on the competition ECG dataset.

Keywords: Electrocardiogram · Deep convolutional neural network · Heart disease diagnosis

1 Introduction

The electrocardiogram (ECG) is a diagnostic tool widely utilized for noninvasive diagnosis of various cardiovascular abnormalities in practice of clinical medicine worldwide. For example, there are approximately 250 million ECG recordings being processed by technicians for the diagnosis and treatment of patients with cardiovascular disease in China. The standard 12-lead electrocardiograms are the records of the heart's electrical activity collected from electrodes on arms/legs (known as limb leads) and torso (known as precordial leads). ECG interpretation plays an central role in the assessment of cardiovascular disease based on either a cardiologist's experience or computer-aided diagnosis systems. In practice, compute-aided interpretation has become increasingly important, since such technique improves the accuracy of diagnosis, facilitates health care decision making and reduces costs [17].

© Springer Nature Switzerland AG 2019
H. Liao et al. (Eds.): MLMECH 2019/CVII-STENT 2019, LNCS 11794, pp. 36–44, 2019.
https://doi.org/10.1007/978-3-030-33327-0_5

Traditionally, non-learning based approaches adopt wavelet, Fourier or other heuristic methods to classify specific abnormalities, but in practice these methods shows substantial rates of misdiagnosis [18]. Recently, deep neural networks (DNNs) [4] have led to great success of machine learning to resolve diversified learning problems, for example, time series classification [3]. There has also been success in applying deep convolutional neural networks (CNN) to detect cardiovascular abnormalities from single-lead ECGs [5] or 12-lead ECGs [9], where end-to-end CNN architectures are applied. On the other hand, we propose a novel deep neural network architecture enhanced by sophisticated hand crafted features, where such features are concatenated to the last fully connected layer in order to aid the activations from the original CNN to classify ECG signals.

Another significant challenge is to train models on the highly heterogeneous ECG dataset. The distribution of cardiovascular abnormalities is highly biased in the dataset, due to the fact that some cardiovascular diseases appear at very low frequencies, while others are relatively common in population. Additionally, even within the ECG signals labeled as the rare abnormal class, the abnormal morphology only appears sporadically. The heterogeneity of the dataset makes sophisticated data preprocessing and augmentation essential to achieve good generalization performance. In attempt to address this issue, we adopt the follow tricks: (i) the weights of different abnormal classes are adjusted according to their frequency; (ii) the noisy ranges of ECGs are removed before applying the CNN model; (iii) the signals are cropped according to a heuristic to augment the training dataset.

The specific contributions of this paper are highlighted as follows:

– A deep CNN model augmented by domain specific features in order to both improve the ability of fitting the ECG training dataset, and reduce the generalization error on the test dataset;
– A group of practical means of data preprocessing and augmentation in attempt to resolve the heterogeneity embedded in the ECG dataset;
– An empirical evaluation to corroborate the effectiveness and efficacy of our architecture on the competition ECG dataset.

In the end, we highlight that our approach achieves promising generalization performance in the First China ECG Intelligent Competition.

2   Dataset

The dataset described in this paper is provided in the rematch stage of the First China ECG Intelligent Competition [1]. ECGs are collected with sample rate of 500 Hz and recorded in a standard 12-lead format including six limb leads (I, II, III, aVL, aVR and aVF) and six precordial leads (V1, V2, V3, V4, V5 and V6). The length of the ECGs varies from 4500 to 30000 representing the record in real time from 9.5 s to 60 s. There are 6500 ECGs in the training dataset, 500 ECGs in the validation dataset, and 7000 ECGs in the test dataset.

The goal of the learning application is to identify 8 cardiovascular abnormalities including atrial fibrillation (AF), first-degree atrioventricular heart block (FDAVB), complete right bundle branch block (CRBBB), left anterior fascicular block (LAFB), premature ventricular contractions (PVC), premature atrial contractions (PAC), early repolarization (ER), T-wave changes (TWC) from the ECGs. Note that the labels of abnormalities are not mutually exclusive; in other word, a multi-label model is required to predict all possible diseases from an ECG. And if no abnormalities are detected, the model should indicate that this ECG is normal.

3   The Architecture

The architecture of our network is summarized in Fig. 1. The original 12-lead ECG signal is first denoised and then passed to the model. Heuristic features including QRS width, PR interval and standard deviation of the signal [8] are abstracted from the ECGs on one side. On the other side, the ECG data batch goes through a 96-layer convolutional neural network with 16 residual basic blocks [6]. Finally, the activations from the deep CNN will be flattened by global pooling layers, where the output will be concatenated with the heuristic features, and then will be utilized by a fully connected layer for the classifying task. Note that we encode a multi-label model where the parameters are shared for each abnormality instead of training 8 independent binary classifiers. We determine the layer number by choosing the shallowest network without compromising the generalization performance. Below we highlight a few important characters of our architecture.

3.1   Heuristic Features

Traditionally, computer-aided interpretation systems substantially depend on the heuristic features, however, these straightforward approaches usually suffer from high misdiagnosis rates. On the other hand, these heuristic features materialize important domain-specific knowledge from the cardiologist's experience. For example, QRS width (in other term of QRS complex) represents the duration of three graphical deflections (known as Q wave, R wave, and S wave) on an ECG, corresponding to the depolarization of the right and left ventricles of the human heart and contraction of the large ventricular muscles; RR interval measures the time elapsed between two successive R waves of the QRS signal on the ECG, representing the intrinsic properties of the sinus node as well as autonomic influences. We find that in practice, end-to-end deep learning approaches can also benefit from such features. In fact, one can view the deep convolutional residual blocks as a magical black box to automatically extract features purely based on the input data and label. As a result, we combine such features with the heuristic features as the input for the last fully connected layer of the classifier in order to further reduce the generalization error.

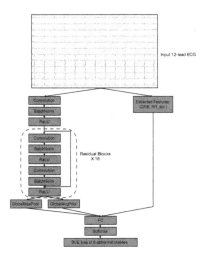

Fig. 1. The architecture of enhanced CNN. The CNN includes 16 residual basic blocks, where each residual blocks include 2 convolutional layers, 2 batch normalization layers [10], and 2 ReLU activation layers [15]. The output activations of the last residual block will be flattened by a global average pooling layer and a global max pooling layer. The concatenation of both global pooling layers and the abstracted features will be used by a fully connected layer. Lastly, the softmax function is applied before computing the binary cross entropy loss with the labels.

3.2 Global Pooling Layer

Global pooling layers are widely used in CNN models, which flatten the activation tensors to two-dimensional before input the activation to afterwards fully connected layers. Different pooling layers tend to preserve different properties from the input activation [2]. In general, max pooling takes the maximum activation in a block, which is good at retaining high frequency characteristics, while average pooling compresses the block by computing the mean of the block, which keeps the low frequency information. However, the detection of different abnormalities relies on different properties. For example, PAV and PVC only occurs in sporadic periods in the ECGs, which relies on infrequent properties, while other abnormalities (AF, FDAVB, CRBBB, LAFB, ER, and TWC) appears in every period in the ECGs. In order to get out of such dilemma, we compute both the global averaging pooling and global max pooling, and concatenate them for the later fully connected layer.

4   Details of Learning

In this section, we discuss the details of the learning procedure, including data preprocessing and augmentation methods, and the optimization hyper parameters applied in the competition.

4.1 Data Preprocessing

Since the abnormalities are substantially heterogenous from the competition dataset, we adjust the weights of each sample according to the frequency in the dataset so that the weighted loss function can emphasize the abnormal classes with less samples. Additionally, the input ECGs are usually interfered by various noises e.g. power line interference, baseline drift, electrode contact noise [11], etc. We apply a wavelet based ECG denoising method [12] to remove the noises from the input ECGs efficiently.

4.2 Data Augmentation

Importantly, the length of ECGs in the dataset varies in the dataset, naive approaches can be padding the short sequences with constant 0, or stochastically cropping the signal to a fixed length. However, padding will include uninformative segments; while random cropping will take the risk of missing the informative parts in the original signal. For example, PAC and PVC only occurs in some periods in each ECG, if such region is not retained, the model can never learn the desired knowledge from the training data. In attempt to address this issue, we propose an innovative **heuristic based cropping** approach aimed at ECG dataset augmentation, where we first locate the QRS complex in the ECGs, according to the power spectrum and a group of bandpass filters [14,16]; then the irregular QRS, T wave and P wave regions are marked as potentially problematic regions; finally only the cropping windows that include the potentially problematic regions for PAC and PVC are accepted, while other cropped ECGs will be rejected. We provide an illustrative example in Fig. 2.

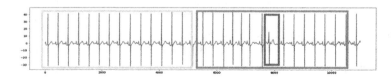

Fig. 2. An illustrative example of heuristic based cropping. The irregular range is marked by the red box, which potentially includes PAC or PVC. In the training phase, random cropping windows are generated, but only the window covers the marked region (eg., the green window above) are included in the training procedure, while the window excluding the marked range will be rejected (like the yellow box above). (Color figure online)

4.3 Optimization

The loss function we apply for optimization is the weighted binary cross entropy between the model's output and the label from the training set. We train our model for 70 epochs using Adam stochastic gradient descent (SGD) optimizer [13] with the batch size of 40, the learning rate of 0.0001 and the weight decay of

0.000001. The learning rate is divided by 5 when the validation error rate stops improving with the current learning rate. Note that we do not apply ensemble learning techniques to obtain the results reported in this paper, which in practice usually further improves the performance, while not preferred when proposing an innovative model.

5   Results

In this section, we will enumerate the detailed results.

Metric. The evaluation metric in the competition is the average F_1 score for 9 labels (8 abnormalities and norm). To be more specific, suppose the true positive, false positive, true negative, and false negative counts for label i are denoted as TP^i, FP^i, TN^i, and FP^i, respectively, then the precision, recall and F_1 score for label i are defined as:

$$Precision^i = \frac{TP^i}{TP^i + FP^i}$$

$$Recall^i = \frac{TP^i}{TP^i + FN^i}$$

$$F_1^i = \frac{2 Precision^i Recall^i}{Precision^i + Recall^i}$$

And the evaluation metric is the average F_1 score:

$$F_1 = \frac{1}{9} \sum_{i=0}^{8} F_1^i$$

The final score our team archives during the rematch stage is 0.879 according to the above definition of the evaluation metric.

Detailed Experimental Comparison. For the purpose of verifying our design, in Table 1, we illustrate the incremental development of our approach with the techniques described in Sects. 3 and 4. We first try an end-to-end deep CNN approach (ResNet with the same residual blocks in Fig. 1, but only including global average pooling before the final fc layer) where the F_1 score is 0.797. Then we augment the CNN architecture with the ECG domain-specific features mentioned in Sect. 3.1 and increase the F_1 score to 0.832. For above two benchmarks, random cropping is utilized to unify the signal length, and no data augmentation techniques are applied. Afterwards, we apply the heuristic data augmentation method introduced in Sect. 4.2 and improve the F_1 score further to 0.853. Finally, with the same data augmentation technique, we switch the global average pooling layer before the last fully connected layer to the combination of global average pooling and global max pooling as we detailed in Sect. 3.2 and achieve the final F_1 score of 0.879.

Table 1. F1 score of incremental development in our approach.

	ResNet	Feature enhanced	Data augmented	Final approach
Normal	0.835	0.873	0.900	0.914
AF	0.902	0.950	0.951	0.962
FDAWB	0.809	0.828	0.876	0.860
CRBBB	0.992	1.000	0.992	1.000
LAFB	0.842	0.812	0.889	0.944
PVC	0.849	0.844	0.915	0.965
PAC	0.625	0.776	0.860	0.874
ER	0.480	0.522	0.412	0.500
TWC	0.839	0.880	0.879	0.892
Average	0.797	0.832	0.853	0.879

Discussion. There are a couple of interesting points we want to emphasize from the above experiments. Firstly, after adopting the ECG domain specific features, we find that the F_1 score for each abnormality increases in general comparing to the naive end-to-end CNN approach, which suggests that such domain specific knowledge does help to extract information difficult to learn by the deep residual blocks. In fact, recent research tends to include more traditional features from signal processing to improve the generalization performance of deep learning models on time series analysis. For example, [19] includes frequency information by considering discrete Fourier transform to enhance LSTM [7].

Secondly, observe that there is a significant improvement of F_1 score for PVC and PAC after applying the heuristic based cropping technique for the training set augmentation, where PVC F_1 score increases from 0.844 to 0.915 and PAC F_1 score increases from 0.776 to 0.860. This confirms the speculation that simple preliminary detection of PVC and PAC abnormalities aids to generate training ECG samples with high quality, so that the learning process can be more effective.

Lastly, the combination of global average pooling and global max pooling layers also introduces a general enhancement of the F_1 score for each abnormality. We ascribe this improvement to the fact that the combination of two global pooling layers preserves more information from the convolution channels. As one can imagine, global pooling dramatically compresses the activations from the preceding residual blocks, which unavoidably losses information. The combination of the two global pooling layers keeps both low frequency information from average pooling and high frequency characteristics from max pooling. As a result, the fully connected layer afterwards can utilize them to improve the prediction accuracy.

6 Conclusion

We recapitulate the main contributions of this paper, where a deep convolutional neural network enhanced by domain specific features is proposed to classify 8 cardiac abnormalities from 12-lead ECGs; practical data preprocessing tricks and a heuristic ECG data augmentation method are introduced to handle the noise and heterogeneousness in the ECG datasets; empirical evaluations corroborating the effectiveness and efficacy of our architecture are enumerated.

In the future, we plan to accumulate more ECG data to validate the robustness of our proposed model so that this technique can be deployed in real clinical settings.

Acknowledgement. Thanks to the committee for their great effort of organizing the First China ECG Intelligent Competition and the anonymous reviewers for their insightful feedback on earlier versions of this paper.

References

1. The first edition of the artificial intelligence competition of cardiovascular disease diagnosis (2019). http://mdi.ids.tsinghua.edu.cn. Accessed 14 July 2019
2. Boureau, Y.L., Ponce, J., LeCun, Y.: A theoretical analysis of feature pooling in visual recognition. In: Proceedings of the 27th International Conference on Machine Learning (ICML-10), pp. 111–118 (2010)
3. Fawaz, H.I., Forestier, G., Weber, J., Idoumghar, L., Muller, P.A.: Deep learning for time series classification: a review. Data Min. Knowl. Discov. 1–47 (2019)
4. Goodfellow, I., Bengio, Y., Courville, A.: Deep Learning. MIT Press, Cambridge (2016)
5. Hannun, A.Y., et al.: Cardiologist-level arrhythmia detection and classification in ambulatory electrocardiograms using a deep neural network. Nat. Med. **25**(1), 65 (2019)
6. He, K., Zhang, X., Ren, S., Sun, J.: Deep residual learning for image recognition. In: Proceedings of the IEEE Conference on Computer Vision and Pattern Recognition, pp. 770–778 (2016)
7. Hochreiter, S., Schmidhuber, J.: Long short-term memory. Neural Comput. **9**(8), 1735–1780 (1997)
8. Holm, H., et al.: Several common variants modulate heart rate, PR interval and QRS duration. Nat. Genet. **42**(2), 117 (2010)
9. Hughes, J.W., Joseph, A.D., Gonzalez, J.E.: Using multitask learning to improve 12-lead electrocardiogram classification. arXiv preprint arXiv:1812.00497 (2018)
10. Ioffe, S., Szegedy, C.: Batch normalization: accelerating deep network training by reducing internal covariate shift. arXiv preprint arXiv:1502.03167 (2015)
11. Joshi, S.L., Vatti, R.A., Tornekar, R.V.: A survey on ECG signal denoising techniques. In: 2013 International Conference on Communication Systems and Network Technologies, pp. 60–64. IEEE (2013)
12. Khan, M., Aslam, F., Zaidi, T., Khan, S.A.: Wavelet based ECG denoising using signal-noise residue method. In: 2011 5th International Conference on Bioinformatics and Biomedical Engineering, pp. 1–4. IEEE (2011)

13. Kingma, D.P., Ba, J.: Adam: a method for stochastic optimization. arXiv preprint arXiv:1412.6980 (2014)
14. Kohler, B.U., Hennig, C., Orglmeister, R.: The principles of software qrs detection. IEEE Eng. Med. Biol. Mag. **21**(1), 42–57 (2002)
15. Nair, V., Hinton, G.E.: Rectified linear units improve restricted Boltzmann machines. In: Proceedings of the 27th International Conference on Machine Learning (ICML-10), pp. 807–814 (2010)
16. Pan, J., Tompkins, W.J.: A real-time QRS detection algorithm. IEEE Trans. Biomed. Eng. **32**(3), 230–236 (1985)
17. Schläpfer, J., Wellens, H.J.: Computer-interpreted electrocardiograms: benefits and limitations. J. Am. Coll. Cardiol. **70**(9), 1183–1192 (2017)
18. Shah, A.P., Rubin, S.A.: Errors in the computerized electrocardiogram interpretation of cardiac rhythm. J. Electrocardiol. **40**(5), 385–390 (2007)
19. Zhang, L., Aggarwal, C., Qi, G.J.: Stock price prediction via discovering multi-frequency trading patterns. In: Proceedings of the 23rd ACM SIGKDD International Conference on Knowledge Discovery and Data Mining, pp. 2141–2149. ACM (2017)

Transfer Learning for Electrocardiogram Classification Under Small Dataset

Longting Chen, Guanghua Xu$^{(\boxtimes)}$, Sicong Zhang, Jiachen Kuang, and Long Hao

Xi'an Jiaotong University, Xi'an 710049, People's Republic of China
ghxu@mail.xjtu.edu.cn

Abstract. The First China ECG Intelligent Competition is held by Tsinghua University. It is aimed to intelligently classify electrocardiogram (ECG) signals into two categories in preliminary and nine categories in rematch. The detailed ECG categories are listed in subsequent section. Our team proposes a deep residual network for diagnosing cardiovascular diseases automatically based on ECG, making full use of the network's hierarchical feature learning and feature representation ability. Considering that the amount of this competition data is small, especially in the stage of preliminary where there are only 600 training samples, while the deep learning-based method is data-hungry. Transfer learning idea is introduced into the training process of proposed deep neural networks. The proposed network is firstly trained on the Physionet/CinC Challenge 2017 dataset that is an open-public ECG data with single lead. Then it is continuously fine-tuned on the competition dataset with 12 leads. The performance of the proposed network is improved a lot. The proposed method achieves F_1 score of 0.89 and 0.86 in the hidden test set of preliminary and rematch, respectively. The research code will be released later.

Keywords: Electrocardiogram classification · Deep residual network · Transfer learning

1 Introduction

Electrocardiogram (ECG) records the electrical activity of heart. It becomes the most significant diagnosis tool for the detection of cardiovascular disease (CVD) that remains the leading cause of human death globally. Therefore, there is an urgent need to interpret ECG with high accuracy and automation.

Recently, many machine learning and pattern recognition based methods have been proposed for the detection and classification of arrhythmia. They are generally involved in three steps, i.e., preprocessing of ECG signal, feature extraction, and classifier construction. The ECG signal is firstly enhanced by removing some background noise or interference, such as the baseline wanders and muscle contraction. Then, the step of feature extraction is implemented on the enhanced ECG, centered on the five waves of ECG. These waves include P, Q, R, S, and T. P wave indicates atria depolarization. T wave represents the depolarization of ventricles. QRS complex describes ventricles depolarization [1]. Some hand-crafted and professional features are extracted on the

H. Liao et al. (Eds.): MLMECH 2019/CVII-STENT 2019, LNCS 11794, pp. 45–54, 2019.
https://doi.org/10.1007/978-3-030-33327-0_6

basis of these waves, such as PQ interval, RR interval, ST interval, TP interval, and so on. Eventually, these features are applied to learn the decision function of a classifier, by the use of support vector machine [2], random forest [3], neural networks [4], and so on. Even though these methods achieve great progress, they still perform not very well on clinical stage. Some cardiovascular diseases have similar ECG findings. Moreover, the ECG signal's amplitude is very small and it is easily contaminated by noise. These problems bring many obstacles to the intelligent diagnosis of cardiovascular diseases based on ECG.

To overcome these problems, our team puts forward an end-to-end deep residual network to classify ECG signals automatically, as a part of the First China ECG Intelligent Competition. The proposed network belongs to convolution neural networks (CNNs), which is one of the mainstream structures of deep neural networks (DNNs). Nowadays, DNNs has achieved great success with highly non-linear learning capacity in many domains, such as image classification [5], text recognition [6], natural language processing [7], as well as ECG classification [8–10]. Hannun et al. [8, 9] build up a 34-layer DNNs to classify 12 rhythm classes using 91232 single-lead ECGs. The performance of this model exceeds that of average cardiologists in terms of specificity and sensitivity. Zihlmann et al. [10] construct a convolution recurrent neural networks to detect atrial fibrillation and three other rhythms on the Physionet/CinC Challenge 2017 dataset that has 8528 single lead ECG recordings, with network input being logarithmic spectrogram of ECG. Eventually, this model obtains an overall F_1 score of 0.82 on these four classes. From these research cases, it is obvious that the above-mentioned deep models are trained and optimized on large ECG datasets. Meanwhile, these datasets contain only single lead ECGs, which is different from the real clinical scene where the collected ECGs are standard 12 leads. In preliminary, the First China ECG Intelligent Competition provides just 600 training samples that are so few that DNNs cannot be trained well from scratch.

Aimed at these issues, our team tries to connect this gap between single lead ECGs and 12 leads ECGs, and further train deep model in the provided small dataset. After all, the depth of representations is of central importance [5]. It is known that the reason why DNNs achieve huge progress in computer vision field is that many large datasets are available, such as Imagenet [11] and MS-COCO [12]. These datasets provide a good entrance to obtain useful pre-trained models that can be generalized well to other visual tasks. Inspired by this, the transfer learning thought is imported in the competition. Firstly, the proposed deep residual network is trained on the Physionet/CinC Challenge 2017 dataset [13], making the deep model have good initial weight parameters. After that, the model is continuously fine-tuned on the target dataset provided by organizing committee. The performance of the proposed deep residual network is enhanced a lot. Taking specificity and sensitivity into consideration simultaneously, the proposed method obtains F_1 score of 0.89 and 0.86 in the hidden test set of preliminary and rematch, respectively.

The rest of paper is organized as follows. The network structure and network training of the proposed deep model are given in Sect. 2. Section 3 describes the information of competition dataset in detail. In Sect. 4, the completion dataset is handled by the proposed method for validation its effectiveness. Finally, the conclusion is drawn in Sect. 5.

2 Methodology

In this section, we describe the network structure of the proposed deep residual network that is used for electrocardiogram classification, as well as training method and evaluation metric of this competition.

2.1 Deep Residual Network for Electrocardiogram Classification

Inspired by the work [8, 9], a novel deep residual network that is aimed at this competition is set up. Figure 1 shows the overall framework of it. The input of this network is the raw ECG signals that are processed by mean subtraction and variance normalization, without any hand-crafted or professional ECG-related features. The processed signal of each lead has zero mean and unit variance. The network input is 12 leads ECG signals, which are very close to standard in-clinic exams. The subsequent 33 convolution layers are applied to do hierarchical feature learning and feature representation of the preprocessed ECG, followed by one average pooling layer and one fully connected (FC) classification layer. The head convolution layer is specially designed because of pre-activation block adopted [14]. It is worth mentioning that the middle part of this network employs 16 residual sub-modules and each module contains one batch normalization layer and two convolution layers. These two technologies, i.e., residual structure [5] and batch normalization [15], can make DNNs deeper and easier to be trained. The former is able to propagate gradient information to more front layers, while the latter is capable of achieving a stable distribution of activation values and reducing internal covariate shift that are generated by the change of network parameters. The length of convolution kernels in all convolution layers is set to 16. The activation function is selected as rectified linear unit (ReLU), i.e., $\sigma(x) = \max(0,x)$.

The optimization of network parameters is driven by predefined cost function. In here, the cross entropy loss is adopted since this competition is aimed at electrocardiogram classification issue. The competition dataset provided by organizing committee is denotes as $\{(x^{(i)}, y^{(i)})|i = 1, 2, 3, \ldots, N\}$. The symbol N represents the number of ECG samples. $\mathbf{x}^{(i)} = (x_1, x_2, x_3, \ldots, x_L)$ and $y^{(i)} \in \{1, 2, \ldots, C\}$. L and C denote the length of ECG and ECG types, respectively. In the stage of preliminary, there are two kinds of ECG. One is the normal, the other is the abnormal. In rematch, there are nine ECG types, i.e., normal (N), atrial fibrillation (AF), first degree atrioventricular block (FDAVB), complete right bundle branch block (CRBBB), left anterior fascicular block (LAFB), premature ventricular contraction (PVC), premature atrial contraction (PAC), early repolarization pattern change (ERPC), and T wave change (TWC). Then the cost function can be expressed as follows:

$$J(\theta) = -\frac{1}{N}\sum_{i=1}^{N}\sum_{j=1}^{C} 1\{y^{(i)} = j\}\log P(\bar{y}^{(i)} = j|\mathbf{x}^{(i)}) + \frac{\lambda}{2}R(\theta) \tag{1}$$

where θ is the weight parameters; $P(\bar{y}^{(i)} = j|\mathbf{x}^{(i)})$ is the estimated probability of $i-th$ ECG sample belonging to j class; $R(\theta)$ is the regularization term of parameters θ; λ is the weight decay factor.

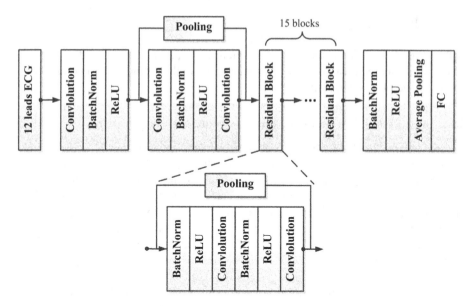

Fig. 1. The proposed deep residual network for electrocardiogram classification.

2.2 Network Training

In general, the whole network is optimized by back propagation (BP) algorithm. It is trained from scratch initially. The weight is initialized by the method described in [16]. The optimizer is selected as Adam and the initial learning rate is set to 0.01 with batch size being 32. The learning rate is decayed by a factor of 0.1 when the cross entropy loss stops falling. In order to choose the best model and avoid overtraining model, the original competition dataset is divided into two parts, i.e., training set and validation set. The ratio between them is 9:1. Consequently, the selected best model performs very well in the divided training set and not well in the validation set. The model is also not in the over-fitting status since the loss of validation set still decreases slowly, which indicates that the model cannot be trained completely in this small dataset.

Aimed at this problem, our team determines to introduce transfer learning idea into the training process of the proposed deep residual network. Firstly, the number of input channels in input layer is change to 1. Then the entire network is trained on the Physionet/CinC Challenge 2017 dataset that is an open-public ECG dataset with single lead. The number of classes in the output layer is set to 2 that corresponds to normal rhythm class and abnormal rhythm class. After that, the number of input channels in input layer is set to 12, matching this competition dataset. The deep model continues to be trained on this competition dataset with weight parameters initialized by the above pre-trained weights. It is worth mentioning that the parameters in the first convolution layer and the last FC layer of pre-trained weights are cut off. Eventually, the performance of this model is improved a lot. The model achieves comparable results on the validation set, compared with that on the training set.

2.3 Evaluation Metric

This competition focuses on ECG classification. Naturally, organizing committee adopts a multi-label classification based scoring method [17]. The phenomenon that one ECG may contain multiple exceptions is taken into consideration. The classification performance is measured using the average F_1 score over all classes. For each class $j \in \{1, 2, \ldots, C\}$, the F_{1j} metric is calculated as follows:

$$P_j = \frac{TP_j}{TP_j + FP_j} \tag{2}$$

$$R_j = \frac{TP_j}{TP_j + FN_j} \tag{3}$$

$$F_{1j} = \frac{2 \times P_j \times R_j}{P_j + R_j} \tag{4}$$

where P and R represent precision and recall, respectively. TP, FP and FN denote true positive, false positive and false negative, respectively. Then, the final score is computed by:

$$F_1 = \frac{1}{C} \sum_{j=1}^{C} F_{1j} \tag{5}$$

3 Dataset

There are some differences between preliminary dataset and rematch dataset. The former just contains two types of ECG signals and each ECG signal is single label, while the latter includes nine ECG classes and some of ECG samples are multi-label. Considering that the rematch dataset is not open-public, our team takes preliminary dataset as an example to evaluate and analyze the performance of the proposed deep model in detail. The result on the rematch dataset is also reported in later section.

In preliminary, there are 1000 conventional resting electrocardiograms collected, with sampling frequency being 500 Hz. Each of them lasts 10 s. The collected ECG signals are 12 leads (I, II, III, aVR, aVL, aVF, V1, V2, V3, V4, V5, V6), which are very close to real clinic practice. Among them, 600 samples are used as training set and 400 samples serve as hidden test set. The number of normal ECG samples and abnormal ECG samples are each half. Every sample is annotated by cardiologists. Figure 2 shows one normal ECG sample and one abnormal ECG sample. The detailed information of this dataset can be found in [18]. The original visible dataset is partitioned into training set and validation set at ratio 9:1.

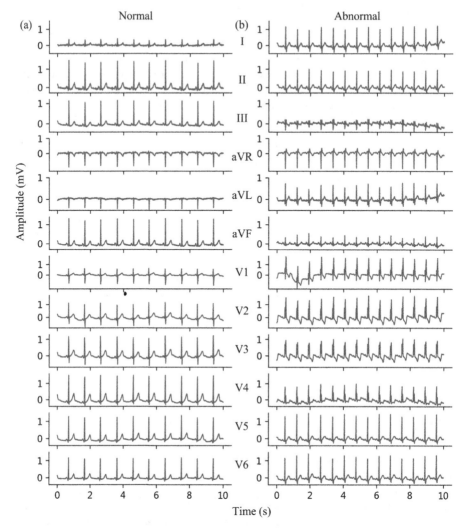

Fig. 2. (a) Normal ECG sample and (b) abnormal ECG sample in preliminary dataset.

The Physionet/CinC Challenge 2017 dataset is also employed for obtaining pre-trained weights. It is made up of 8528 ECG records with single lead. The sampling frequency is 300 Hz. The duration of these records varies largely, from 9 s to 30 s. There are 4 ECG classes contained in this dataset, i.e., noisy, normal, atrial fibrillation and other rhythms. More information about this dataset can be known in [13]. The noisy records are removed out, and the atrial fibrillation records and other rhythms records are considered to be abnormal class in the first pre-training stage.

4   Results

Based on the structural parameters described in Sect. 2, the proposed deep residual network is built up. Firstly, this network is trained from scratch on the divided training set of the First China ECG Intelligent Competition. Figure 3 shows the cross entropy loss of training set and validation set in red solid line and black solid line, respectively. It is clear that the performance of the model varies greatly between these two datasets, and the loss of validation set cannot be decreased even though the learning rate is decayed continuously, which indicates that the model is in a state of incomplete training. After all, the amount of training samples is too small to train such a deep model.

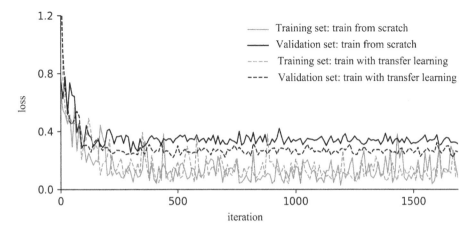

Fig. 3. The proposed deep residual network is trained on the divided training set and evaluated on the validation set. The solid lines represent cross entropy loss obtained by the model that is trained from scratch, while the dotted lines denote cross entropy loss obtained by the model that is trained with transfer learning. (Color figure online)

To weaken above-mentioned problem, the training approach with transfer learning that is stated in Sect. 2.2 is employed. Figure 3 plots the changes of cross entropy loss of training set and validation set in dotted lines. It is obvious that the loss of validation set is reduced a lot. The best models that are trained by above two ways are selected based on maximizing F_1. Figure 4 shows the precision-recall curves of them. It can be seen that the model trained with transfer learning achieves high precision while achieving high recall. The final scores on validation set are listed in Table 1. The performance of the proposed deep model increases by 4% points in terms of F_1 and 5% points considering accuracy. Finally, the proposed model obtains F_1 score of 0.89 and 0.86 in the hidden test set of preliminary and rematch, respectively. Detailed scores on hidden test set of rematch are listed in Table 2.

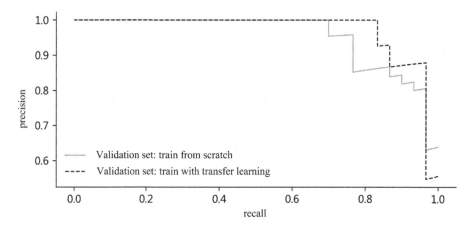

Fig. 4. The precision-recall curves of the best models on the validation set. The red solid line represents the precision-recall curve of the best model that is trained from scratch, while the black dotted line denotes the precision-recall curve of the best model that is trained with transfer learning. (Color figure online)

Table 1. Final scores on the validation set.

	Accuracy	P	R	F_1
Train from scratch	0.87	0.84	0.90	0.87
Train with transfer learning	0.92	1.00	0.83	0.91

Table 2. Final scores on the hidden test set of rematch.

N	AF	FDAVB	CRBBB	LAFB	PVC	PAC	ER	TWC	F_1
0.85	0.98	0.92	0.98	0.74	0.96	0.91	0.70	0.74	0.86

5 Conclusion

In order to improve the recognition accuracy of electrocardiogram under small dataset and take fully advantage of deep model, our team proposes a deep residual network and introduces transfer learning idea into the training process of this network. The input of this network is just raw ECG signals that are processed by standard normalization, without any hand-crafted and professional features. The effectiveness of the model and the training approach is verified on the First China ECG Intelligent Competition dataset. It is worth mentioning that the pre-trained weight is obtained on the single lead ECG dataset and it works on the standard 12 leads competition dataset that is very close to realistic clinical setting. This research shortens the gap between single lead ECG and standard 12 lead ECG, and provides a promising idea to solve ECG recognition problem with small samples.

Acknowledgements. This research is supported by grant with number 51775415, 2017YFC1308500, and 2018ZDCXL-GY-06-01. Thank Tsinghua University and other member of the organizing committee for providing ECG dataset and platform.

References

1. Warrick, P., Homsi, M.N.: Cardiac arrhythmia detection from ECG combining convolutional and long short-term memory networks. In: 2017 Computing in Cardiology (CinC), pp. 1–4. IEEE (2017)
2. Khazaee, A., Ebrahimzadeh, A.: Classification of electrocardiogram signals with support vector machines and genetic algorithms using power spectral features. Biomed. Signal Process. Control **5**, 252–263 (2010)
3. Li, T., Zhou, M.: ECG classification using wavelet packet entropy and random forests. Entropy **18**(8), 285 (2016)
4. Jadhav, S.M., Nalbalwar, S.L., Ghatol, A.: Artificial neural network based cardiac arrhythmia classification using ECG signal data. In: International Conference on Electronics and Information Engineering (ICEIE), pp. V1-228–V1-231 (2010)
5. He, K., Zhang, X., Ren, S., Sun, J.: Deep residual learning for image recognition. In: Proceedings of the IEEE Conference on Computer Vision and Pattern Recognition, pp. 770–778 (2016)
6. Shi, B., Bai, X., Yao, C.: An end-to-end trainable neural network for image-based sequence recognition and its application to scene text recognition. IEEE Trans. Pattern Anal. Mach. Intell. **39**(11), 2298–2304 (2017)
7. Young, T., Hazarika, D., Poria, S., Cambria, E.: Recent trends in deep learning based natural language processing. IEEE Comput. Intell. Mag. **13**(3), 55–75 (2018)
8. Hannun, A.Y., et al.: Cardiologist-level arrhythmia detection and classification in ambulatory electrocardiograms using a deep neural network. Nat. Med. **25**(1), 65–69 (2019)
9. Rajpurkar, P., Hannun, A.Y., Haghpanahi, M., Bourn, C., Ng, A.Y.: Cardiologist-level arrhythmia detection with convolutional neural networks. arXiv preprint arXiv:1707.01836 (2017)
10. Zihlmann, M., Perekrestenko, D., Tschannen, M.: Convolutional recurrent neural networks for electrocardiogram classification. In: 2017 Computing in Cardiology (CinC), pp. 1–4. IEEE (2017)
11. Deng, J., Dong, W., Socher, R., Li, L.-J., Li, K., Fei-Fei, L.: ImageNet: a large-scale hierarchical image database. In: Proceedings of the IEEE Conference on Computer Vision and Pattern Recognition, pp. 248–255 (2009)
12. Lin, T.-Y., et al.: Microsoft COCO: common objects in context. In: Fleet, D., Pajdla, T., Schiele, B., Tuytelaars, T. (eds.) ECCV 2014. LNCS, vol. 8693, pp. 740–755. Springer, Cham (2014). https://doi.org/10.1007/978-3-319-10602-1_48
13. Clifford, G.D., et al.: AF Classification from a short single lead ECG recording: the PhysioNet/computing in cardiology challenge 2017. In: 2017 Computing in Cardiology (CinC), pp. 1–4. IEEE (2017)
14. He, K., Zhang, X., Ren, S., Sun, J.: Identity mappings in deep residual networks. In: Leibe, B., Matas, J., Sebe, N., Welling, M. (eds.) ECCV 2016. LNCS, vol. 9908, pp. 630–645. Springer, Cham (2016). https://doi.org/10.1007/978-3-319-46493-0_38
15. Ioffe, S., Szegedy, C.: Batch normalization: accelerating deep network training by reducing internal covariate shift. arXiv preprint arXiv:1502.03167 (2015)

16. He, K., Zhang, X., Ren, S., Sun, J.: Delving deep into rectifiers: surpassing human-level performance on imagenet classification. In: Proceedings of the IEEE International Conference on Computer Vision, pp. 1026–1034. IEEE (2015)
17. Zhang, M., Zhou, Z.: A review on multi-label learning algorithms. IEEE Trans. Knowl. Data Eng. **26**(8), 1819–1837 (2014)
18. The First China ECG Intelligent Competition dataset, http://mdi.ids.tsinghua.edu.cn. Accessed 1 July 2019

Multi-label Classification of Abnormalities in 12-Lead ECG Using 1D CNN and LSTM

Chengsi Luo, Hongxiu Jiang, Quanchi Li, and Nini Rao$^{(\boxtimes)}$

School of Life Science and Technology,
University of Electronic Science and Technology of China,
Chengdu, Sichuan, People's Republic of China
raonn@uestc.edu.cn

Abstract. In this study, we proposed a method based on Convolutional Neural Network (CNN) and Long Short-Term Memory (LSTM) to classify 12-lead ECG into 9 categories (1 normal, 8 abnormal). The only preprocessing techniques we used are the baseline drift removal based on median filtering and signal segmentation. Then an 18-layer deep 1D CNN consisting of residual blocks and skip architectures that is followed by a bi-directional LSTM layer was developed. During the training session, we suggested a new strategy to compute the Dice loss for multi-label classification. The average F1-score we achieved on the hidden testing dataset of the First China ECG Intelligent Competition (FCEIC) is 85.11%. With the same model, we achieved 82.21% (5-fold cross-validation) on the Chinese physiological signal challenge 2018 (CPSC2018) training dataset.

Keywords: ECG classification · Convolutional Neural Network · Dice loss · Long Short-Term Memory

1 Introduction

Cardiovascular disease (CVD) is one of the main causes of premature deaths and disabilities in the world, accounting for 44% of all noncommunicable diseases (NCDs) deaths according to World Health Organization (WHO) [1]. Recently, many studies have been using deep learning technology in signal modalities from cardiology due to its high accuracy and effectiveness [2]. Gotlibovych et al. [3] designed a convolutional-recurrent neural network architecture with LSTM to detect atrial fibrillation in multi-channel photoplethysmography (PPG) data. There are others [4, 5] who also used CNN with LSTM to classify the arbitrary-length or real-time physiological signals. The 1D CNN with residual blocks has been used in this field as well [6–8]. Hannun et al. [8] is a pioneer among them. They developed a 34-layer end-to-end deep 1D CNN with residual blocks to classify 12 rhythms, including 10 arrhythmias from single-lead ECG, and the results they achieved exceeded cardiologists.

Inspired by the studies mentioned above, we proposed a deep neural network architecture that combines 1D CNN with bi-directional LSTM layer to classify 9 types of the 12-lead ECG signals. This work was done and evaluated in the FCEIC [9].

© Springer Nature Switzerland AG 2019
H. Liao et al. (Eds.): MLMECH 2019/CVII-STENT 2019, LNCS 11794, pp. 55–63, 2019.
https://doi.org/10.1007/978-3-030-33327-0_7

Since it's an online competition, the training dataset could only be accessed on the Cloud Desktop. In order to further validating our work, we also used the dataset provided by the CPSC2018 [10, 11].

2   Methods

2.1   Data Description

The training set in the FCEIC contains 6500 recordings, ranging from 10 to 91 s, sampled at 500 Hz. The hidden testing set contains 8000 similar recordings. There are 9 categories of ECG to be classified: (1) Normal (N), (2) Atrial fibrillation (AF), (3) First-degree atrioventricular block (AVB), (4) Complete right bundle branch block (CRBBB), (5) Left anterior fascicular block (LAFB), (6) Premature ventricular contraction (PVC), (7) Premature atrial contraction (PAC), (8) Early repolarization (ER), (9) T wave changes (TWC), and each recording might have more than one label. The CPSC2018 training dataset has 9 categories as well, the differences are: (1) length of recordings in CPSC2018 are ranging from 6 to 60 s; (2) instead of CRBBB, LAFB, ER mentioned above, the CPSC2018 have Left bundle branch block (LBBB), Right bundle branch block (RBBB), and the TWC is divided into ST-segment depression (STD) and ST-segment elevated (STE).

2.2   Architectures

The architecture of our approach consists of four parts: (1) data preprocessing, removing baseline drift and slicing the arbitrary-length ECG to a fixed number of segments with equal length of 2048; (2) weight-sharing CNN to extract the features of each segment; (3) a bi-directional LSTM followed by global pooling to integrate the features across time; (4) fully connected layer with sigmoid for predicting the class label. Figure 1 illustrates an overview of our approach.

Preprocessing. We first used the median filter to remove baseline drift from raw ECG data before the signal segmentation. Even though Gotlibovych et al. [3] found the first convolutional layer can perform as a high-pass filter, we believe in multi-lead situation the convolutional layer can also combine different leads, in which using removal of baseline drift can make it more efficient and preserve more information. The window size is a crucial factor of the median filter since windows of short duration can deliver an estimation that is a mixture of true ECG and baseline [12]. We chose 501 as the window size, which approximately equal to the sampling rate.

The left part of Fig. 1 provides an illustration of signal segmentation. The number of segments N and the length of each segments l is fixed. Since the length of the ECG L is arbitrary, the intervals between adjacent segments were calculated by Eq. 1 to cover as many signal areas as possible.

$$\left\lfloor \frac{(L-l)}{N-1} \right\rfloor \tag{1}$$

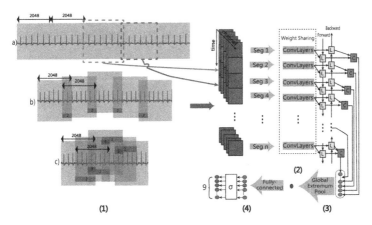

Fig. 1. Overview of our approach: (1) Signal segmentation with or without overlaps for 12-lead ECG. (2) Weight-sharing CNN. (3) Features integration by a bi-directional LSTM and global pooling. (4) Fully connected layer with sigmoid.

There are three cases of signal segmentation: (a) there is no overlap between signal segments; (b) only adjacent segments overlap; (c) the same overlap exists in three or more continuous signal segments. Obviously, the smaller the length of ECG, the larger the overlap area, which could be seen as data augmentation for short ECG.

Weight-Sharing CNN. The CNN is for feature extraction. Each segment from the previous step is fed to the 1D CNN sharing the same parameters. The network architecture has 18 layers and 4 residual blocks, the latter was constructed in a way similar to Hannun et al. [8]. Except that the first residual block contains 2 convolutional layers, the rest of three blocks contain 4 convolutional layers. The width of filters is fixed with 4 throughout the whole network. The number of filters per convolutional layer begins with 12, and after the first residual block, it doubles at the second convolutional layers in every residual block. The subsampling rates of the first and last layers of the network are 2. In addition, except the first residual block, the sub-sampling rates of the first and second convolutional layers in every residual block are 2 as well. We applied ELU [13] as activation function for convolutional layers without batch normalization. The dropout layers with rate of 0.2 were used to prevent overfitting.

As can be seen from Fig. 2, the first convolutional layer consists of 3 concatenated separable convolution layers with different dilation rate of 1, 4 and 8 respectively, and each of them contains 3 filters. The separable convolution, performing a spatial (temporal) convolution independently over each channel of input, followed by a pointwise convolution, can be seen as extreme form of an Inception module [14]. However, as for 12-lead ECG, we can understand it in a different view. It is well known that there is information redundancy in the standard 12-lead ECG, and Vectorcardiography (VCG) is superior to ECG in the diagnosis. Edenbrand et al. [15] found a way to synthesize a12-lead ECG into 3-lead VCG by Inverse Dower Matrix, which can be seen as a linear combination of different leads, sharing the characteristic of separable convolution layers. Thus, we can implicitly treat the separable convolution layers as a linear adder to synthesize 12-lead ECG, with an extra function of filtering.

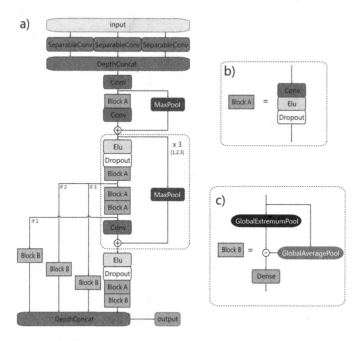

Fig. 2. The proposed 1D CNN architecture: (a) The whole architecture. (b) Structure of Block A. (c) Structure of Block B.

The abnormalities in ECG can be fine (i.e. R-wave morphology) or coarse (i.e. f waves in atrial fibrillation). Then, drawing inspiration from FCN [16], there are skip architectures in our network as well. Structures of Block B between low layers to the output layers, play the roles of skips. In Block B, we defined a new global pooling strategy, we call this "GlobalExtremumPool (GEP)", which could refer from the study by Saeedan et al. [17]. Slightly different from them, GEP in our study selects the extremum that stands out most from zero globally. Moreover, Clevert et al. [13] implied ELU could saturate the degree of presence of particular phenomena of input to negative value with smaller arguments, and the GEP can obtain this information. However, the whole Block B is similar to the ExtremumPool described by Saeedan, where the output of GEP subtracts the output of GlobalAveragePool, following by dimension reduction procedure that is the fully connected layer with 6 neurons. In ECG, there are many similarities between signals, we assume this subtraction strategy would alleviate the effect of it by automatically masking the insignificant value. The output layer consists of 4 concatenated output of fully connected layer, which would feed to the input of LSTM cell.

Features Integration. Studies [3–5, 18] have shown LSTM could be a good solution for integrating the features across time for physiological signals. Further, bi-directional

LSTM [19] could be a better solution for our study, since each cell of it can concatenate hidden states with past and future information through forward and backward streams. Subsequently, GEP mentioned above would synthesize the hidden states over all time steps.

2.3   Training

We implemented our network in Keras [22] framework. The Adam optimizer was employed during the training session, and the batch size was 64.

Loss Function. We employed the Dice loss that is mathematically equivalent to the F1 measure, can alleviate the class imbalance issue without sample weighting, which is suitable for multi-label classification. However, it is particularly sensitive to the category with small sample size and consequently causes the instability during training. Unlike some studies handled this issue by combining it with other loss [20, 21], we proposed a simple strategy to compute it by combining the sample-wise Dice loss with class-wise Dice loss inside a mini-batch. If there are J classes and the number of samples in each mini-batch is I, the proposed Dice loss can be written as:

$$L = -\frac{1}{I}\sum_{i=1}^{I}\frac{\sum_{j=1}^{J}p_{ij}g_{ij}}{\sum_{j=1}^{J}\left(p_{ij}+g_{ij}\right)} - \frac{1}{J}\sum_{j=1}^{J}\frac{\sum_{i=1}^{I}p_{ij}g_{ij}+s}{\sum_{i=1}^{I}\left(p_{ij}+g_{ij}\right)+s} \tag{2}$$

Where p_{ij} is the predicted label of i-th sample that belongs to the j-th class, g_{ij} is the ground-truth label of i-th sample, which means the real labels of i-th sample contain the j-th class or not. And s is a small number ($s = 1e{-}07$) to prevent division by zero. The right part of Eq. 2 is the combination of class-wise and sample-wise Dice loss, the latter can be seen as a smoother way to calculate by averaging each sample's Dice loss, which may alleviate the instability of the class-wise while keeping the nature of it.

3   Results

The label-based metric, macro-averaging F_1, was used to measure the classification performance, the detail of which can be found in [9, 23]. Table 1 shows the results obtained from the FCEIC's hidden testing dataset and CPSC2018 (using 5-fold cross validation). Considering the length of recordings, there is a slight difference between the models we used on two datasets. The average length of recordings in the first dataset are longer, so we set the N (described in the Preprocessing, Sect. 2.2) to 22, resulting in the bi-directional LSTM have 22 time steps. As for the second one, we set N to 16.

Table 1. The macro-averaging F_1 (in %) in two different dataset.

Dataset	N	AF	AVB	CRBB	LAFB	PVC	PAC	ER	TWC	Avg
FCEIC	85.3	97.0	91.6	97.7	66.4	95.3	90.0	72.3	70.4	85.1
CPSC2018	–	–	–	LBBB	RBBB	–	–	STD	STE	–
	80.6	91.8	88.1	90.0	92.5	84.5	72.7	78.2	61.5	82.2

Comparison Between Different Methods. We also used the F_1' defined in CPSC2018 [11] to evaluate our performance, which only takes one predicting label for each recording into account, that is, when a recording has multiple labels, either of these was correctly identified would be seen as a True Positive prediction. Under the criteria of this, we compared our methods with Liu et al. [7] and He et al. [11]. The former assembled handcrafted features and CNN features together to do classification, while the latter is the top scorer in CPSC2018. The results of Liu et al. obtained by 5-fold cross validation on CPSC2018 training dataset, which was the same as us, whereas He et al. was on the public validation set of CPSC2018. Even so, it can be deduced from Table 2 that our method is robust under this criteria.

Table 2. Comparison between different methods using the F_1' (in %) defined in CPSC2018.

Methods	N	AF	AVB	LBBB	RBBB	PVC	PAC	STD	STE	Avg
Liu	**82.0**	91.0	87.0	87.0	91.0	82.0	63.0	81.0	60.0	81.0
He	74.8	**92.0**	88.2	88.9	88.3	85.1	**78.7**	78.0	**78.0**	83.6
Ours	81.0	**92.0**	**88.5**	**91.5**	**93.4**	**86.6**	74.5	**81.7**	65.5	**83.9**

Experimental Results. We conducted four controlled experiments to evaluate the effectiveness of GEP, the subtraction operation of two global pools and loss function we proposed, respectively. Four of the conditions were all estimated on the CPSC2018 training dataset. As shown in Table 3: condition 1 used the GEP without the subtracting operation; condition 2 was using the GlobalMaxPool instead of GEP with the subtracting operation; condition 3 only used the GlobalAveragePool. Three conditions above were all applied inner Block B. Condition 4 used the ordinary Dice loss. The results support our claim about the benefit of these proposed methods.

Table 3. The macro-averaging F_1 (in %) under different conditions

Condition	N	AF	AVB	LBBB	RBBB	PVC	PAC	STD	STE	Avg
1	80.1	91.7	87.0	89.2	**92.5**	81.9	70.3	78.0	58.2	81.0
2	**81.5**	90.7	87.1	86.6	**92.5**	83.5	70.0	77.9	60.2	81.1
3	80.7	**91.9**	87.2	88.9	92.4	83.4	70.4	78.0	56.0	81.0
4	80.4	91.1	87.1	89.5	92.1	82.7	**73.4**	77.7	58.8	81.4
Full model	80.6	91.8	**88.1**	**90.0**	92.5	**84.5**	72.7	**78.2**	**61.5**	**82.2**

According to the definition of our Dice loss in Eq. 2, the impact of the batch size on the performance might be significant. Therefore, we chose the batch size of 16, 32, 64, 96 and 128 to investigate it. As illustrated by Fig. 3, the best performance is achieved at the batch size of 32, where F_1 and F_1' are 82.5% and 84.2% respectively, which is better than the 64 used before. And when batch size is larger than 32, the scores decrease as batch size increases. We thought that the increase of batch size would create the over-smooth caused by the sample-wise Dice loss, and we may tackle this issue by decreasing the weight of it. Conversely, samples from small classes may not be included in the mini-batch if the batch size is too small, causing performance degradation, as in the case of 16.

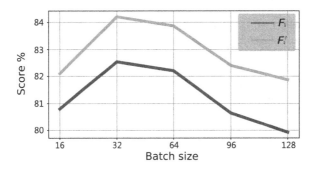

Fig. 3. Performances of using different batch size

4   Conclusion and Discussion

We developed a deep neural network architecture for multi-label classification of abnormalities in 12-lead ECG. As two important parts, 1D CNN for feature extraction and bi-directional LSTM for feature integration, constitute the network. Several approaches, such as GEP, subtraction operation of two global pools and modified Dice loss, were used to improve the performance of our work. The evaluations we did on two datasets and in several controlled experiments are showing the effectiveness of our approaches. In addition, it is worth to mention that the number of parameters in our network is only 183,954, which is quite competitive compared to the previous studies.

However, some approaches used in this study have not yet been verified. Such as the separable convolution in 12-lead ECG, could it be a more effective way to transform the 12-lead ECG rather than the Dower Matrix? And the dilation rate larger than one might cause gridding artifacts, is there a better way to do? These all could be our future directions for improvement.

Acknowledgments. This work was supported by National Natural Science Foundation of China (Grant No. 61872405 and 61720106004), Key Project of Natural Science Foundation of Guangdong province (2016A030311040), Sichuan Science and Support Program (Grant No. 2015SZ0191) and Chengdu Science and Technology Benefit Plan (2015-HM01-00528-SF).

References

1. World Health Organization: World health statistics 2018: Monitoring Health for the SDGs sustainable development goals. WHO (2018)
2. Bizopoulos, P., Koutsouris, D.: Deep learning in cardiology. IEEE Rev. Biomed. Eng. **12**, 168–193 (2019). https://doi.org/10.1109/RBME.2018.2885714
3. Gotlibovych, I., et al.: End-to-end deep learning from raw sensor data: atrial fibrillation detection using wearables. arXiv preprint arXiv:1807.10707 (2018)
4. Zihlmann, M., Perekrestenko, D., Tschannen, M.: Convolutional recurrent neural networks for electrocardiogram classification. In: 2017 Computing in Cardiology Conference (CinC) (2017)
5. Bashivan, P., Rish, I., Yeasin, M., Codella, N.: Learning representations from EEG with deep recurrent-convolutional neural networks. arXiv preprint arXiv:1511.06448 (2015)
6. Sellami, A., Hwang, H.: A robust deep convolutional neural network with batch-weighted loss for heartbeat classification. Expert Syst. Appl. **122**, 75–84 (2019). https://doi.org/10.1016/j.eswa.2018.12.037
7. Liu, Z., Meng, X.A., Cui, J., Huang, Z., Wu, J.: Automatic identification of abnormalities in 12-lead ECGs using expert features and convolutional neural networks. In: 2018 International Conference on Sensor Networks and Signal Processing (SNSP), pp. 163–167. IEEE (2018)
8. Hannun, A.Y., et al.: Cardiologist-level arrhythmia detection and classification in ambulatory electrocardiograms using a deep neural network. Nat. Med. **25**, 65–69 (2019). https://doi.org/10.1038/s41591-018-0268-3
9. The First China ECG Intelligent Competition (2019). http://mdi.ids.tsinghua.edu.cn/
10. Liu, F.F., et al.: An open access database for evaluating the algorithms of electrocardiogram rhythm and morphology abnormality detection. J. Med. Imaging Health Inform. **8**, 1368–1373 (2018). https://doi.org/10.1166/jmihi.2018.2442
11. The China Physiological Signal Challenge (2018). http://2018.icbeb.org/Challenge.html
12. Lenis, G., Pilia, N., Loewe, A., Schulze, W.H., Dossel, O.: Comparison of baseline wander removal techniques considering the preservation of ST changes in the ischemic ECG: a simulation study. Comput. Math. Methods Med. **2017**, 9295029 (2017)
13. Clevert, D.-A., Unterthiner, T., Hochreiter, S.: Fast and accurate deep network learning by exponential linear units (ELUs). arXiv preprint arXiv:1511.07289 (2015)
14. Chollet, F.: Xception: deep learning with depthwise separable convolutions. In: Proceedings of the IEEE Conference on Computer Vision and Pattern Recognition, pp. 1800–1807 (2017)
15. Edenbrandt, L., Pahlm, O.: Vectorcardiogram synthesized from a 12-lead ECG: superiority of the inverse Dower matrix. J. Electrocardiol. **21**, 361–367 (1988)
16. Long, J., Shelhamer, E., Darrell, T.: Fully convolutional networks for semantic segmentation. In: Proceedings of the IEEE Conference on Computer Vision and Pattern Recognition, pp. 3431–3440 (2015)
17. Saeedan, F., Weber, N., Goesele, M., Roth, S.: Detail-preserving pooling in deep networks. In: 2018 Proceedings of the IEEE Conference on Computer Vision and Pattern Recognition, pp. 9108–9116 (2018)
18. Tan, J.H., et al.: Application of stacked convolutional and long short-term memory network for accurate identification of CAD ECG signals. Comput. Biol. Med. **94**, 19–26 (2018). https://doi.org/10.1016/j.compbiomed.2017.12.023

19. Dyer, C., Ballesteros, M., Ling, W., Matthews, A., Smith, N.A.: Transition-based dependency parsing with stack long short-term memory. arXiv preprint arXiv:1505.08075 (2015)
20. Zhu, W., et al.: AnatomyNet: deep learning for fast and fully automated whole-volume segmentation of head and neck anatomy. Med. Phys. **46**, 576–589 (2019). https://doi.org/10.1002/mp.13300
21. Wong, K.C.L., Moradi, M., Tang, H., Syeda-Mahmood, T.: 3D segmentation with exponential logarithmic loss for highly unbalanced object sizes. In: Frangi, A.F., Schnabel, J. A., Davatzikos, C., Alberola-López, C., Fichtinger, G. (eds.) MICCAI 2018. LNCS, vol. 11072, pp. 612–619. Springer, Cham (2018). https://doi.org/10.1007/978-3-030-00931-1_70
22. Chollet, F., et al.: Keras (2015). https://keras.io
23. Zhang, M.L., Zhou, Z.H.: A review on multi-label learning algorithms. IEEE Trans. Knowl. Data Eng. **26**, 1819–1837 (2014)

An Approach to Predict Multiple Cardiac Diseases

Guanghong Bin, Yongyue Sun, Jiao Huang, and Guangyu Bin[✉]

Beijing University of Technology, Pingleyuan 100, Beijing, China
guangyubin@bjut.edu.cn

Abstract. The First China ECG Intelligent Competition launched ECG challenge to classify 8 kinds of abnormalities from uneven 12-lead ECGs. These abnormalities can be classified into two categories according to morphology and rhythm, four in each group. In this paper, for morphology tasks neural network is applied mainly with input median wave extracted from raw data, while traditional methods are executed and promoted by machine learning to achieve rhythm classification. Non-coexistence relationship is taken into consideration to fit in clinical significance better. The final average F1 score is 0.886 on test set, which certificates these are effective methods for ECG auto detection.

Keywords: ECG abnormalities · Deep learning · Machine learning

1 Introduction

1.1 Background

As ECG signal acquisition equipment getting more accurate, medical engineers are devoted to replace manual discrimination of abnormalities in ECG signals with medical device, which is also demanded clinically because of lacking enough senior cardiac surgeons and specialists. Meanwhile, Appearance of Artificial Intelligence (short for AI) technology shows possibilities to extract features automatically for ECG recognition and is widely applied recently [1]. To encourage the development of algorithms, The First China ECG Intelligent Competition co-sponsored by Tsinghua University Clinical Medical College and Data Science Research Institute and several key hospitals came into being and officially launched the intermediary ECG challenge. Challenge aims to identify 8 kinds rhythm/morphology abnormalities from 12-lead ECGs. This paper will give a detailed introduction of algorithm which combined traditional method, machine learning and AI, and hope to contribute to other's follow-up research.

1.2 Project Introduction

This ECG challenge launched a task to classify 8 kinds of ECG abnormalities including Atrial fibrillation (AF), First degree atrioventricular block (FDAVB), Complete right bundle branch block (CRBBB), Left anterior fascicular block (LAFB), Premature ventricular contraction (PVC), Premature atrial contraction (PAC), Early rise repolarization change (ER) and T-wave change (TWC). Database includes 7000 records of 12-

H. Liao et al. (Eds.): MLMECH 2019/CVII-STENT 2019, LNCS 11794, pp. 64–71, 2019.
https://doi.org/10.1007/978-3-030-33327-0_8

lead ECGs together with sex and age information. Data sequences are sampled as 500 Hz with unit of 1 mV, and unequal sample time of each ranges from 9 s to 91 s. All of 7000 records are divided into 6500 training set and 500 test set. Labels of test set are hidden for online ranking assessment. Taking the rest training set as the foundation of algorithm development, numbers of different abnormalities are summarized as Table 1 alone with mutually exclusive relationships.

Table 1. Numbers of different abnormalities in training set.

Cardiac diseases type	Numbers in training set/records	Not simultaneous with others
AF	504	FDAVB, PAC
FDAVB	534	AF
CRBBB	826	ER
LAFB	180	–
PVC	654	–
PAC	672	AF
ER	224	CRBBB
TWC	2156	–
Normal	1953	–

2 Methods

2.1 QRS Detection and Median Complex

QRS detector uses a filter and template matching techniques to both detect and group the QRS complexes. The beat type that computer considers to be most informative of normal conduction is often referred to as the "primary beat". After a primary beat type has been chosen, each of its associated beats is used in generating a representative (median) complex for each lead. The representative complex is then generated with the median voltages from this aligned group of beats.

The beat position and type of QRS is used for detection of rhythm abnormalities, and the median complex is used for detection of morphology abnormalities.

2.2 Detection of Morphology Abnormalities

CRBBB, LAFB, ER and TWC are branded into morphology abnormalities. The diagnosis of these abnormalities can be analyzed by the median complex. Determination of morphological abnormalities is based on the first or second derivative characteristics of wavelength and elevation within ECG beats in traditional methods, calculation of which depends on the accurate extraction of key points. In the research of Muthuvel et al. [2], a hybrid feature extractor based on morphology, Haar wavelet and Tri-spectrum is used to extract morphological features and frequency domain characteristic parameters of each wave in ECG for classification. Better yet, neural network can more intelligently describe a waveform trend with perceptual field. In order to eliminate uncertainty of noise and baseline interference, neural network uses the median complex extracted from raw data as input, which also solves problem of unequal data length. Median complex represents morphological features of ECG segments including P wave, QRS complex, ST-T segment, and T wave. Multi-label structure uses the same feature extraction part while different diseases focus on different parts. The final model will be better selected in multi-label structure and multi-binary classification model.

CRBBB. Main clinical criteria are QRS complex duration (>120 ms) and morphology in each single lead. Convolutional Neural Network can be used to process continuous signals to obtain their morphological information according to characteristics of convolution core. Feature extraction on QRS waveform can be realized by fitting actual tags. Compared with method of intercepting data, extracting median wave as neural network input can preserve morphological information of the whole beat while dealing with problem of unequal data length.

LAFB. Clinical judgement also refers to QRS complex morphology in each single lead, besides the left deviation of electric axis (generally $>-45°$) is a crucial part of criteria. Neural network is suitable for this case, but we will contrast with other way basing on calculating electric axis. Direction of electric axis is a complex morphological feature obtained by further calculation on basis of accurately extracting amplitude of QRS wave in lead I and III. At present, judgment of electric axis by neural network can't reach the accuracy of traditional methods. Considering that small amplitude deviation of QRS wave will lead to large fluctuation of electric axis, feature extracted by convolutional neural network is fused with electric axis calculated by traditional method before entered into classifier to improve accuracy.

ER. Abnormality in early stage of cardiac repolarization reflects in ST segment backward from J point, especially in V3 lead. The miniature of ST segment morphological amplitude change compared with R-wave peak and vulnerability to noise and baseline wandering makes morphological recognition a tough task. To exclude this effect, 400 ms from J-point to back are intercepted based on the median waveform as the input of neural network to enhance the saliency of ST-segment. Considering fewer samples, data balance algorithm is to be applied.

TWC. T wave change reflects influences by blood vessels (especially coronary artery), nerves and myocardium that supply heart on cardiac repolarization process. Usually manifested as T-wave low flat, bidirectional, inverted or high-pointed. To be more consistent with locality that T-wave changes occur only on some leads, 12 single channels will be trained as separately input.

2.3 Detection of Rhythm Abnormalities

AF, FDAVB, PVC and PAC are branded into rhythm abnormalities. Rhythm abnormalities focus more on indicators showing pathological significance between beats like heart rate, R-R interval or P-R interval. Sarfraz et al. [3] proposed an independent component analysis algorithm to obtain reliable ECG feature space which includes R-R interval exactly for classification of arrhythmias. Sensitivity to waveform morphology of convolutional neural networks will lead to misjudgment that does not depend on the relationship between beats. Traditional methods are more directional with locating key point for indicator measurement.

AF. Local atrial activation induced by multiple inconsistent reentry rings is characterized by rapid changes of AF wave instead of P wave. Mainly is diagnosed by absolutely uneven R-R interval rating at 350–600 times per minute. Misjudgment of fibrillation wave as scattered P wave poses difficulty for convolutional neural network. Thus, classification criteria based on clinical experience is set for locating P and R waves in the absence of normal ECG waveforms. In addition to R-R interval, other indicators describing P-R wave inner heartbeat relations and P-P, R-R relations between heartbeats also have strict reference value. XGBoost based on these extracted accurate discrete features will be tried to verify whether the performance is improved or not.

FDAVB. Any part of the conduction system from the sinoatrial node to Purkinje fibers can cause a prolonged P-R interval. Rules that P-R interval exceeds 200 ms threshold and not coexists with AF determines FDAVB. XGBoost applied as optimization of traditional method employs the same classification dependencies as AF.

PVC. Rhythmically, sinus rhythm and stable P-P interval are present, rather than the drastic change of AF. The abnormal ventricular depolarization caused by ventricular pacing points is characterized by abnormal QRS complex waves after long intervals. Separating independent beats from raw data and aligning them according to P-wave position, frequency up to 3 times per minute for QRS complex deformity and P-R interval abnormalities is considered to be the presence of PVC.

PAC. QRS complex presents sinus rhythm, while deformed P wave appears irregularly with uneven R-R interval. Method is same to PVC. Difference is that beats are aligned according to the position of R wave and presence of pathological P wave or P' wave is observed.

2.4   CNN Model

Many researchers are digging in ECG signal auto recognition with neural network. Kiranyaz et al. [4] proposed one-dimensional convolution depth neural network for single-lead ECG signal, which achieves good classification performance for arrhythmias, and confirms the ability of convolution neural network to process ECG signal. Acharya et al. [5] extend it to multi-lead. Ng et al. [6] researched to classify cardiac arrhythmia via 34 layers convolutional neural network, which is even more accurate than a cardiologist.

Convolutional neural network extracts the high-level semantic information from original data layer by layer through stacking a series of operations such as convolutional operation, pooling operation and non-linear activation mapping. This process is called "feedforward operation". Different types of operations are commonly called layers in convolution neural networks, namely "convolution layer", "pooling layer", "activation layer" and so on. The last layer of convolutional neural network formalizes its target task as an objective function. By calculating the error and loss between predicted value and actual value, back-propagation algorithm feeds back the error or loss from the last layer one by one, updates parameters of each layer, and so on, until the network converges, so as to achieve purpose of model training.

Basic module of the network architecture proposed in this study consists of four parts: one-dimensional convolution layer, Relu activation layer, batch normalization layer and maximum pooling layer. 4 basic modules are connected to build the CNN feature extractor, and adding different classifier to achieve the recognition target. A basic binary-classification model is shown in Fig. 1.

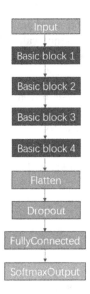

Fig. 1. A basic binary-classification CNN model

In this study, we have made some comparisons of the methods, here is a brief introduction.

Single Label. The most basic model to achieve each single task using full connection layer activating by Softmax function [1] as classifier. Yu et al. [7] extracted features by independent component analysis, added R-R interval features to form feature vectors, and used probabilistic neural networks and back propagation neural networks as classifiers. So as some features need to be added, concatenate them before Dropout layer.

Multilabel. Way to classify multiple type [8] cardiac abnormalities using the same feature extractor. In the multi-label model, sigmoid activation function is used to map each neuron to a probability value of 0 to 1, and the result is obtained by threshold. Model summary refers to Table 2.

Table 2. Multi label model summary.

Layer (type)	Output shape	Param #
Input	(None, 250, 12)	0
conv1d_1 (Conv1D)	(None, 98, 256)	9472
batch_normalization_1	(None, 98, 256)	1024
max_pooling1d_1	(None, 49, 256)	0
conv1d_2 (Conv1D)	(None, 45, 128)	163968
batch_normalization_2	(None, 45, 128)	512
max_pooling1d_2	(None, 22, 128)	0
conv1d_3 (Conv1D)	(None, 19, 32)	16416
batch_normalization_3	(None, 19, 32)	128
max_pooling1d_3	(None, 9, 32)	0
conv1d_4 (Conv1D)	(None, 7, 16)	1552
batch_normalization_4	(None, 7, 16)	64
max_pooling1d_4	(None, 3, 16)	0
flatten_1 (Flatten)	(None, 48)	0
dropout_1 (Dropout)	(None, 48)	0
dense_1 (Dense)	(None, 4)	196

Single Channel. A 12 inputs model that separate each lead to convolve and concatenate before entering the classifier. Liu et al. [9] proposed a multi-channel convolution neural network (ML-CNN), which consists of two-dimensional convolution layer, lead asymmetric pooling layer (LAP) and full connection layer. It is used to detect myocardial infarction from ECG beats led by V2, V3, V5 and aVL. This method can learn the characteristics of each lead by avoiding averaging the convolution results of each channel in the convolution layer.

2.5 Machine Learning Model

For the classification of discrete features, multiple kinds of machine learning methods represent strong applicability. Li et al. [10] compared SVM, C4.5, Naive Bayes, Logistic, Random Forest and XGBoost algorithms, and found that tree-based model classifier is the best fit to predict arrhythmia. Chen et al. [11] achieved average 81% F1 score applying it to AF classification in PhysioNet Challenge 2017. Extreme gradient boosting (XGBoost) is a lifting tree-based hierarchical classification method [12]. This method bases on CART regression tree model, and fundament ethical is to fit the residual of the last prediction by adding a tree, that is, learning a new function. Basic idea is to optimize object function (formula 1) with approximating $\widehat{y}_i$ by Taylor expansion.

$$Obj = \sum_{i=1}^{n} l(y_i, \widehat{y}_i) + \sum_{k=1}^{K} \Omega(f_k) \tag{1}$$

Where $l(y_i, \widehat{y}_i)$ is training loss and $\Omega(f_k)$ is complexity of trees.

3   Results

In this experiment, we contrast different method for each task, and evaluate using the criteria given by the sponsor. Each group predicts 500 samples on test set and calculates them on the ranking website. F1 score is calculated as formula 2.

$$F_1 = \frac{2 \cdot Precision \cdot Recall}{Precision + Recall} \tag{2}$$

According to official instructions, this challenge is a multilabel task, so multilabel model is executed on CRBBB, LAFB, ER and TWC as baseline to compare with. Results of rhythm abnormalities summarized in Table 3, morphological in Table 4.

Table 3. Rhythm abnormalities results.

F1 score	Traditional method	XGBoost
AF	0.913	0.938
FDAVB	0.773	0.851
PVC	0.852	–
PAC	0.887	–

Table 4. Morphological abnormalities results.

F1 score	Multi label	Single label	New method
CRBBB	0.960	0.980	–
LAFB	0.682	0.774	0.852 (Single label with feature)
ER	0.670	0.702	0.706 (Single label on ST segment)
TWC	0.859	0.854	0.831 (Multi channel)

The final average F1 score of all eight tasks is 0.866. Median wave is proved to have strong representation in morphology classification. For ER, it can be seen that recognizing ST segment abnormality is a tough task in deep learning with some important features are easily overlooked in process of automatic learning. But there is still some promotion space if intercept a more reasonable part of wave. Rhythm abnormalities classification seems more reliable with traditional method, and adding some machine learning part will get a certain promotion. Besides considering non-coexistence relationship can help to make a better prediction. From results of LAFB and ER, adequate data volume is a significant condition when training neural network which is irreplaceable by data balancing algorithm.

Acknowledgement. This work is supported by program ykj-2018-00393 of Technology foundation of Beijing University of Technology.

References

1. Rahhal, M.M.A., Bazi, Y., Alhichri, H., Alajlan, N., Melgani, F., Yager, R.R.: Deep learning approach for active classification of electrocardiogram signals. Inf. Sci. **345**(1), 340–354 (2016)
2. Muthuvel, K., Suresh, L.P., Alexander, T.J., Veni, S.H.K.: Classification of ECG signal using hybrid feature extraction and neural network classifier. In: Kamalakannan, C., Suresh, L.P., Dash, S.S., Panigrahi, B.K. (eds.) Power Electronics and Renewable Energy Systems. LNEE, vol. 326, pp. 1537–1544. Springer, New Delhi (2015). https://doi.org/10.1007/978-81-322-2119-7_150
3. Sarfraz, M., Khan, A.A., Li, F.F.: Using independent component analysis to obtain feature space for reliable ECG Arrhythmia classification. In: 2016 IEEE International Conference on Bioinformatics and Biomedicine (BIBM), pp. 62–67. IEEE (2016)
4. Kiranyaz, S., Ince, T., Gabbouj, M.: Real-time patient-specific ECG classification by 1-D convolutional neural networks. IEEE Trans. Biomed. Eng. **63**(3), 664–675 (2016)
5. Acharya, U.R., Fujita, H., Oh, S.L., et al.: Application of deep convolutional neural network for automated detection of myocardial infarction using ECG signals. Inf. Sci. **415–426**, 190–198 (2017)
6. Rajpurkar, P., Hannun, A.Y., Haghpanahi, M., et al.: Cardiologist-level arrhythmia detection with convolutional neural networks (2017)
7. Yu, S.N., Chou, K.T.: Integration of independent component analysis and neural networks for ECG beat classification. Expert Syst. Appl. **34**(4), 2841–2846 (2008)
8. Zhang, M.L., Zhou, Z.H.: A review on multi-label learning algorithms. IEEE Trans. Knowl. Data Eng. **26**(8), 1819–1837 (2014)
9. Liu, W., Zhang, M., Zhang, Y., et al.: Real-time multilead convolutional neural network for myocardial infarction detection. IEEE J. Biomed. Health Inform. **22**(5), 1434–1444 (2018)
10. Li, H., Pu, B., Kang, Y., Lu, C.Y., et al.: Research on massive ECG data in XGBoost. J. Intell. Fuzzy Syst. **36**(2), 1161–1169 (2019)
11. Chen, Y., Wang, X., Jung, Y.H., et al.: Classification of short single-lead electrocardiograms (ECGs for atrial fibrillation detection using piecewise linear spline and XGBoost. Physiol. Meas. **39**(10), 104006 (2018)
12. Shi, H.T., Wang, H.R., Huang, Y.X., et al.: A hierarchical method based on weighted extreme gradient boosting in ECG heartbeat classification. Comput. Methods Program. Biomed. **171**, 1–10 (2019)

A 12-Lead ECG Arrhythmia Classification Method Based on 1D Densely Connected CNN

Chunli Wang$^{(\boxtimes)}$, Shan Yang$^{(\boxtimes)}$, Xun Tang$^{(\boxtimes)}$, and Bin Li$^{(\boxtimes)}$

Chengdu Spaceon Electronics Co., Ltd., Chengdu, China
llwung001@163.com, yangshanbuaa@163.com,
petertangxun@126.com, lbspaceon@163.com

Abstract. In this work, we have proposed an electrocardiogram (ECG) arrhythmia classification method for short 12-lead ECG records to identify nine types (one normal type and eight abnormal types), using a 1D densely connected CNN which is a relatively novel convolutional neural network (CNN) model and shows outstanding performance in the field of pattern recognition. Firstly, noticing that ECG records are one dimensional time series with different noise levels, several wavelet-based shrinkage filtering methods were adopted to the ECG records for data augmentation. Secondly, each ECG record was divided into segments with a fixed length of 10 s, and the total number of segments for an ECG record is 10. And then, 10 segments were fed into an optimized 1D densely connected CNN for training. And lastly, a threshold vector was trained for the multi-label classification since each record may have more than one abnormal types. The approach has been validated against The First China ECG Intelligent Competition data set, obtaining a final F1 score of 0.873 and 0.863 on the validation set and test set, respectively.

Keywords: Electrocardiogram (ECG) · Arrhythmia · CNN

1 Introduction

We consider the task of arrhythmia classification from 12-lead electrocardiogram (ECG) records, as proposed by The First China ECG Intelligent Competition [1], which aims to encourage the development of algorithm to identify the rhythm/morphology abnormalities from 12-lead ECGs, lasting seconds to tens of seconds. The 12-lead ECGs include one normal type and eight abnormal types, which are detailed as: atrial fibrillation (AF), first-degree atrioventricular block (FDAVB), complete right bundle branch block (CRBBB), left anterior fascicular block (LAFB), premature ventricular contraction (PVC), premature atrial contraction (PAC), early repolarization (ER) and T wave changes (TWC). It should be noted that each record may contain more than one abnormality, so actually we need to deal with a multi-label classification problem.

Recently, the arrhythmia detection algorithm based on deep learning has achieved outstanding performance [2, 3]. In [2], Rajpurkar et al. proposed a 1D CNN classifier that used a 34-layer convolutional neural network which maps a sequence of ECG samples to a sequence of rhythm classes. By testing their model against board—certified cardiologists, they concluded that the CNN-based model exceeds the individual expert

© Springer Nature Switzerland AG 2019
H. Liao et al. (Eds.): MLMECH 2019/CVII-STENT 2019, LNCS 11794, pp. 72–79, 2019.
https://doi.org/10.1007/978-3-030-33327-0_9

performance on both recall, and precision on the test set. In [3], the authors proposed an ECG arrhythmia classification method using deep two-dimensional CNN with grayscale ECG images by transforming 1D ECG signals into 2D ECG images.

In this paper, we presented a 1D densely connected CNN-based algorithm for identifying the rhythm/morphology abnormalities from short 12-lead ECG records. The proposed method contained shorter connections between layers close to the input and those close to the output, which make the substantially deeper convolutional networks more accurate and efficient to train. The main contributions in this paper are: (1) adopting several wavelet-based shrinkage filtering methods for data enhancement (Sect. 2.1). (2) dividing the records into segments with a fixed length of 10 s, and the total number of segments for an ECG record is 10 (Sect. 2.2). This is crucial because the length of records varies from 9 s to 91 s, while generally the input of CNN should be of equal length. (3) following the basic structure of DenseNet and optimizing CNN model to show optimal performance for ECG arrhythmia classification (Sect. 2.3). (4) training a threshold vector for the multi-label classification (Sect. 2.4) noting that the final outputs of neural network are probabilities of each class.

In Sect. 3, the proposed method is validated against The First China ECG Intelligent Competition data set and the results are discussed, and Sect. 4 is the conclusions.

2 Methods

The First China ECG Intelligent Competition [1] was a sequential classification task where multi-labels were required for each individual input signal. The training set for the competition consisted of 6,500 12 leads ECG record ranging from 9 to 91 s in length. Manual classification by a team of experts for the ECG data contained nine classes: Normal, AF, FDAVB, CRBBB, LAFB, PVC, PAC, ER and TWC. The validation set consisted of 500 samples similar to the training set (Fig. 1), and the samples of online hidden testing set is unknown.

Train		Validation
6500		500

Type	Class	Number of Records
	Normal	1953
	AF	504
Block	FDAVB	534
	CRBBB	826
	LAFB	180
Premature Contraction	PVC	654
	PAC	672
ST-Segment Abnormalities	ER	224
	TWC	2156

Fig. 1. The distribution of training and validation set samples.

To reduce the computational burden, we down-sampled all signals to 256 Hz while noting that the ECG records were originally sampled as 500 Hz and this sampling rate is high for our application.

2.1 Data Augmentation

A total of 6,500 12-lead ECG records were provided in the training set of The First China ECG Intelligent Competition [1]. This data set could be further extended by the means of data augmentation, which is a regularization technique that is used to avoid over-fitting and maintain a balanced distribution between classes. This advantage is particularly important in medical data analysis because most medical data are normal and only a few data are abnormal [3].

Data augmentation is very common in computer vision and some of the common techniques used in data augmentation include: flip, shift, rotation and so on. Notice that ECG records are one dimensional (1D) time series with different noise levels, several wavelet-based shrinkage filtering methods were adopted to the ECG records.

Shrinkage filtering method was used in wavelet domain to smooth out or to remove some coefficients of wavelet transform sub signals of the measured signal, which has been proved to work well for a wide class of one-dimensional and two-dimensional signals, such as ECG [4, 5].

In this work, three types of wavelets were adopted to filter the ECG records: Daubechies 4 wavelet (db4), Daubechies 6 wavelet (db6) and Symlets 8. In this way, the training set was expanded to about three times the original size.

2.2 Data Segmentation

The length of records varies from 9 s to 91 s, while generally the input of CNN should be of equal length. In previous works, the CNN input was mostly based on heart beats or short clips (such as 1 s, etc.) [3]. To make the records equal in length, zero padding and resampling are the optional solutions, which, however, have a certain destructive effect on the ECG information. In addition, more convolution kernels are needed in order to extract as much information as possible when processing a long record, which will cause the whole network to be very bloated and is not conducive to focusing on the local part of the record, while the abnormality of ECG is sometimes characterized through some local changes. So splitting the records into small segments helps ensure the streamlining of the network and also strengthen the local features.

The specific method of data segmentation is explained in Fig. 2. We broke up each record into 10 segments with a fixed length of 10 s, based on the attributes that the length of the longest (91 s) is about 10 times of the shortest (9 s) in the competition database [1]. The records less than 10 s were padded by zeros to a size of 10 s. For the other records, there was an overlap between segments and the start point x for each segment can be calculated from formula (1), where L is the length of the record specified in seconds, fs is the sampling rate.

$$x = \left\lfloor \frac{(L-10) * fs}{9} * (i-1) \right\rfloor, where\ i = 1, 2, \ldots, 10 \tag{1}$$

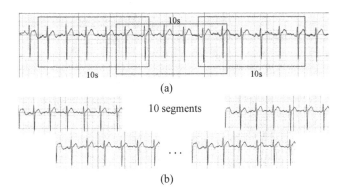

(a)

(b)

Fig. 2. The specific method of data segmentation

2.3 Model Architecture and Training

In this study, we have developed and compared three deep learning approaches: 1D residual CNN, Attention Long Short Term Memory (LSTM), and 1D densely connected CNN for the ECG classification task.

1D Residual CNN. A 18 layers 1D residual CNN modified on the basis of the ResNet, was trained to detect arrhythmias in arbitrary length ECG time-series [2, 6]. To make the optimization of such a deep model tractable, the residual connections and batch-normalization were used. The shortcut connections between neural network layers optimize training by allowing information to propagate well in very deep neural networks.

Attention Long Short Term Memory. The network architecture of this method consists of four stacked one dimensional convolutional blocks and attention LSTM block [8]. Each convolutional block is accompanied by Rectified linear activation (ReLU) function and dropout layer. Finally, an attention LSTM block was designed following the final stacked convolutional blocks.

1D Densely Connected CNN. The network architecture of this method consists of four stacked one dimensional convolutional blocks and attention LSTM block [7]. Each convolutional block is accompanied by Rectified linear activation (ReLU) function and dropout layer. Finally, an attention LSTM block was designed following the final stacked convolutional blocks. A 12-layer one dimensional densely connected convolutional network was proposed for the 12-lead ECG classification challenge (Fig. 3).

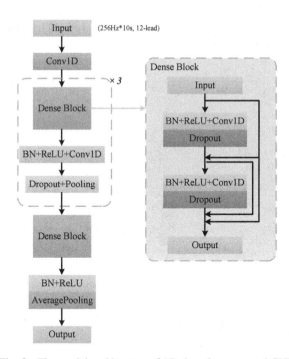

Fig. 3. The model architecture of 1D densely connected CNN

The architecture mainly consisted of four dense blocks. In each block, the same operations were performed.

The proposed 1D densely connected CNN was designed according to DenseNet [8]. One dimensional dense convolutional block was the major component of the proposed network, which proposed a different connectivity pattern introducing direct connections from any layer to all subsequent layers, in order to further improve the information flow between layers. Consequently, the lth layer receives the feature maps of all preceding layers.

To normalize the batch at each layer, the batch-normalization [9] was performed to ensure the numerical values throughout the network were scaled to the same magnitude. Rectified linear activation (ReLU) units [10] were applied to speed up training by further normalizing the values. Dropout [11] was then used to reduce overfitting of the CNN on the training data before the convolution layer.

Pooling layers were added to down sample the signal by taking every two values in a vector and reducing it to 1 value by average pooling. This forced the CNN to keep only the most relevant features and also decreased the memory burden. Pooling layers were also used on the skip connections to maintain dimensional consistency when the two separate paths joined back together at each block [12].

By providing the proposed 1D densely connected CNN model with multi-labeled data, the model was able to learn the significant features that characterize different classes.

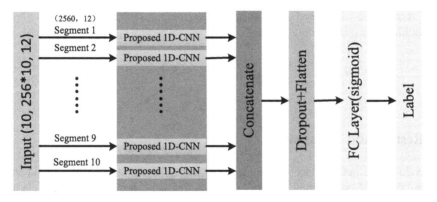

Fig. 4. The architecture of our proposed network

As is shown in Fig. 4, to produce a prediction, the network outputs of 10 segments were concatenated, then the dropout layer and flatten layer were designed following concatenate output. Finally, a fully connected layer with sigmoid function was designed which transformed the output from the flatten layers to a 9x1 vector of numerical values corresponding to the outputs for each class.

The network took 10 segments with 10 s long and 12-lead ECG records as input, and produced a multi-label prediction for each ECG record. The training set was randomly split into 80% training and 20% validation for 5-fold cross validation. The adaptive momentum estimation (Adam) optimizer, with a constantly decreasing learning rate according to the assessment criteria, was used to optimize the network parameters.

2.4 Multi-label Classification

There are two main methods for tackling a multi-label classification problem discussed in the literatures: [13, 14] problem transformation methods and algorithm adaptation methods. Problem transformation methods transform the multi-label problem into a set of binary classification problems. This method has the obvious downside of training too many classifiers and ignores possible correlation between each label. Algorithm adaptation methods adapt the algorithms to directly perform multi-label classification. In this work, we fitted the neural network to perform multi-label classification by replacing the final softmax (which often allows the neural network to run a multi-class function) layer with a sigmoid layer and then using Binary Cross Entropy to optimize the model. This way we got a probability associated with each label such that their sum across labels no longer need to add to unity.

A threshold vector was trained for the multi-label classification since each record may have more than one abnormal types. The threshold vector was calculated to achieve the highest Matthews correlation coefficient on the training set. Final label for each record was calculated by comparing the output probabilities to the trained threshold vector (see formula (2)).

$$label_i = \begin{cases} 1, & if\ prob_i \geq thr_i \\ 0, & if\ prob_i < thr_i \end{cases}, \quad where\ i = 0, 1, 2, \ldots, 8 \tag{2}$$

3 Results and Discussion

To evaluate the performance of the algorithm, we followed the challenge guidelines and metrics. The competition adopted a scoring method based on multi-label classification [1], which measures the prediction accuracy of the algorithm on each category. The final score takes the arithmetic mean of all categories. The Precision, Recall, and F1 scores for each class were calculated according to the following formulas, where $0 \leq j \leq 8$,

$$Precision_j = \frac{TP_j}{TP_j + FP_j} \tag{3}$$

$$Recall_j = \frac{TP_j}{TP_j + FN_j} \tag{4}$$

$$F_{1j} = \frac{2 * Precision_j \cdot Recall_j}{Precision_j + Recall_j} \tag{5}$$

The average F1 score is the arithmetic mean of the above 9 scores. Table 1 shows the results that the proposed method is able to achieve using 5-fold cross-validation. In Methods column, 1D-ResNet, AT-LSTM and the proposed stand for the results achieved by three network frames: 1D residual CNN, Attention Long Short Term Memory and the proposed 1D densely connected CNN, respectively. The preprocess for the ECG records is performed according to the methods detailed in Sect. 2.

Table 1. Results of different methods.

Dataset	Methods	F_{Normal}	F_{AF}	F_{FDAWB}	F_{CRBBB}	F_{LAFB}	F_{PVC}	F_{PAC}	F_{ER}	F_{TWC}	F_1
Validation	1D-ResNet	0.91	0.96	0.89	0.99	0.78	0.90	0.83	0.45	0.86	**0.841**
	AT-LSTM	0.92	0.97	0.82	0.99	0.81	0.94	0.84	0.50	0.88	**0.852**
	The proposed	0.92	0.95	0.86	0.99	0.84	0.94	0.89	0.59	0.88	**0.873**
Test	The proposed	0.87	0.98	0.92	0.98	0.70	0.96	0.91	0.67	0.78	**0.863**

The proposed method based on 1D densely connected CNN can achieve a final F1 of 0.873 on the validation set and the F1 score on the hidden test set is 0.863. It can be observed that the method yields a high F1 score in classifying Normal, AF, CRBBB and PVC records.

4   Conclusions

In this paper, we have proposed a method based on 1D densely connected CNN for identifying the rhythm/morphology abnormalities from short 12-lead ECG records. We preprocessed the training data by adopting different wavelet filtering methods and dividing the records into 10 segments where each has a fixed length of 10 s. Following the basic structure of DenseNet, we optimized CNN model to show optimal performance for ECG arrhythmia classification. The present method achieved a final F1 score of 0.863 on the hidden test set.

The following aspects could be considered in the future study to further improve the performance: (1) increasing the amount of record for some categories for data augmentation, such as ER and LAFB category, (2) introducing some machine learning features to improve performance, (3) combining RNN with CNN to further curve the features of ECG record.

References

1. The First China ECG Intelligent Competition. http://mdi.ids.tsinghua.edu.cn. Accessed 12 July 2019
2. Rajpurkar, P., Hannun, A.Y., Haghpanahi, M., et al.: Cardiologist-level arrhythmia detection with convolutional neural networks. arXiv preprint arXiv:1707. 01836 (2017)
3. Jun, T.J., Nguyen, H.M., Kang, D., et al.: ECG arrhythmia classification using a 2-d convolutional neural network. arXiv preprint arXiv:1804.06812 (2018)
4. Donoho, D.L.: Denoising by soft thresholding. IEEE Trans. Inf. Theory **41**, 613–627 (1995)
5. Alfaouri, M., Daqrouq, K.: ECG signal denoising by wavelet transform thresholding. Am. J. Appl. Sci. **5**(3), 276–281 (2008)
6. He, K., Zhang, X., Ren, S., Sun, J.: Deep residual learning for image recognition. In: 2015 IEEE Conference, pp. 770–778 (2015)
7. Mostayed, A., Luo, J., Shu, X., et al.: Classification of 12-lead ECG signals with bi-directional LSTM network. arXiv preprint arXiv:1811.02090 (2018)
8. Huang, G., Liu, Z., van der Maaten, L., Weinberger, K.Q.: Densely connected convolutional networks. In: 2017 IEEE Conference on Computer Vision and Pattern Recognition (CVPR), pp. 2261–2269 (2017)
9. Ioffe, S., Szegedy, C.: Batch normalization: accelerating deep network training by reducing internal covariate shift. In: 2013 IEEE Conference, pp. 448–456 (2013)
10. He, K., Zhang, X., Ren, S., Sun, J.: Identity mappings in deep residual networks. In: Leibe, B., Matas, J., Sebe, N., Welling, M. (eds.) ECCV 2016. LNCS, vol. 9908, pp. 630–645. Springer, Cham (2016). https://doi.org/10.1007/978-3-319-46493-0_38
11. Srivastava, N., Hinton, G.E., Krizhevsky, A., et al.: Dropout: a simple way to prevent neural networks from overfitting. J. Mach. Learn. Res. **15**(1), 1929–1958 (2014)
12. Xiong, Z., Stiles, M.K., Zhao, J.: Robust ECG signal classification for detection of atrial fibrillation using a novel neural network. In: 2017 Computing in Cardiology (CinC), pp. 24–27 (2017)
13. Zhang, M.-L., Zhou, Z.-H.: A review on multi-label learning algorithms. IEEE Trans. Knowl. Data Eng. **26**(8), 1819–1837 (2014)
14. Tsoumakas, G., Katakis, I.: Multi-label classification: an overview. Int. J. Data Warehous. Min. **3**(3), 1–13 (2007)

Automatic Multi-label Classification in 12-Lead ECGs Using Neural Networks and Characteristic Points

Zhourui Xia[1], Zhenhua Sang[2(✉)], Yutong Guo[3], Weijie Ji[2], Chenguang Han[2], Yanlin Chen[1], Sifan Yang[1], and Long Meng[4]

[1] Shenzhen International Graduate School, Tsinghua University, Shenzhen, China
[2] Beijing Tsinghua Changgung Hospital, Beijing, China
sangzhenhua@btch.edu.cn
[3] School of Information and Electronics, Beijing Institute Technology, Beijing, China
[4] Shandong Mingjia Technology Co., Ltd., Tai'an, China

Abstract. Electrocardiogram (ECG) signals are widely used in the medical diagnosis of heart disease. Automatic extraction of relevant and reliable information from ECG signals is a tough challenge for computer systems. This study proposes a novel 12-lead electrocardiogram (ECG) multi-label classification algorithm using a combination of Neural Network (NN) and the characteristic points. The proposed model is an end-to-end model. CNN extracts the morphological features of each ECG. Then the features of all the beats are considered in the context via BiRNN. The proposed method was evaluated on the dataset offered by The First China Intelligent Competition, and results were measured using the macro F1 score of all nine classes. Our proposed method obtained a macro F1 score of 0.878, which is excellent among the competitors.

Keywords: ECG Classification · Characteristic points · Multi-label

1 Introduction

ECG is a standard measurement method widely used in the diagnosis and monitoring of cardiovascular diseases. It can reflect the electrophysiological process of the heart to a certain extent and assist the doctors to diagnose diseases accordingly [7]. Moreover, the automatic classification of arrhythmias is a challenging task because ECG signals based on different patients vary significantly under different conditions.

The deep-learning-based approaches have been applied in many fields, as well as the field of ECG classification. Inspired by this method, Kiranyaz et al. [3] developed an adaptive implementation of one-dimensional convolutional neural

This work is partially supported by The National Key Research and Development Program of China No. 2017YFB1401804.

H. Liao et al. (Eds.): MLMECH 2019/CVII-STENT 2019, LNCS 11794, pp. 80–87, 2019.
https://doi.org/10.1007/978-3-030-33327-0_10

network (1D-CNN). It adopts CNN for feature extraction and classification and achieved excellent results. Although CNN is suitable for extracting internal morphological features, it cannot learn to take advantage of the information between beats. Researchers tried to apply different methods to improve the performance and concern more about features among adjacent beats. Zhang et al. [9] proposed a method of combining recurrent neural networks (RNN) and clustering techniques to classify ECG beats. The representative training data set is obtained by the clustering technique, and the beat morphology information is directly fed into the RNN to obtain the classification results.

In this work, we propose a novel end-to-end multi-label classification model based on a combination of Neural Network (NN) and the characteristic points. The ECG waveforms from all 12 leads will first be fed into the CNN to extract internal morphological features, which are then placed into the BiRNN to learn the relationship between the current beat and the adjacent beats. Besides, the Median Beat and the normalized coordinates of each characteristic point would be put into other two input channels to extract more relevant features. The experimental results on The First China ECG Intelligent Competition demonstrate that our proposed scheme achieves superior multi-label classification performance.

2 System Framework

The framework of our proposed system is shown in Fig. 1. Firstly the raw ECG data is denoised and then normalized. Next, we use the DPI algorithm [5] to detect the positions of R_{peak}. Afterward, with the help of the random walk algorithm [8] we designed earlier, we can obtain other characteristic points with high precision. Meanwhile, the normalized data would be realigned according to the coordinate of the first R_{peak}. Then if the length of this record is more extended than 10000, we cut the extra tail off; else we pad the front part of the record to the tail. Thus we have got three input channels for the classification model. These precessed data is randomly divided into a training set, a testing set, and a validation set. Finally, our model is trained and then evaluated on the validation set, respectively.

2.1 Denosing

Wavelet method is used to filter the noise of the raw ECG data. Firstly, the raw ECG signal is decomposed into nine scales using the Dual-Tree Complex Wavelet Transform (DTCWT) proposed by Selesnick [6]. Then only the information in three to eight levels is retained to reconstruct the signal, while other information is treated as noise and discard.

2.2 Alignment and Padding

We chose the DPI algorithm to detect the R_{peak} position of each beat. Furthermore, all leads of the normalized ECG data is realigned according to the

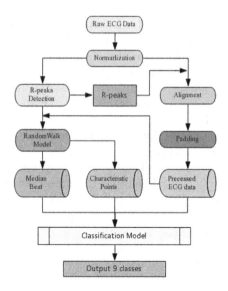

Fig. 1. The framework of the whole algorithm.

position of the first R_{peak} (R_0). Points before R_0 are abandoned. And then, we pad the head of the signal to the tail for each lead to make the signal up to a 10000×12-dim vector when the original length of the record is less than 10000. Otherwise, the redundant points over the tail would be discarded.

2.3 Characteristic Points Detection

In our previous work [8], we proposed a fast ECG delineation scheme by leveraging wavelet transform and machine learning techniques to detect characteristic points in ECG waveforms. With the RSWT (randomly selected wavelet transform) feature pool, we build a random forest regressor for each type of characteristic point. The regression tree is then trained to estimate the probability distribution to the direction toward the target point, relative to the current position. Then we devise a random walk testing scheme to refine the final positions of each ECG characteristic point.

Our trained model on QT database [4] can infer eight types of ECG characteristic points: P_{onset}, P_{peak}, P_{offset}, R_{onset}, R_{peak}, R_{offset}, T_{peak}, and T_{offset} (T_{onset} wave isn't included in QT database). Thus, we adopt the random walk algorithm to generate other seven characteristic points with the processed ECG data. We would collect 160 points of 20 continuous beats, and each point contains two features which are the normalized abscissa and ordinate.

2.4   Median Beat Extraction

For each person, the ECG waveform has a particular specificity. The waveforms presented in the static ECG have their own unique morphological laws. We hope to extract the most representative heartbeat as a simple reference.

The United States General Electric Company (GE) has conducted in-depth research on this issue [2], and the final solution aims to the median heartbeat algorithm. The basic idea of this algorithm is to use the pre-detected R_{peak}s to cut out each heartbeat in a record, and then align all the obtained heartbeats according to their R_{peak}s. For each point in the time series, the median of the amplitude values corresponding to the point in each heartbeat is taken as the final amplitude value at the same timing point of the median heartbeat. Thus, a representative median beat is generated, which could characterize the current record for later processing (Fig. 2).

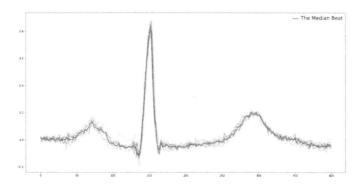

Fig. 2. Example of the Median Beat.

2.5   Classification

We create an end-to-end model to accomplish the multi-label classification task. There are three input channels of our model: ECG channel, median beat channel, and characteristic points channel. The ECG channel learns the overall morphological features in the ECG waveform. The median beat channel focuses on the most significant and representative feature in each lead. Most of the clinically useful information in ECG can be inferred from the intervals and amplitudes of the ECG characteristic points. So we establish a new input channel sending the position and amplitude information of 8 characteristic points (P_{onset}, P_{peak}, P_{offset}, R_{onset}, R_{peak}, R_{offset}, T_{peak}, and T_{offset}) to improve the performance.

The final classification result is acquired from the features offered by all three input channels. More details about our model would be presented in the following part.

3   Classification Model

This model is used for both feature extraction and classification of all 12 lead ECG signals. The network architecture of our model is shown in Fig. 3. The network takes three input channels as input data and outputs a vector of multi-label prediction.

At the final dense layer, in order to achieve multi-label classification, we choose the sigmoid function rather than the softmax function as the activation of the final dense layer. Because it is hoped that sigmoid function will activate the value of each node once, thus outputting the probability of 1 for each node respectively. Moreover, the binary cross-entropy loss function is used, which makes the model continuously reduce the cross-entropy between output and label during the training process. It is equivalent to make the output value of the node with label one closer to one, and the output value of the node with label zero closer to zero.

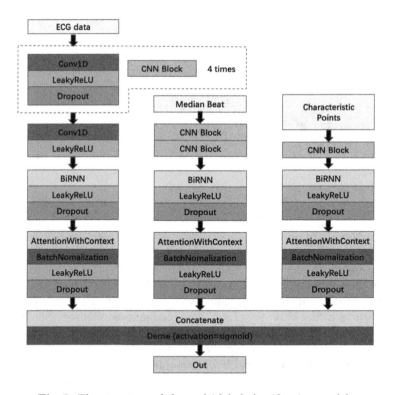

Fig. 3. The structure of the multi-label classification model.

In the ECG channel, the shape of the input data is N × 10000 × 12 (N refers to the number of records). The input data would firstly be fed into the four sequential CNN blocks which can effectively extract the interior morphological features of the12-lead ECG. As Fig. 3 shows, the CNN block is built by a 1-D convolution layer, a leaky ReLu layer, and a dropout layer. The reason why we design it in this way is that this structure has a stronger ability to learn interior features. After the CNN block, another convolution layer with large kernel size follows it, since it helps to enhance the relevance between those interior features. Next, these features would be sent to the BiRNN layer, which could consider the above features in the context, thus represent more relevant information between adjacent beats. Finally, we set up an AttentionWithContext layer to balance the weights between different combinations of features and focus more on the essential parts.

In the median beat channel, the input shape is $N \times 400 \times 12$. This input data is relatively tiny that it will only get through 2 CNN blocks to learn the most representative features of each lead. Similarly, it follows a BiRNN layer and an AttentionWithContext layer. This input channel may pay more attention to the relevance between those 12 leads and the implied information behind some specific groups of certain leads.

In the characteristic points channel, the input shape is $N \times 320 \times 12$. This input data is extracted by only one CNN block and then directly connected to the BiRNN layer and the AttentionWithContext layer. The feature of the characteristic points could help consider the intervals between different waveforms and some sudden change of the amplitudes. It is quite efficient for identifying certain diseases.

4   Results and Discussion

The First China ECG Intelligent Competition [1] has offered us a dataset of 6500 records digitized at 500 Hz with 12-lead (I, II, III, aVR, aVL, aVF, V1, V2, V3, V4, V5, and V6) with corresponding multi-labels. Each record may contain more than one arrhythmia, and there are eight arrhythmias (AF, FDAVB, CRBBB, LAFB, PVC, PAC, ER, and TWC) at all. We randomly split the dataset into 5000, 1000, and 500 as the training set, testing set, and validation set. The distribution of each arrhythmia is kept similar for the three datasets. Note that all of the following experimental results are the final averaging of the experiments repeated ten times of randomly splitting datasets.

Our proposed algorithm has achieved excellent performance on the validation dataset. For classification performance measured, four standard metrics are used: classification accuracy ($Acc.$), sensitivity ($Sen.$), positive predictivity ($Ppr.$), and f1 score ($F1$). Using true positive (TP), false positive (FP), true negative (TN), false negative (FN), $Acc.$, $Sen.$, $Ppr.$, and $F1$ are defined as follows. $Acc.$ is the ratio of the number of correctly classified patterns to the total number of patterns classified: $Acc. = (TP+TN)/(TP+TN+FP+FN)$. $Sen.$ is the rate of correctly classified events among all events: $Sen. = TP/(TP + FN)$. $Ppr.$ is the rate of correctly classified events in all detected events: $Ppr. = TP/(TP + FP)$. $F1$ is the harmonic mean of the $Sen.$ and the $Ppr.$: $F1 = 2*Sen.*Ppr./(Sen.+Ppr.)$. The result is shown in Table 1. As can be seen from the table, we find that the

Table 1. Evaluation Results on the Validation Set

Metrics	Normal	AF	FDAVB	CRBBB	LAFB	PVC	PAC	ER	TWC	All
Acc.	0.943	0.993	0.978	**0.996**	0.987	0.985	0.971	0.954	0.943	0.836
Sen.	0.946	0.957	0.885	**0.989**	0.630	0.921	0.865	0.631	0.790	0.846
Ppr.	0.850	0.973	0.958	0.973	0.953	**0.980**	0.930	0.907	0.781	0.932
*F*1	0.892	0.965	0.920	**0.981**	0.759	0.950	0.897	0.744	0.786	0.878

[1] Column *All* refers to the macro average result of all classes.
[2] Bold fonts indicate that this class performs best in that metric.

Table 2. Control Experiments for the Median Beat and Characteristic Points

Component	Normal	AF	FDAVB	CRBBB	LAFB	PVC	PAC	ER	TWC	All
Baseline	0.810	0.934	0.871	0.957	0.502	0.933	0.839	0.549	0.734	0.792
MB	0.879	0.937	0.909	0.977	0.507	0.947	0.879	0.728	0.768	0.836
CP	0.872	0.944	0.911	**0.982**	0.512	**0.961**	0.882	0.693	0.783	0.838
MB&CP	**0.892**	**0.965**	**0.920**	0.981	**0.759**	0.950	**0.897**	**0.744**	**0.786**	**0.878**

[1] The metric used is F1 score only.
[2] Baseline represents that the model only contains ECG channel.
[3] MB represents that the model contains Median Beat and ECG channel.
[4] CP represents that the model contains Characteristic Points and ECG channel.
[5] MB&CP represents that the model contains Median Beat, Characteristic Points, and ECG channel.
[6] Bold fonts indicate that this component performs best in that class.

overall performance of our algorithm is superior, and the performance of CRBBB is particularly outstanding.

In order to show the significance of the median beat channel and the characteristic points channel, we trained four models with different configurations. The result of the control experiments is shown in Table 2. Several observations could be made from this table. First, with the median beat embedded separately, the overall *F*1 score improved a lot. Note that the performance on Normal and ER is exceptionally better than CP. We argue that it is because the characteristics of the median beat can distinguish between normal and abnormal ECG waveforms. The results of the characteristic points embedded separately are also gratifying. For instance, results on CRBBB and PVC are even a little better than the result of the combination of these two channels. Moreover, like PVC and TWC, because the characteristic points of certain diseases possess distinguishing features, the results on them are better as expected. The result of the combined model achieved a sharp increase than the baseline, which fully demonstrates that the median beat and characteristic points have excellent performance on the work of multi-label ECG classification.

5   Conclusion

In this paper, we firstly propose a novel end-to-end ECG classification model with extra input channels of the median beat and characteristic points. We use CNN to extract interior morphological features, and the features between beats are considered in the context via BiRNN. The median beat could help represent the most significant features between adjacent beats and leads. The position and amplitude information of characteristic points could enhance the associations between features. Moreover, it performs better on some arrhythmias, which relies more on the interval and amplitude changes during the waveform. The evaluation results on The First China ECG Intelligent Competition show that our proposed system achieves superior multi-label ECG classification performance.

References

1. The first China ECG intelligent competition. http://mdi.ids.tsinghua.edu.cn/#/
2. Kaiser, W., Findeis, M.: Method and system for measuring T-wave alternans by alignment of alternating median beats to a cubic spline. US Patent 6,668,189, 23 December 2003
3. Kiranyaz, S., Ince, T., Gabbouj, M.: Real-time patient-specific ecg classification by 1-D convolutional neural networks. IEEE Trans. Biomed. Eng. **63**(3), 664–675 (2015)
4. Laguna, P., Mark, R.G., Goldberg, A., Moody, G.B.: A database for evaluation of algorithms for measurement of QT and other waveform intervals in the ECG. In: Computers in Cardiology 1997, pp. 673–676, September 1997. https://doi.org/10.1109/CIC.1997.648140
5. Ramakrishnan, A., Prathosh, A., Ananthapadmanabha, T.: Threshold-independent QRS detection using the dynamic plosion index. IEEE Signal Process. Lett. **21**(5), 554–558 (2014)
6. Selesnick, I.W., Baraniuk, R.G., Kingsbury, N.G.: The dual-tree complex wavelet transform. IEEE Signal Process. Mag. **22**(6), 123–151 (2005)
7. Taylor, G.J.: 150 Practice ECGs: Interpretation and Review. Wiley, Hoboken (2008)
8. Xia, Z., et al.: Real-time ECG delineation with randomly selected wavelet transform feature and random walk estimation. In: 2018 40th Annual International Conference of the IEEE Engineering in Medicine and Biology Society (EMBC), pp. 1–4. IEEE (2018)
9. Zhang, C., Wang, G., Zhao, J., Gao, P., Lin, J., Yang, H.: Patient-specific ECG classification based on recurrent neural networks and clustering technique. In: 2017 13th IASTED International Conference on Biomedical Engineering (BioMed), pp. 63–67. IEEE (2017)

Automatic Detection of ECG Abnormalities by Using an Ensemble of Deep Residual Networks with Attention

Yang Liu[1], Runnan He[1], Kuanquan Wang[1], Qince Li[1], Qiang Sun[5],
Na Zhao[1], and Henggui Zhang[1,2,3,4($\boxtimes$)]

[1] School of Computer Science and Technology,
Harbin Institute of Technology (HIT), Harbin 150001, China
[2] School of Physics and Astronomy, The University of Manchester,
Manchester M13 9PL, UK
henggui.zhang@manchester.ac.uk
[3] SPACEnter Space Science and Technology Institute, Shenzhen 518117, China
[4] International Laboratory for Smart Systems and Key Laboratory of Intelligent
of Computing in Medical Image, Ministry of Education, Northeastern University,
Shenyang 110004, China
[5] The Department of Pharmacology, Beijing Electric Power Hospital,
Beijing 100073, China

Abstract. Heart disease is one of the most common diseases causing morbidity and mortality. Electrocardiogram (ECG) has been widely used for diagnosing heart diseases for its simplicity and non-invasive property. Automatic ECG analyzing technologies are expected to reduce human working load and increase diagnostic efficacy. However, there are still some challenges to be addressed for achieving this goal. In this study, we develop an algorithm to identify multiple abnormalities from 12-lead ECG recordings. In the algorithm pipeline, several preprocessing methods are firstly applied on the ECG data for denoising, augmentation and balancing recording numbers of variant classes. In consideration of efficiency and consistency of data length, the recordings are padded or truncated into a medium length, where the padding/truncating time windows are selected randomly to suppress overfitting. Then, the ECGs are used to train deep neural network (DNN) models with a novel structure that combines a deep residual network with an attention mechanism. Finally, an ensemble model is built based on these trained models to make predictions on the test data set. Our method is evaluated based on the test set of the First China ECG Intelligent Competition dataset by using the F_1 metric that is regarded as the harmonic mean between the precision and recall. The resultant overall F_1 score of the algorithm is 0.875, showing a promising performance and potential for practical use.

Keywords: Heart disease · Electrocardiogram · Automatic diagnosis · Deep neural networks

---

Y. Liu and R. He—Joint first author.

H. Liao et al. (Eds.): MLMECH 2019/CVII-STENT 2019, LNCS 11794, pp. 88–95, 2019.
https://doi.org/10.1007/978-3-030-33327-0_11

1 Introduction

Heart diseases, mainly manifested as disordered patterns of atrial and ventricular electrical excitation activity, have been regarded as the leading cause of morbidity and mortality. Electrocardiogram (ECG) is a common and noninvasive tool that can be used for diagnosing heart conditions. However, it is time consuming and error-prone to analyze ECGs in practice, therefore, computer-aided algorithms may offer a promising way to improve the efficiency and accuracy of ECG analyzing.

The algorithms for ECG analyzing typically contain three steps, which are pre-processing, feature extraction and classification [1–5]. Among these, the feature extraction is a critical step, for which many methods have been proposed, such as morphology information [2], temporal and frequency features [3], high order statistical features [4] and wavelet features [5]. However, these algorithms still have shortcomings to achieve a good performance for the detection of abnormalities in ECGs. Recently, deep convolutional neural networks (DNNs) showed outstanding performance in automatic feature extraction, leading to a dramatic breakthrough in a range of fields associated with computer vision [6]. Therefore, in the field of ECG analysis, many studies have attempted to apply DNNs, such as convolutional neural network (CNN) [7], deep residual network [6], and recurrent neural network (RNN) [8], to address the problem of heart diseases detection, all of which have achieved some impressive results. However, due to the long recording length, low signal quality and pathological diversity of ECG recordings, it is still a challenge for accurate feature extraction.

In this study, we propose a novel deep residual neural network with attention mechanism to detect a series of abnormalities from 12-lead ECG recordings. The deep residual neural network is used to learn local features from the ECG waveforms, while the attention mechanism determines the relevance of features from each part and summarizes them into a single feature vector that is used for the classification. This combination demonstrates to be effective for feature learning in a long ECG recording, and robust when the signal is partially corrupted.

2 Materials

The First China ECG Intelligent Competition dataset contains about 15000 12-lead ECG recordings, among which 6,500 for training and 8,500 for testing respectively. The recordings are in different lengths, ranging from 9 to 90 s sampled at 500 Hz (Fs = 500 Hz). Each recording is labeled with one or more types including normal, atrial fibrillation (AF), first degree atrioventricular block (FDAVB), complete right bundle branch block (CRBBB), left anterior fascicular block (LAFB), premature ventricular contraction (PVC), premature atrial contraction (PAC), early repolarization pattern changes (ER) and T-wave changes (TWC).

3 Method

3.1 Preprocessing

Baseline Wander Removal. Baseline wander results from low-frequency noise in the ECG signal. It can influence the diagnosis of many diseases that manifest as low-frequency changes in the ECG signals, e.g., S-T segment changes. We remove the baseline wander by first estimating it and then subtracting it from the original signal. The estimating is based on moving average which is a windowed low-pass filter with the cut-off frequency calculated by

$$f_{co} = 0.443 \times \frac{f_s}{N} \tag{1}$$

where f_{co} indicates the cut-off frequency, f_s indicates the sampling frequency, and N indicates the window size. Generally, the cut-off frequency shouldn't be less than the slowest heart rate which is typically 40 beats/minute, i.e., 0.67 Hz. But, considering the fluctuation of heart rate, the cut-off frequency should be slightly lower, approximately 0.5 Hz.

Powerline Interference and Muscle Noise Removal. Powerline interference generally resulted from the alternating current (AC) in the environment. Thus, its frequency is usually 50/60 Hz depending on the specific standard of the AC power supply system. Muscle noise, i.e., electromyographic noise, is caused by the electrical activity produced by muscle contraction. Different from the powerline interference, muscle noise is much more irregular, due to the randomness of muscle activities. The frequency components of muscle noise have a wide overlap with those of the ECG, and can be even higher. In this work, we remove both these noises by wavelet denoising based on 5-level 'db4' wavelet transform and soft-thresholding [9].

Padding or Truncating Signals to the Same Length. The lengths of ECG recordings in the dataset is in a high variety, ranging from 9 s to 90 s. For batch processing of a DNN model, the recordings in a batch should be in the same length. To address this problem, there are three ways:

- Padding all recordings into the longest length. This method avoids the loss of information during the length-unifying process. But, for most of the recordings, the new length is several times longer than their original lengths, which will result in the significant increase in processing time of a DNN model.
- Truncating signals into the shortest length. On the contrary to the padding method, this method can reduce the processing time significantly. However, the truncating process will inevitably lead to the loss of information, especially when the truncated part is in a large proportion of the original signal.
- Grouping the recordings that have the same length. Compared to the above two methods, this method doesn't change the original signals and thus won't cause any loss or distortion to their information. But, as the distribution of the recording lengths is extremely uneven, a group may contain just one or two recordings,

resulting in a big variety of batch sizes. Besides, there is some uncertainty in the prediction by a DNN model when it receives a recording with an unknown length.

In this work, we try to make a trade-off between the recording integrity and computing complexity by padding or truncating the signals into a medium length. As more than 90% of recordings in the dataset is no longer than 30 s, we choose 30 s (i.e., 15000 sampling points) as the target length. To minimize the effect of padding on the following interpretations, the value for padding is set to zero which is equal to the baseline of the ECG signals. The obvious difference between the padded part and the original part will help a machine learning model to detect the original part from the whole recording. However, the padding and truncating operations can be done in different positions, which may lead to different impacts on the interpretation by a DNN model. We will discuss this in the following section about data augmentation and balancing.

Redistribution of Signal Lengths. Even though the recordings are padded or truncated into the same length, the difference of original length distributions between data classes can still induce a bias to the discrimination of a DNN model. For example, the recordings longer than 20 s only account for a proportion less than 1% in the normal class, but account for more than 10% in the PAC class. As a result, a DNN model may recognize the padding length as a feature to distinguish between these classes, which is clearly unreasonable. Therefore, we propose a method to organize the recordings into the same distribution of recording lengths among all the classes. We first make a distribution statistics of recording lengths in the whole dataset. Because of the truncating operation in our pipeline as stated above, recordings longer than 30 s are all counted as that of 30 s. Then, the global distribution is used as the target distribution, and recordings in each class are augmented to have the same distribution. For lengths that exist in the target distribution but not exist in the original distribution of a class, we truncate the longer recordings to make recordings with these lengths.

Data Augmentation and Balancing. As discussed above, there are different ways for padding or truncating a recording in terms of time windows. In order to make a DNN model insensitive to the timing positions of padding or truncating, we pad or truncate each recording at different positions to create more samples for training. In other words, we augment the dataset by different padding and truncating ways. The selection for padding or truncating way is random in our study. For a recording shorter than the target length, we can pad it at both the ends with various of schemes to specify the padding length at each end. This method introduces more randomness to the positions of padding, which would help a DNN model learn to ignore the padded parts and focus the original parts of the recordings. And for the truncated recordings, this method generates more training samples with different parts of the original recordings that would contribute to better use of the limited data and enhance the model's discrimination ability. Besides, in terms of recordings' numbers, the dataset is very imbalanced between classes. The data augmentation method can also be used to balance the dataset. Generally speaking, recordings with short class length will be augmented more times than those with long class length, allowing each class have approximately the same number of recordings.

3.2   Model Architecture

Due to the automatic feature-learning ability, DNNs can reduce human working load in extracting features from the raw ECGs. A DNN model is supposed to learn a brief, robust but comprehensive representation from a raw ECG recording. In this work, we propose a novel DNN architecture that combines a residual convolutional network and an attention mechanism, as shown in Fig. 1.

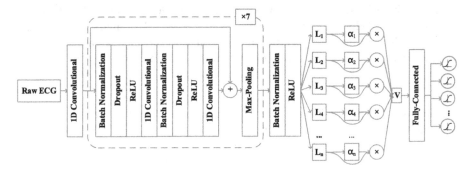

Fig. 1. The architecture of proposed deep residual network with attention mechanism. L_i indicates the i-th local feature vector. α_i indicates the attention value for the i-th local feature vector. V indicates the global feature vector.

In our proposed architecture, the feature learning process can be divided into two stages: local features learning stage and global features learning stage. A local feature vector learned by a stack of residual convolutional modules characterizes a short fragment of a ECG recording, while the global feature vector learned by an attention mechanism is a summary of the sequence of local-feature vectors. After the feature learning, the global feature vector is input into a fully-connected layer to predict the probabilities that a recording belongs to each class. We will give more details about this architecture in the following section.

In the local features learning stage, a raw ECG recording is first input into a 1D convolutional layer. The output feature map is then processed sequentially by 7 residual convolutional modules which are considered having good properties to avoid the degradation problem in DNNs [6]. Each residual model is constructed by 9 layers: 2 batch normalization layers, 2 dropout layers, 2 ReLU activation layers, 2 1D-convolutional layers and an addition-based merging layer, in the order shown in Fig. 1. The kernel size of each convolutional layer is 16. The kernel number in the first convolutional layer is 16, and it grows by 16 for every two residual modules. There is also a max-pooling layer following each residual module for compression of intermediate feature maps. As a result, the length of a feature map output by the local feature learning part will be $1/2^7$ of the input length.

In the global features learning stage, an attention mechanism is utilized to learn an attention distribution on the sequence of local features. Due to the possible paroxysm of diseases, padding parts and noise effects, only a few episodes in a ECG recording may be relevant for the diagnosis. In view of this, the attention distribution is supposed to manifest the relevance of each part in the ECG recordings for the classification. Then, the local features are summed, weighted by the attention, into a single feature vector. Finally, a fully-connected layer is used to learn a classifier based on the global features. This layer contains 9 cells corresponding to the 9 categories respectively. As a record may belong to more than one category, the output of each cell is processed by a sigmoid activation function to make prediction independently.

3.3 Model Training

Based on the architecture stated above, we train a series of models with different procedures. As shown in Fig. 2, there are 4 different pipelines (labeled with numbers) are used in our research for model training. Most of the differences between pipelines are present in the preprocessing steps, including data normalization, denoising, data augmentation and balancing between classes. The window size for baseline wander removal is 250 ($f_{co} = 0.886\,\text{Hz}$) in pipeline 1, while it is 500 ($f_{co} = 0.443\,\text{Hz}$) in other pipelines for denoising. In the pipeline 2, recordings from the CPSC 2018 dataset are mixed into the training dataset of this challenge to enhance the robustness and generalization ability of the trained models. Besides, as the recordings of training set and test set are in the same distribution which is imbalanced among data classes, the balancing operations to the training set may cause a bias to the trained models and hence reduce the classification accuracy. Therefore, we utilize a two-stage (balance and imbalanced) strategy to address this problem. Specifically, in pipelines 3, the models trained with balanced data (from pipeline 2) are retrained with imbalanced data which is in the same distribution with the original training set. The balanced data helps the model to learn more distinguishing features, while the data in the independent identically distribution with the test set helps to improve the classification accuracy. In pipeline 4, the input data is not denoised but normalized to have zero mean and unit variance. The model training steps in these pipelines are all in a 10-fold cross-validation manner. Furthermore, the training/testing samples division in each fold is also in the same scheme among these pipelines, which can especially avoid overlap between training and testing samples in the two-stage model training. At the final step, an ensemble model is built by averaging the probabilistic predictions of models from all these pipelines.

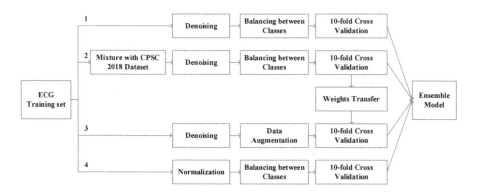

Fig. 2. The model training workflow that combines models from different pipelines to make an ensemble model.

4   Results and Discussion

The metrics are designed based on the evaluation of multi-label classification, where a single recording may belong to more than one class. The predictive accuracy of the algorithm for each class is measured by the F_1 score. Besides, an overall F_1 score is also calculated by averaging all the categorical sub-scores. The formulas for calculation of these metrics are described in the following.

For each class $(0 \le j \le 8)$, there are four values counting samples with different prediction results, namely true positive (TP), false positive (FP), true negative (TN) and false negative (FN):

$$TP_j = \left| \{x_i | y_j \in Y_i, y_j \in f(x_i), 1 \le i \le N\} \right|, \tag{2}$$

$$FP_j = \left| \{x_i | y_j \notin Y_i, y_j \in f(x_i), 1 \le i \le N\} \right|, \tag{3}$$

$$TN_j = \left| \{x_i | y_j \notin Y_i, y_j \notin f(x_i), 1 \le i \le N\} \right|, \tag{4}$$

$$FN_j = \left| \{x_i | y_j \in Y_i, y_j \notin f(x_i), 1 \le i \le N\} \right|. \tag{5}$$

where x_i indicates a sample for prediction, y_j is the label for the class j, Y_i is the annotated label set of x_i, and $f(x_i)$ is the predicted label set of x_i. The precision, recall and F_1 of each class can be calculated by

$$Precision_j = \frac{TP_j}{TP_j + FP_j}, \tag{6}$$

$$Recall_j = \frac{TP_j}{TP_j + FN_j}, \tag{7}$$

$$F_{1j} = \frac{2 \cdot Precision_j \cdot Recall_j}{Precision_j + Recall_j}. \tag{8}$$

The overall F_1 score is the arithmetic mean value of that of the nine classes.

$$F_1 = \frac{1}{9} \sum F_{1j} \tag{9}$$

The results show that the overall F_1 score of the proposed classifier on the hidden test set is 0.875, with the detailed scores shown in Table 1.

Table 1. Results of the ECG abnormalities classification on the entire test set.

	Normal	AF	FDAVB	CRBBB	LAFB	PVC	PAC	ER	TWC	Total
F_1	0.875	0.974	0.901	0.983	0.747	0.971	0.926	0.736	0.757	0.875

Results shown in Table 1 demonstrate that the classifier achieves a good performance for AF, FDAVB, CRBBB, PVC and PAC, which are all above 0.9. However, the identification of LAFB, ER and TWC are less good, which are just over 0.7 due to relatively few data.

5   Conclusions

In this paper, two contributions have been made for ECG automatic classifications. (1) The random padding/truncating method is a simple strategy that not only helps to balance the processing efficiency and recordings integrity, but also provides ways to augment and balance the dataset. Furthermore, the randomness involved by this method in the padding/truncating positions can prevent a DNN overfitting the padding/truncating manner. (2) The proposed workflow that combines different pipelines of model training to make an ensemble model achieved better results than each of the separated pipelines. Classification results showed that the proposed algorithm may provide a potential way of computer-aided diagnosis for clinical applications.

Acknowledgements. The work is supported by the National Science Foundation of China (NSFC) under Grant Nos. 61572152 (to HZ), 61571165 (to KW), 61601143 (to QL) and 81770328 (to QL), the Science Technology and Innovation Commission of Shenzhen Municipality under Grant Nos. JSGG20160229125049615 and JCYJ20151029173639477 (to HZ), and China Postdoctoral Science Foundation under Grant Nos. 2015M581448 (to QL).

References

1. Ari, S., Das, M.K., Chacko, A.: ECG signal enhancement using S-transform. IEEE Trans. Biomed. Eng. **43**(6), 649–660 (2013)
2. De Chazal, P., Reilly, R.B.: A patient-adapting heartbeat classifier using ECG morphology and heartbeat interval features. IEEE Trans. Biomed. Eng. **53**(12), 2535–2543 (2006)
3. Yang, H., Kan, C., Liu, G., Chen, Y.: Spatiotemporal differentiation of myocardial infarctions. IEEE Trans. Autom. Sci. Eng. **10**(4), 938–947 (2013)
4. Dima, S.-M., et al.: On the detection of myocadial scar based on ECG/VCG analysis. IEEE Trans. Biomed. Eng. **60**(12), 3399–3409 (2013)
5. Yu, S.N., Chou, K.T.: Integration of independent component analysis and neural networks for ECG beat classification. Expert Syst. Appl. **34**, 2841–2846 (2008)
6. He, K., Zhang, X., Ren, S., Sun, J.: Deep residual learning for image recognition. In: 2016 IEEE Conference on Computer Vision and Pattern Recognition (CVPR), pp. 770–778. IEEE, Las Vegas, NV, USA (2016)
7. He, R., et al.: Automatic detection of atrial fibrillation based on continuous wavelet transform and 2D convolutional neural networks. Front. Physiol. **9**, 1206 (2018)
8. Oh, S.L., Ng, E.Y., San Tan, R., Acharya, U.R.: Automated diagnosis of arrhythmia using combination of CNN and LSTM techniques with variable length heart beats. Comput. Biol. Med. **102**, 278–287 (2018)
9. Donoho, D.L.: De-noising by soft-thresholding. IEEE Trans. Inform. **41**(3), 613–627 (1995)

Deep Learning to Improve Heart Disease Risk Prediction

Shelda Sajeev[1]([✉]), Anthony Maeder[1], Stephanie Champion[1], Alline Beleigoli[1],
Cheng Ton[2], Xianglong Kong[3], and Minglei Shu[3]

[1] Flinders Digital Health Research Centre, School of Nursing and Health Sciences,
Flinders University, Adelaide, Australia
shelda.sajeev@flinders.edu.au
[2] Department of Big Data Engineering Technology
Research Center of E-Government, Jinan, Shandong, China
[3] Shandong Computer Science Center,
Shandong Provincial Key Laboratory of Computer Networks,
Qilu University of Technology, Jinan, China

Abstract. Disease prediction based on modeling the correlations between compounded indicator factors is a widely used technique in high incidence chronic disease prevention diagnosis. Predictive models based on personal health information have been developed historically by using simple regression fitting over relatively few factors. Regression approaches have been favored in previous prediction modeling approaches because they are simplest and do not assume any nonlinearity in the model for contributions of the chosen factors. In practice, many factors are correlated and have underlying non-linear relationships to the predicted outcome. Deep learning offers a means to construct a more complex modeling approach, along with automation and adaptation. The aim of this paper is to assess the ability of a deep learning model to predict the heart disease incidence using a common benchmark dataset (University of California, Irvine (UCI) dataset). The performance of deep learning model has been compared with four popular machine learning models (two linear and two nonlinear) in predicting the incidence of heart disease using data from 567 participants from two cohorts taken from UCI database. The deep learning model was able to achieve the best accuracy of 94% and an AUC score of 0.964 when compared to other models. The performance of deep learning and nonlinear machine learning models was significantly better compared to the linear machine learning models with increase in the dataset size.

Keywords: Cardiovascular disease · Risk factors · Risk prediction · Machine learning · Deep learning

This research was funded by the Government of South Australia and Shandong Provincial Government, China.

H. Liao et al. (Eds.): MLMECH 2019/CVII-STENT 2019, LNCS 11794, pp. 96–103, 2019.
https://doi.org/10.1007/978-3-030-33327-0_12

1   Introduction

Cardiovascular disease (CVD) is the leading cause of death worldwide (30%) and is regarded as highly preventable (90%) [14]. Coronary heart disease also known as heart disease is the most common form of CVD [1]. Primary prevention is thus, a high priority and requires screening for severity of the risk factors, and generally addressing these with medication or health behavior changing interventions. Likelihood of heart disease is conventionally assessed from known highly indicative risk factors using compound formulas based on underlying Cox regression analysis methods [8]. A major longitudinal study (Framingham) conducted in USA has provided evidence for risk factor effects contributing to these formulas [4]. Several CVD risk prediction models to estimate an individual's risk of a CVD event within a given period are available [11]. However, the existing models are limited to the use of clinical decision (or prediction) rules in the form of simple heuristics and scoring systems. These models use a small set of variables (risk factors) that are easily observable, known to be clinically relevant and therefore easily incorporated into calculations. In addition, the traditional models do not assume any non-linear relationships between the predictors and the outcome measure and suffer from generalization and lacks the ability to be updated as new information becomes available.

Deep learning/machine learning is an emerging computational technique that can address the issues of multiple and correlated predictors, nonlinear relationships and interactions between the predictors and outcome, better than the traditional approach [6]. A recent investigation within a UK population found machine learning approaches predicted cardiac events more accurately, compared to conventional models [13]. The aim of the work reported here was to investigate plausibility of using deep learning/machine learning approach, by demonstrating its ability to derive prediction models for heart disease. This study discusses variations that can arise in the performance of some typical linear and more sophisticated non-linear machine learning prediction methods on a case study for heart disease, using data from the well-known public domain UCI dataset. The effects of different underlying populations on predictive performance, and the impact of combining cohorts to mimic a more general population, are considered.

2   Materials and Methods

2.1   Dataset

The dataset used for this study was taken from the University of California, Irvine (UCI) machine learning repository. A detailed information of the database can be found in the literature [2]. As a result of the small sample sizes in the available datasets, two datasets (cohorts) with 13 common risk factors/variables and no overlap in data instances were combined for the purposes of the machine learning analysis, in addition to analyzing each cohort individually. The two datasets used were the Statlog heart dataset (270 participants) and Cleveland heart disease dataset (303 participants). Six participants were excluded from Cleveland dataset due to missing values, reducing the total sample to 567. The risk factors and the outcome variable used in the machine learning analysis are listed in Table 1.

2.2   Multi-Layer Perceptron - A Deep Learning Model

Multi-Layer Perceptron (MLP) is a traditional deep learning architecture [7]. It uses supervised learning called back propagation to train the model. It is a feed forward network consists of three types of layers (input, hidden and output). There could be one input layer, multiple hidden layers and one output layer. Nodes in each layer connected to every node in the previous and following layer. Nodes are not connected with any other node in the same layer. These connections carry a weight which represents the strength of the connection, typically initialized randomly. Learning is summarized by an attempt to determine which network connection weights best reduce the difference between predicted and true outputs. Activation function used on the node describes the nonlinear relationship between input of the node to the node output.

A basic MLP approach with 4 layers was used in this study: input layer, 2 hidden layers and output layer with 12, 8, 4 and 1 hidden units respectively. ReLU was used as the activation function for input and hidden layers. Sigmoid was the activation function used for the output layer. Loss function used was *binary-cross entropy* and *Adam* as optimizer. Deep learning environment used includes Python (3.6.6), Anaconda (5.3.0), Keras (2.2.4) and Tensorflow (1.11.0).

3   Experimental Setup and Performance Measures

In addition to MLP, four popular machine learning models (logistic regression (LR) [9], linear discriminant analysis (LDA) [10], support vector machine (SVM) with RBF kernel [12], and random forest (RF) [3]) were used for comparison. LR and LDA are simple linear classifiers, while SVM and RF are more advanced machine learning models that support non-linear classification. All the machine learning algorithms code was implemented in Python using the Scikit-learn library.

After removing missing values, the data was randomly divided into training and testing data. The training data consisted of 454 samples (80% of total data) and the remaining 113 samples (20%) were used for testing. Before feeding the data to the machine learning algorithms, some preprocessing was necessary. The data was normalized to zero mean and unit variance, to have each variable same influence on the cost function in designing the classifier.

In machine learning, a confusion matrix calculates the actual and predicted classifications for each class, measuring the accuracy of the algorithm and identifying the type of errors being made by the classifier. In this study, a confusion matrix was used to review the performance of the classification algorithm. The two-class confusion matrix reports four outcomes; true positives (TP) for subjects with heart disease, correctly classified as cases, false positives (FP) for healthy subjects incorrectly classified as cases, true negatives (TN) for healthy subjects correctly classified as healthy, and false negatives (FN) for subjects with heart disease incorrectly classified as healthy. The performance measures extracted from the confusion matrix were sensitivity, specificity, precision and accuracy and that are calculated as follows: $Sensitivity = \frac{TP}{TP+FN}$, $Specificity = \frac{TN}{TN+FP}$, $Precision = \frac{TP}{TP+FP}$ and $Accuracy = \frac{TP+TN}{TP+TN+FN+FP}$.

To visualize the performance of the classification algorithm, a receiver operating characteristic (ROC) curve was used. The curve is calculated by plotting the TP rate against the FP rate for every possible threshold. The area under the curve was used as a measure of the accuracy of the classification algorithm, an accepted approach for evaluating classification performance. Additionally, to ensure stable classification results, the overall process was repeated 50 times for each machine learning model. Performances results reported in Tables 2 and 3 are the average score from 50 iterations.

4   Results

4.1   Study Population Characteristics

The characteristics of the study population are reported in Table 1. The average age of the participants was 54 years. There were substantially fewer women than men (32% women, 68% men). Of the participants, 14% had diabetes and 52% had high cholesterol (above 240). In addition, 51% exhibited an abnormality in ECG results and 31% exhibited major vessel calcification in fluoroscopy, while 33% experienced exercise induced angina. There were 257 (45%) cases of heart disease, from 567 participants. In Statlog cohort, there were 120 cases out of 270 (44%) and in Cleveland 137 cases out of 297 (46%).

4.2   Prediction Accuracy

Tables 2 and 3 show the performance comparison of deep learning model and four machine learning models for predicting heart disease incidence for individual cohort and combined cohort respectively. As mentioned previously, the performance of the predictive models was accessed using sensitivity, specificity, precision, accuracy and AUC score. For individual cohort analysis, the machine learning model achieved an accuracy up to 0.838 and an AUC score up to 0.913 for Statlog cohort and an accuracy up to 0.840 and an AUC score up to 0.912 for Cleveland cohort. The results of the modeling indicated that the performance of the linear and nonlinear classifiers was similar in both cohorts.

For combined cohort analysis, deep learning model MLP obtained the highest scores (sensitivity = 0.932, specificity = 0.957, precision = 0.942, accuracy = 0.940 and an AUC score of 0.964). The next highest performance was achieved

Table 1. List of all 13 variables and the outcome variable that were used for machine learning analysis and their characteristics for combined cohort (Statlog and Cleveand).

Variables	Description	Values
Age	-	54.49 ± 9.06
Sex	Male	384 (68%)
	Female	183 (32%)
Cp	Chest pain type	
	Typical angina	43 (7.5%)
	Atypical angina	91 (16%)
	Non-anginal pain	162 (28.5%)
	Asymptomatic	271 (47.8%)
Trestbps	Resting blood pressure	131 ± 17.8
Chol	Serum cholesterol	248 ± 51.8
Fbs	Fasting blood sugar > 120 mg/dl) (1 = true; 0 = false)	
	Diabetics	83 (14.6%)
	Non-diabetics	484 (85.4%)
Restecg	Resting electrocardiographic results	
	Normal	278 (49%)
	Having ST-T wave abnormality	6 (1%)
	Showing probable or definite left ventricular Hypertrophy by Estes criteria	283 (50%)
Thalach	Maximum heart rate achieved	149 ± 23
Exang	Exercise induced angina (1 = yes; 0 = no)	
	No	381 (67%)
	Yes	186 (33%)
Oldpeak	ST depression induced by exercise relative to rest (0–6.2)	1.05 ± 1.15
Slope	The slope of the peak exercise ST segment	
	Upsloping	269 (47.4%)
	Flat	259 (45.7%)
	Down sloping	39 (6.9%)
Ca	Number of major vessels (0–3) colored by fluoroscopy	
	0	334 (58.9%)
	1	123 (21.7%)
	2	71 (12.5%)
	3	39 (6.9%)
Thal	Thallium stress test	
	Normal	316 (55.7%)
	Fixed defect	32 (5.6%)
	Reversible defect	219 (38.7%)
Presence of heart disease		257 (45%)

by RF (sensitivity = 0.890, specificity = 0.955, precision = 0.943, accuracy = 0.933 and an AUC score of 0.963). It can be seen that deep learning approach gives the best results in all performance measures except precision, where it is comparable with random forest. Further, the nonlinear models (MLP, RF and SVM) showed considerably superior results than the linear ones (LR and LDA).

Table 2. Comparison of the performance of deep learning and four machine learning models using thirteen risk factors predicting heart disease incidence for individual cohorts (Statlog and Cleveland). The reported values are the average of 50 iterations. DL represents deep learning.

Algorithms	Sensitivity	Specificity	Precision	Accuracy	AUC
Statlog heart dataset					
Logistic regression	**0.807**	0.859	0.821	0.836	0.910
Linear discriminant analysis	0.798	0.870	0.830	**0.838**	0.909
Support vector machine - RBF	**0.807**	0.849	0.849	0.830	0.907
Random Forest	0.788	0.879	0.838	0.836	**0.913**
DL - Multi-Layer Perceptron	0.701	**0.907**	**0.856**	0.814	0.881
Cleveland heart dataset					
Logistic regression	**0.794**	0.869	0.841	0.834	0.903
Linear discriminant analysis	0.789	**0.886**	0.858	**0.840**	0.904
Support vector machine - RBF	0.773	0.867	**0.867**	0.828	0.900
Random forest	0.778	0.883	0.853	0.832	**0.912**
DL - Multi-Layer Perceptron	0.780	0.879	0.850	0.833	0.861

Table 3. Comparison of the performance of deep learning and four machine learning models using thirteen risk factors predicting heart disease incidence for *combined* cohort (Statlog and Cleveand). The reported values are the average of 50 iterations. DL represents deep learning.

Algorithms	Sensitivity	Specificity	Precision	Accuracy	AUC
Logistic regression	0.817	0.873	0.844	0.848	0.913
Linear discriminant analysis	0.800	0.888	0.857	0.848	0.911
Support vector machine - RBF	0.866	0.906	0.885	0.888	0.943
Random forest	0.890	0.955	**0.943**	0.933	0.963
DL - Multi-Layer Perceptron	**0.932**	**0.957**	0.942	**0.940**	**0.964**

Figure 1 shows the ROC curves for all the five predictive models for combined cohort. The ROC curves have been drawn for one of the best cases of the 50 iterations. An AUC score 0f 0.988 was achieved using MLP. This indicates that the deep learning have the potential to build highly accurate prediction system that could give a second opinion in clinical decision making.

5 Discussion

In this study we presented deep learning and machine learning methodologies for predicting the presence of heart disease. Results for predictive accuracy obtained from deep learning model is compared with two popular linear (LR

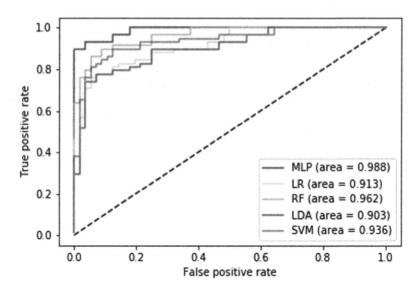

Fig. 1. ROC curves for MLP, LR, RF, LDA, SVM models for UCI study participants (Statlog and Cleveland cohorts combined). ROC is drawn for one of the 50 iterations.

and LDA) and non-linear machine learning models (SVM and RF). The models were applied on 13 highly indicative factors in the datasets, comparable with factors used in standard Framingham derived models. Evidence of heart disease diagnosis was available within the datasets through clinical history of chest pain, resting and exercise electrocardiogram, myocardial scintigraphy or angiogram tests (45% of cases). The results for application to two cohorts from different sources show that even for a small dataset, machine learning models can produce good results and variations in comparable cohorts do not affect this adversely. Furthermore, when the cohorts are combined, the overall non-linear model's performance increases significantly, while the results from linear models remain similar. The reason for superior performance could be due to its flexibility and non-linear function. Our train/test technique with 50 iterations assured the independence of the testing samples from training samples and validation of the model effectiveness.

As the deep learning model was created and tested on 2 small datasets, we have plans to validate the model in larger cohorts that will enable us to investigate the potential of deep learning with multiple layers and explore its suitability for general population heart disease risk prediction.

The availability of larger datasets from the electronic health records would allow deep learning/machine learning to discover unseen relationship and find new risk factors previously not identified as highly relevant. In addition, it could lead to the development of better cohort-based risk models and perhaps even individually tailored risk profiles. Finally, in this study we have not compared the proposed approach with the popular CVD risk prediction model: the American College of Cardiology/American Heart Association (ACC/AHA) model [5], as the information to compute the AHA model was not available in UCI dataset.

6   Conclusion

This work demonstrates value in considering deep learning method for disease prediction modeling, and the potential for modeling performance to improve as dataset size increases. This suggests that the deep learning approach may be more effective for maintaining prediction accuracy for datasets which change over time, as well as for specialized cohorts within the overall population, for which prediction may be less accurate due to deviation from the standard model. It provides an exciting prospect for achieving better and more specific disease risk assessment that may assist the drive towards personalised medicine.

References

1. AIHW: Cardiovascular disease: Australian facts 2011. Cardiovascular disease series. Cat. no. CVD 53. Canberra. Australian Institute of Health and Welfare (2011)
2. Bache, K., Lichman, M.: UCI Machine Learning Repository Irvine. University of California, School of Information and Computer Science, Oakland (2013). http://archive.ics.uci.edu/ml
3. Breiman, L.: Random forests. Mach. Learn. **45**(1), 5–32 (2001)
4. D'Agostino, R.B., et al.: General cardiovascular risk profile for use in primary care. Circulation **117**(6), 743–753 (2008)
5. Goff, D.C., et al.: 2013 ACC/AHA guideline on the assessment of cardiovascular risk: a report of the American College of Cardiology/American Heart Association task force on practice guidelines. J. Am. Coll. Cardiol. **63**(25 Part B), 2935–2959 (2014)
6. Goldstein, B.A., Navar, A.M., Carter, R.E.: Moving beyond regression techniques in cardiovascular risk prediction: applying machine learning to address analytic challenges. Eur. Heart J. **38**(23), 1805–1814 (2016)
7. Goodfellow, I., Bengio, Y., Courville, A.: Deep Learning. MIT Press, Cambridge (2016)
8. Hlatky, M.A., et al.: Criteria for evaluation of novel markers of cardiovascular risk: a scientific statement from the American Heart Association. Circulation **119**(17), 2408–2416 (2009)
9. Hosmer Jr., D.W., Lemeshow, S., Sturdivant, R.X.: Applied Logistic Regression, vol. 398. Wiley, Hoboken (2013)
10. Mika, S., Ratsch, G., Weston, J., Scholkopf, B., Mullers, K.R.: Fisher discriminant analysis with kernels. In: Neural Networks for Signal Processing IX: Proceedings of the 1999 IEEE Signal Processing Society Workshop (Cat. No. 98th8468), pp. 41–48. IEEE (1999)
11. Sajeev, S., Maeder, A.: Cardiovascular risk prediction models: a scoping review. In: Proceedings of the Australasian Computer Science Week Multiconference, p. 21. ACM (2019)
12. Van Gestel, T., et al.: Benchmarking least squares support vector machine classifiers. Mach. Learn. **54**(1), 5–32 (2004)
13. Weng, S.F., Reps, J., Kai, J., Garibaldi, J.M., Qureshi, N.: Can machine-learning improve cardiovascular risk prediction using routine clinical data? PLoS ONE **12**(4), e0174944 (2017)
14. WHO: Prevention of cardiovascular disease : guidelines for assessment and management of total cardiovascular risk. World Health Organization (2007)

LabelECG: A Web-Based Tool for Distributed Electrocardiogram Annotation

Zijian Ding[1], Shan Qiu[1], Yutong Guo[2], Jianping Lin[3,4], Li Sun[3],
Dapeng Fu[5], Zhen Yang[6], Chengquan Li[4], Yang Yu[7], Long Meng[8],
Tingting Lv[4,9], Dan Li[9], and Ping Zhang[4,9(✉)]

[1] Department of Electronic Engineering, Tsinghua University, Beijing, China
[2] School of Information and Electronics, Beijing Institute of Technology,
Beijing, China
[3] Xinheyidian Co. Ltd., Beijing, China
[4] School of Clinical Medicine, Tsinghua University, Beijing, China
zhpdoc@126.com
[5] Chinese Academy of Sciences Zhong Guan Cun Hospital, Beijing, China
[6] ECG Center, Tianjin Wuqing District People's Hospital, Tianjin, China
[7] The Affiliated Hospital of Qingdao University, Qingdao, China
[8] Shandong Mingjia Technology Co., Ltd., Taian, China
[9] Department of Cardiology, Beijing Tsinghua Changgung Hospital,
Beijing, China

Abstract. Electrocardiography plays an essential role in diagnosing and
screening cardiovascular diseases in daily healthcare. Deep neural networks
have shown the potentials to improve the accuracies of arrhythmia detection
based on electrocardiograms (ECGs). However, more ECG records with ground
truth are needed to promote the development and progression of deep learning
techniques in automatic ECG analysis. Here we propose a web-based tool for
ECG viewing and annotating, LabelECG. With the facilitation of unified data
management, LabelECG is able to distribute large cohorts of ECGs to dozens of
technicians and physicians, who can simultaneously make annotations through
web-browsers on PCs, tablets and cell phones. Along with the doctors from four
hospitals in China, we applied LabelECG to support the annotations of about
15,000 12-lead resting ECG records in three months. These annotated ECGs
have successfully supported the First China ECG intelligent Competition.
LabelECG will be freely accessible on the Internet to support similar researches,
and will also be upgraded through future works.

Keywords: Cardiovascular disease · Electrocardiograms · Distributed
annotation

1 Introduction

Electrocardiography is a common approach to diagnose and screen cardiovascular
diseases in clinic. Due to its characteristics including non-invasive, easy-to-operate and
economical, it's the most widely adopted clinical detection to diagnose arrhythmia,
myocardial ischemia and myocardial infarction [1]. In order to deal with large amounts

© Springer Nature Switzerland AG 2019
H. Liao et al. (Eds.): MLMECH 2019/CVII-STENT 2019, LNCS 11794, pp. 104–111, 2019.
https://doi.org/10.1007/978-3-030-33327-0_13

of electrocardiograms (ECGs), computerized interpretations aim to improve the correctness of ECG diagnose and alleviate the workloads of physicians [2]. Though there are dozens of computerized interpretation systems for ECGs, e.g. GE Marquette system [3] and Glasgow system [4], computerized interpretation are still suffered from the limited diagnostic accuracies [2].

As the fast growth and huge success of deep neural networks in computer vision and natural language processing, etc. [5], these computational techniques are expected to impact the area of precision cardiovascular medicine, including automatic ECG interpretation [6]. Recently Hannun et al. published their work on detecting and classifying arrhythmia based on single-lead ECG data [7]. The deep ResNet network achieved better results compared to several technicians, which was trained on almost 91,232 records and tested on 328 records from unique patients. Similarly, Attia et al. reported that a neural network, trained on 35,970 ECG-echocardiogram pairs and tested on 52,780 ECG records, can screen for asymptomatic left ventricular dysfunction [8]. These works show that deep neural networks are able to improve the diagnostic accuracies based on large collections of ECG records.

However, almost all ECG databases with careful annotations are small in sample sizes, which might inhibit the application and progression of deep neural networks. The application of an image annotation tool named LabelMe [9] laid the foundation of the well-known ImageNet dataset [10] that flourish the research of deep learning. Similarly, an ECG annotation tool can help build large collections of ECG records with ground truth. As a result, ECG databases with large sample sizes will promote the research of deep learning in the computerized analysis.

In this paper, we present a web-based tool for distributed ECG annotation named LabelECG. Physicians and technicians can annotate ECG records with various time lengths and number of leads, through the web-browsers on desktops, laptops, tablets and cell phones at anytime and anywhere. What's more, ECG datasets are under unified management, and can be accessed by several doctors simultaneously. Four doctors used LabelECG to annotate almost 15,000 12-lead resting ECG records. The resulting database has supported the First China ECG AI Challenge [11]. LabelECG will be accessible online to support similar researches.

2 Related Work

ECG annotating often requires expert knowledge and laborious work. Considering the tedious clinical workload of doctors, the manipulations should take up less time and improve efficiency. For example, the tool should provide a convenient way to access such that doctors can use spare time to annotate data. What's more, the tool should be responsible for data management such that doctors can focus on the data annotation. However, most previous tools fail to fulfill these requirements.

Most tools are used off-line (see Table 1). As a result, computers with installed tools and user manuals should be provided for doctors, who have to spend time to learn and use these tools. Among all tools shown in Table 1, WaveformECG [16] is the only web-based tool. However due to unknown reasons, the tool is not accessible currently.

For most off-line tools, the problem is that doctors have to be responsible for data management.

The major difference between LabelECG and these previous tools is on two aspects. First of all, LabelECG is a web-based tool for distributed ECG annotation. Several doctors can access LabelECG through web-browsers on desktops, laptops, tablets and even cell phones. Compared to WaveformECG, LabelECG is easier to deploy since it's based on docker. As a result, LabelECG is more suitable when doctors cannot upload data to the Internet and have to make annotations in a local area network. Secondly, LabelECG is responsible for data management. Doctors can ignore the manipulation of data and focus on ECG annotation.

Table 1. Tools for ECG annotation.

Name	Access	Functions
SigViewer [12]	Off-line	Multi-lead viewing, diagnose annotating
EcgEditor [13]	Off-line	Multi-lead viewing, QRS detection, diagnose annotating
ECG Viewer [14]	Off-line	QRS detection, diagnose annotating
BSS_ECG [15]	Off-line	QRS detection, diagnose annotating
WaveformECG [16]	Online	Multi-lead viewing, QRS detection, diagnose annotating

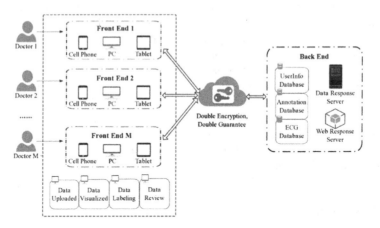

Fig. 1. The organization of LabelECG. Multiple doctors can upload, visualize, annotate and review ECG records through the frontends. The backend support these functions through three databases and two servers. LabelECG can be deployed on any cloud systems to connect the frontend and the backend.

3   LabelECG

LabelECG is a web-based tool for distributed ECG annotation (see Fig. 1). Through the web browsers of desktops, laptops, tablets and cell phones, multiple doctors can collaborate on annotating the diagnoses of ECG records at any time and any place.

With the help of unified data management, doctors are able to focus on annotation without manipulating hundreds of ECG records.

The distributed system consists of a frontend, a backend and a communicating cloud server. To explicitly explain the usage and deployment of LabelECG, we introduce the functions and architecture in the following two sections. Firstly, we mainly discuss how to login LabelECG, choose a dataset, visualize and annotate an ECG record, and revise the personal annotated records. Secondly, we mainly discuss how LabelECG is organized to support the above mentioned functions.

Fig. 2. The functions of LabelECG. (A) Register and login; (B) Select a dataset to ECG annotating; (C) Visualize and annotate diagnoses; (D) Personal accounts.

3.1 Functions

LabelECG is able to help users upload, visualize, annotate and revise their ECG records. To make these manipulations, the functions of LabelECG is designed to include four parts, including making registration and login, choosing a dataset, annotating the diagnoses, and revising all personal annotations (see Fig. 2).

First of all, the establishment of personal accounts makes it possible to track all annotations of each user. One character is that in consideration of data security, a system administrator needs to provide a verification code to each user to complete registration. This manipulation aims to ensure that only the specific users can have access to their ECG data.

Secondly, LabelECG offers almost all open source datasets from Physionet [17], as well as the user uploaded datasets. Users can choose their own dataset and begin ECG annotating. One characteristic of LabelECG is that when entering the dataset, users can begin with the last record in their last or previous annotation. LabelECG introduces the Lightwave system [17] to visualize any ECG records with various time lengths and number of leads. Meanwhile users can hide specific leads in order to facilitate the observation of certain leads. Three dialog boxes above the visualization are used to help make annotations: the box on the left side provides ECG parameters such heart rate, the one in the middle provides automatic diagnoses, and the one on the right is for writing annotations. Another characteristic of LabelECG is that users can label one record as either "confirmed" or "unsure", since some ECG records may be too ambiguous to annotate.

Furthermore, as multiple users can collaborate on annotating one dataset, LabelECG gives rights to advanced and experienced experts to verify all annotations among these users. Besides, LabelECG enhances intra-group communication by making the unsure ECG data visible for all group members.

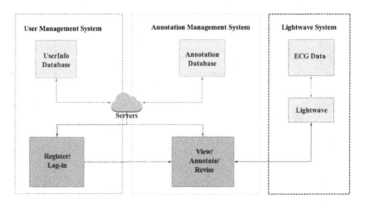

Fig. 3. The architecture of LabelECG. A user management system, an annotation management system and the Lightwave system support all the functions of LabelECG.

3.2   Architecture

To support the above mentioned functions, LabelECG is built upon three systems, including a user management system, an annotation management system and a Lightwave system (see Fig. 3). The user management system supports the function of user registration and user information management. The annotation management system supports the function of uploading and storing ECG data and their corresponding parameters, automatic diagnoses and user annotations. The Lightwave system supports the function of ECG visualization.

User Management System. This system mainly supports the function of user registration and user information storage. It includes a web page for registration and login, a user information database to store personal accounts, and a server to connect the front web page and the user information database.

To be specific, users need to register their accounts for ECG annotation. We have set "Password" etc. as the required information. After registration, users can login to enter their accounts. The log-in web page sends a login request to the server, and it will check the input information. It will reflect a successful connected prompt if the user's information is found. Otherwise, it will ask the user to check the fill-in information. The frontend of LabelECG offers an online working environment on computers, tablets, or cell phones. The backend server uses the framework of node.js and Express as the Common Gateway Interface (CGI). By keeping abreast with the request from the front end, the back end will return the corresponding data and information.

Annotation Management System. This system mainly supports the function of annotating and revising ECG records. It includes an annotation web page, a database to store ECG data and corresponding parameters, automatic diagnoses and user annotations, and a server to connect the frontend annotation web page with the backend database.

To be specific, if users have their ECG data to annotate, there exists an interface to transfer data into the backend ECG signal database. There is a backend server to decode and transfer the raw ECG data into the form fitting the standard of LabelECG. Users are also able to view ECG data from Physionet [17]. After entering the annotation page, the first-time users need to choose the first data to annotate. After the first-time annotation, the system automatically shows the record next to the ones they previously annotated.

In the annotation web page, users can visualize their ECG data and make annotations. We designed a "confirm" button and an "Unsure" button for annotation. After writing annotations into the right side box and pressing the "confirm" button, the server sends this message into the client's list of the Diagnosis Info database. If users press the "Unsure" button, this particular data is stored into a particular list in the Diagnosis Info database. Once users have clicked on one of the mentioned buttons, the interface would automatically turn to the next record. Moreover, we design "Next One" or "Previous One" button for users to view the nearby data.

In order to review the personal annotations, users can press the "Account" button and enter the review pattern. As for regular users, the labeled ECG data and annotation are shown in order. They can click on the data number and enter the annotation page to make revises. If a user has an expert account, s/he can also check other users' annotations.

Lightwave System. This system mainly supports the function of ECG data visualization. Physionet provides this system online [17]. We run this system as a CGI application. Once the front end sends requests to the back end, a web server collects and forwards them to the Lightwave system. Afterwards, the Lightwave system will parse the requests and access to the corresponding database in order to obtain data.

4   Supporting the First China ECG Intelligent Competition

The First China ECG Intelligent Competition aims to encourage the development of algorithms to classify, from 12-lead resting ECGs with various time lengths, whether an ECG record shows normal, atrial fibrillation, early repolarization and T wave change, etc. [11]. In order to ensure the data quality, doctors who come from Beijing Tsinghua Changgung hospital, Chinese Academy of Sciences Zhong Guan Cun Hospital, Tianjin Wuqing District People's Hospital, and the Affiliated Hospital of Qingdao University, used LabelECG to visualize, annotate and review about 15,000 records. LabelECG helped pair four doctors as two teams, and gave rights to two experienced doctors to review and revise all annotated records. With the assistances of LabelECG, these doctors finished annotations in about three months which guaranteed the success of the competition.

5   Discussion

LabelECG is a web-based tool for distributed ECG annotation. Multiple doctors can upload, visualize, annotate and revise ECG records via web browsers through desktops, laptops, tablets and cell phones. LabelECG is able to distribute one dataset to several doctors for collaborative annotation. It is also responsible for unified data management such that doctors can focus on data annotation. With doctors as first users, LabelECG supported the First China ECG Intelligent Competition. Our doctors annotated about 15,000 12-lead resting ECG records in about three months.

The current version of LabelECG can make annotations on diagnoses but lacks the ability to annotate local information such as beats and waves. We will add functions including beats annotation and fiducial point annotation, and add more automatic analysis functions, in order to reduce burden and improve efficiency. In addition, since the current version supported the Competition, LabelECG was presented in Chinese. We will distribute this version of LabelECG in English.

Acknowledgement. This work is supported by The National Key Research and Development Program of China (2017YFB1401804) and The Medicine-Engineering Innovation Support Program of Tsinghua University (IDS-MSP-2019003).

References

1. Clifford, G.D., Azuaje, F., McSharry, P.: Advanced Methods and Tools for ECG Data Analysis. Artech House, Boston (2006)
2. Schläpfer, J., Wellens, H.J.: Computer-interpreted electrocardiograms: benefits and limitations. J. Am. Coll. Cardiol. **70**(9), 1183–1192 (2017)
3. Marquette 12SL ECG Analysis Program, Statement of Validation and Accuracy. http://gehealthcare.com. Accessed 13 July 2019
4. Macfarlane, P.W., Devine, B., Clark, E: The university of Glasgow (Uni-G) ECG analysis program. In: Computers in Cardiology, 2005, pp. 451–454. IEEE (2016)
5. LeCun, Y., Bengio, Y., Hinton, G.: Deep learning. Nature **521**(7553), 436 (2015)

6. Krittanawong, C., Zhang, H., Wang, Z., Aydar, M., Kitai, T.: Artificial intelligence in precision cardiovascular medicine. J. Am. Coll. Cardiol. **69**(21), 2657–2664 (2017)
7. Hannun, A.Y., et al.: Cardiologist-level arrhythmia detection and classification in ambulatory electrocardiograms using a deep neural network. Nat. Med. **25**(1), 65 (2019)
8. Attia, Z.I., et al.: Screening for cardiac contractile dysfunction using an artificial intelligence–enabled electrocardiogram. Nat. Med. **25**(1), 70 (2019)
9. Russell, B.C., Torralba, A., Murphy, K.P., Freeman, W.T.: LabelMe: a database and web-based tool for image annotation. Int. J. Comput. Vis. **77**(1–3), 157–173 (2008)
10. Deng, J., Dong, W., Socher, R., Li, L.J., Li, K., Fei-Fei, L.: ImageNet: a large-scale hierarchical image database. In: 2009 IEEE Conference on Computer Vision and Pattern Recognition, pp. 248–255 (2009)
11. The First China ECG Intelligent Competition. http://mdi.ids.tsinghua.edu.cn/#/. Accessed 13 July 2019
12. Lin, Y., Brunner, C., Sajda, P., Faller, J.: SigViewer: visualizing multimodal signals stored in XDF (Extensible Data Format) files. arXiv preprint arXiv:1708.06333. 12 Aug 2017
13. EcgEditor. https://github.com/Unisens/EcgEditor. Accessed 13 July 2019
14. ECG Viewer. https://github.com/jramshur/ECG_Viewer. Accessed 13 July 2019
15. BSS_ECG. https://github.com/AdnanHidic/bss_ecg. Accessed 13 July 2019
16. Winslow, R.L., Granite, S., Jurado, C.: WaveformECG: a platform for visualizing, annotating, and analyzing ECG data. Comput. Sci. Eng. **18**(5), 36 (2016)
17. Goldberger, A.L., et al.: PhysioBank, PhysioToolkit, and PhysioNet: components of a new research resource for complex physiologic signals. Circulation **101**(23), e215–e220 (2000)

Particle Swarm Optimization for Great Enhancement in Semi-supervised Retinal Vessel Segmentation with Generative Adversarial Networks

Qiang Huo[1,2], Geyu Tang[1,2], and Feng Zhang[1,2(✉)]

[1] Institute of Microelectronics of Chinese Academy of Sciences,
Beijing 100029, China
zhangfeng_ime@ime.ac.cn
[2] University of Chinese Academy of Sciences, Beijing 100049, China

Abstract. Retinal vessel segmentation based on deep learning requires a lot of manual labeled data. That's time-consuming, laborious and professional. In this paper, we propose a data-efficient semi-supervised learning framework, which effectively combines the existing deep learning network with generative adversarial networks (GANs) and self-training ideas. In view of the difficulty of tuning hyper-parameters of semi-supervised learning, we propose a method for hyper-parameters selection based on particle swarm optimization (PSO) algorithm. This work is the first demonstration that combines intelligent optimization with semi-supervised learning for achieving the best performance. Under the collaboration of adversarial learning, self-training and PSO, we obtain the performance of retinal vessel segmentation approximate to or even better than representative supervised learning using only one tenth of the labeled data from DRIVE.

Keywords: Generative adversarial networks · Retinal vessel segmentation · Particle swarm optimization · Semi-supervised learning

1 Introduction

Retinal vessel segmentation is very important for assistant diagnosis, treatment and surgical planning of fundus diseases. Retinal vessel segmentation is also a necessary step for accurate visualization and quantification of retinal diseases. Changes of vascular morphology, such as shape, tortuosity, branch and width, provide a powerful reference to ophthalmologists in early diagnosis of retinal diseases [1]. Automatic vessel segmentation is of great value to improve work efficiency and reduce errors caused by fatigue and non-uniform illumination.

Conventional automatic retinal vessel segmentation includes supervised and unsupervised methods. Usually, most of unsupervised methods are rule-based technologies, including traditional matched filtering [2], morphological processing [3], vessel tracing [4], thresholding [5], etc. Although unsupervised learning usually has the advantage of high speed and low computational complexity, it requires hand-crafted feature extraction, which needs professional knowledge and is difficult to achieve high accuracy. Supervised

© Springer Nature Switzerland AG 2019
H. Liao et al. (Eds.): MLMECH 2019/CVII-STENT 2019, LNCS 11794, pp. 112–120, 2019.
https://doi.org/10.1007/978-3-030-33327-0_14

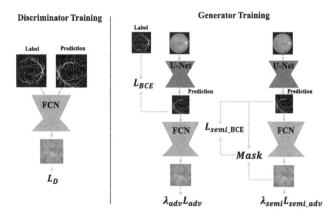

Fig. 1. Visualization of training of discriminator and segmentation networks for proposed semi-supervised learning.

methods are to train a series of gold standard data for pixel-level classification. Gold standard images are usually labeled by experienced ophthalmologists [6]. Supervised methods are widely used because of its better performance than unsupervised method without tricky manual feature engineering. However, little work about retinal vessel segmentation has been done under the semi-supervised learning framework.

In recent years, convolutional neural network (CNN) has been successfully applied in computer vision. Some studies have also extended it to the field of retinal vessel segmentation and achieved similar or even more than human segmentation results. However, these methods require huge number of artificial labeled images. Fundus images are not only difficult to obtain, but also require enormous efforts from ophthalmologists. There are obstacles in the wide application of supervised retinal vessel segmentation based on CNN [7, 8]. GAN has excellent ability to learn potential distribution and has been successfully used in unsupervised and semi-supervised learning [9]. GAN consists of generator and discriminator. Generators try to generate distributions close to the original data, while discriminators try to distinguish the original data from the generated data [10].

Particle swarm optimization (PSO) algorithm is an intelligent optimization algorithm based on the idea that the social sharing of information among the same species can bring benefits. Because of its concision, easy implementation, no need gradient information and few parameters, PSO has shown good results in continuous optimization problems and discrete optimization problems, especially its natural real coding characteristics are suitable for solving the problems of real optimization [11]. PSO has been applied to the selection of hyper parameters of deep neural networks and achieved excellent results [12].

In this paper, we replace the original generation network of GAN with segmentation network. The discriminator network uses the fully convolutional neural network with the confidence map as output instead of the discriminator which only outputs a single probability value. We introduce self-training scheme to construct semi-supervised learning framework with GAN for unlabeled data. PSO is proposed to select semi-supervised learning parameters to avoid its own noise. The scheme can greatly improve the effect of semi-supervised learning, save a lot of time and reduce the technical threshold compared with manual tuning.

2   Proposed Methods

2.1   Network Architecture

U-Net has the structure that initial convolutional feature maps are skip-connected to up-sampling layers from bottleneck layers. The structure can transfer the low-level features such as edges and lines of the original feature maps to the up-sampling layers, which makes the segmentation network better recognize the details, especially in the medical field with little data [13]. Therefore, we adopt U-Net as our segmentation network in our work, which is given a fundus image labeled or unlabeled and generates a probability map with the same size as input. The probability map shows the probability that each pixel belongs to the vessel.

We adopt the simplified fully convolutional network as our discriminator network. It consists of 5 convolution layers with 4×4 kernel and {64, 128, 256, 512,1} channels in the stride of 2 followed by a Leaky-ReLU parameterized by 0.2 except the last layer and an up-sampling layer to get the probability map with the size of the input map. Figure 1 shows our proposed algorithm framework.

2.2   Loss Function

The fundus images can be recognized as X_n with three channels. The output probability map of segmentation network can be regarded as function $S(X_n)$. $S(X_n)^{(h,w)}$ indicates the probability value of each pixel derived from the vessel. The discriminator network $D(\cdot)$ takes the output probability map $S(X_n)$ and the ground truth label map Y_n as input. The loss function L_{SEG} of our segmentation network can be defined as,

$$L_{SEG} = L_{BCE} + \lambda_{adv}L_{adv} + \lambda_{semi\_adv}L_{semi\_adv} + \lambda_{semi\_BCE}L_{semi\_BCE} \tag{1}$$

where,

$$L_{BCE} = -\frac{1}{nhw}\sum_{n,h,w} y_n^{(h,w)} log\left(S(X_n)^{(h,w)}\right) + (1 - y_n^{(h,w)})log\left(1 - S(X_n)^{(h,w)}\right) \tag{2}$$

$$L_{adv} = -\frac{1}{nhw}\sum_{n,h,w} log\left(D(S(X_n))^{(h,w)}\right) \tag{3}$$

$$L_{semi\_BCE} = -\frac{1}{nhw}\sum_{n,h,w} I\left(D(S(X_n))^{(h,w)} > T_{semi\_mask}\right)\left(\hat{y}_n^{(h,w)} log\left(S(X_n)^{(h,w)}\right) + (1 - \hat{y}_n^{(h,w)})log\left(1 - S(X_n)^{(h,w)}\right)\right) \tag{4}$$

The components of the loss function are:

i. L_{BCE} is the usual binary cross entropy loss of labeled fundus images. The target of this is to maximize the predicted probability over the correct class label.

ii. L_{adv} and L_{semi_adv} are the adversarial losses of predicted probability map generated from labeled and unlabeled fundus images by segmentation network. They have the same expression except for the different input sources. λ_{adv} and λ_{semi_adv} are coefficients of L_{adv} and L_{semi_adv} respectively.

iii. L_{semi_BCE} are the binary cross entropy loss of unlabeled fundus images based on a self-training semi-supervised learning framework. As shown in the indicator function $I(D(S(X_n))^{(h,w)} > T_{semi\_mask})$, the main idea of self-training is that the discriminator estimates the probability map of unlabeled data and selects the most assured pixels to participate in the construction of loss function. Then the label of selected pixels with high confidence is element-wise set with $\hat{y}_n^{(h,w)} = 1$ if $S(X_n)^{(h,w)} > 0.5$, and $\hat{y}_n^{(h,w)} = 0$ otherwise. λ_{semi_BCE} is the coefficient of L_{semi_BCE}.

The loss function L_D of our discriminator can be defined as,

$$L_D = -\frac{1}{nhw}\sum_{n,h,w} log\left(1 - D(S(X_n))^{(h,w)}\right) + log\left(D(Y_n)^{(h,w)}\right) \qquad (5)$$

where Y_n represents the vessel ground truth label map of fundus image. The adversarial loss is similar with traditional GAN in which target is to enhance the ability of discriminator to distinguish positive samples or others.

2.3 Hyper-parameter Selection for Semi-supervised Learning

Since self-training based semi-supervised learning is sensitive to hyper-parameters, it is easy to recognize unlabeled data as noise without refined parameter options. However, manual tuning will take a lot of time and be confusing. We deploy PSO as a wrapper to excavate hyper-parameters that make full use of unannotated fundus images, including λ_{semi_adv}, λ_{semi_BCE} and T_{semi_BCE}. Algorithm 1 shows the complete step of hyper-parameter selection for semi-supervised learning.

3 Implementation Details

3.1 Evaluation Datasets and Metric

We conduct experiments on DRIVE datasets [14]. DRIVE dataset has a clear demarcation of training and test set with 20 images in each category. The first manual annotator's images are used to train and test our proposed model. During training, we use the random scaling and cropping operations with size 512 × 512. We train all our models on this dataset for 20K iterations with batch size 2. We evaluate our methods with Area Under Curve for Receiver Operating Characteristic (ROC AUC), Area Under Curve for Precision and Recall curve (PR AUC) and the mean of them (Score).

3.2 Training Details

Our methods are implemented based on PyTorch library. We train the proposed model on a single GTX 1080Ti GPU with 11 GB memory. To train our U-Net, we use the Adam optimizer with fixed learning rate of 1e−4 and $\beta_1 = 0.5$, $\beta_2 = 0.9$. For hyper-parameters in L_{SEG}, we set λ_{adv} as 0.1. λ_{semi_adv}, λ_{semi_BCE} and T_{semi_BCE} are determined by PSO. To train the discriminator, we also adopt the Adam optimizer with $\beta_1 = 0.5$, $\beta_2 = 0.9$. Unlike U-Net, the learning rate is fixed as 0.01e−4 to balance adversarial learning.

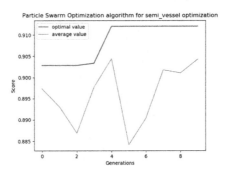

Fig. 2. The results of PSO for selecting the semi-supervised learning hyper-parameters when using 0.5 labeled images.

Algorithm 1 PSO for selecting the hyper-parameters of semi-supervised learning.

Input: b_l, b_u, G, S, ϕ_p, ϕ_g, ω **Output:** $\hat{P}$.

begin

    $f(P^S) \leftarrow -\infty$

for each particle $i = 1, \dots, S$ do

    Initialize the particle's position with a uniformly distributed random vector: $P_i \sim U(b_l, b_u)$

    Initialize the particle's best position to its initial position: $P_i^* \leftarrow P_i$

    if $f(P_i^*) > f(P^S)$ then

        Update the swarm's best position: $P^S \leftarrow P_i^*$

    Initialize the particle's velocity: $v_i \sim U(-|b_u - b_l|, |b_u - b_l|)$

while $g \leq G$ do

    for each particle $i = 1, \dots, S$ do

        Pick random numbers: $r_p, r_g \sim U(0,1)$

        Update the particle's velocity: $v_i \leftarrow \omega v_i + \phi_p r_p (P_i^* - P_i) + \phi_g r_g (P^S - P_i)$

        Update the particle's position: $P_i \leftarrow P_i + v_i$

        if $f(P_i) > f(P_i^*)$ then

            Update the particle's best position: $P_i^* \leftarrow P_i$

            if $f(P_i^*) > f(P^S)$ then

                Update the swarm's best position: $P^S \leftarrow P_i^*$

        $g \leftarrow g + 1$

        $\hat{P} \leftarrow P^S$

end

$\hat{P} = (\lambda_{semi\_adv}, \lambda_{semi\_BCE}, T_{semi\_BCE})$: outputs vector of hyper-parameters for semi-supervised learning.

b_l, b_u: the lower and upper limits. G: number of iterations.

S: population size. ϕ_p, ϕ_g: the acceleration coefficients.

ω: inertia weight.

Table 1. Progressive comparison of our semi-supervised retinal vessel segmentation model on DRIVE dataset with respect to Area Under Curve (AUC) for Receiver Operating Characteristic (ROC), Precision and Recall (PR).

Case I			
Model (Data Amount)	AUC (ROC)	AUC (PR)	Score
U-Net (0.1 labeled)	0.9391	0.8051	0.8721
U-Net+L_{adv} (0.1 labeled)	0.9496	0.8290	0.8893
U-Net+L_{adv}+L_{semi} (0.1 labeled + 0.9 unlabeled)	0.9550	0.8419	0.8985
Case II			
Model (Data Amount)	AUC (ROC)	AUC (PR)	Score
U-Net (0.5 labeled)	0.9554	0.8508	0.9031
U-Net+L_{adv} (0.5 labeled)	0.9650	0.8547	0.9099
U-Net+L_{adv}+L_{semi} (0.5 labeled + 0.5 unlabeled)	0.9681	0.8676	0.9179

Table 2. Comparison of our semi-supervised retinal vessel segmentation model with other classical methods on DRIVE datasets with respect to Area Under Curve (AUC) for Receiver Operating Characteristic (ROC), Precision and Recall (PR). Note that our model uses only 0.1 labeled images and 0.9 unlabeled images from DRIVE.

Method	AUC (ROC)	AUC (PR)	Score
Kernel Boost [6]	0.9306	0.8464	0.8885
Wavelets [16]	0.9436	0.8149	0.8793
HED [15]	0.9696	0.8773	0.9234
DRIU [8]	0.9793	0.9064	0.9428
Ours	0.9550	0.8419	0.8985

The discriminator and the U-Net are trained alternatively in every iteration until all of them converge. The typical maximum number of iterations is set as 20K. For our proposed semi-supervised learning, it is noted that λ_{semi_BCE} is set to 0 before 5000 iterations for the loss function L_{SEG} of U-Net in order to eliminate the noise introduced by immature U-Net and discriminator. The noise can be expressed as unreliable $I(D(S(X_n))^{(h,w)} > T_{semi\_mask})$ and $\hat{y}_n^{(h,w)}$ in Eq. 4. Besides, our proposed PSO method for hyper-parameters selection of semi-supervised learning can remove some noises further.

3.3 Hyper-parameter Selection Details

For hyper-parameters selection based on PSO, the main procedure is depicted in Algorithm 1. b_l and b_u determine the lower and upper bounds of vector P_i of hyper-parameters for semi-supervised learning respectively. According to prior knowledge of our work, we set $b_l = (0, 0, 0)$ and $b_u = (0.01, 0.3, 0.5)$. The number of total iterations G and the population size S of particle swarm are set to 10 and 3 after considering the trade off between time complexity and performance. The acceleration coefficients ϕ_p and ϕ_g are set as 1. Inertia weight ω plays an important role in the convergence of PSO. We use time-varying weight to avoid crossing the global optimum due to the narrow range of particle positions and too fast flight speed. ω_g can be expressed as,

$$\omega_g = \omega_{max} - \frac{\omega_{max} - \omega_{min}}{N_{iter}} \times g$$

where g is the number of iteration, ω_{max} is set as 0.5 and ω_{min} is set as 0.1.

We randomly choose two images from train dataset used to evaluate our fitness function $f(\cdot)$, that is, the score of our proposed model on retinal vessel segmentation. To reduce time of optimization and ensure optimal effect, the number of total iterations of each particle is modified to 1000 from 20000. Reference output vectors of hyper-parameters for semi - supervised learning are available after 16 h of optimizing and training on a single GTX 1080Ti GPU. The optimal and average scores for each generation of our proposed models are shown in Fig. 2. In this work, the optimal $\hat{P}$ is about (0.004, 0.1, 0.1).

4   Experimental Results

4.1   Progressive Comparison of Our Own Models

We randomly select 0.1 and 0.5 images from DRIVE dataset respectively as labeled data and the others as unlabeled data for training our semi-supervised retinal vessel segmentation framework. Case I and case II in Table 1 shows the progressive comparison of our own model. For our baseline, the U-Net achieves lowest score trained on 0.1 or 0.5 labeled images from DRIVE dataset. If combining adversarial learning with U-Net, the score will increase slightly because adversarial loss helps U-Net to generate probability map approximate to labeled data in details. After adding our semi-supervised loss, performance will be enhanced further to verify the effect of our proposed methods.

4.2   Comparison of Different Models

The comparison between our semi-supervised retinal vessel segmentation model and other representational methods is depicted in Table 2. Although only 0.1 labeled data is used, we have achieved similar or even better results compared with supervised learning using all labeled data from DRIVE.

5   Conclusions

In this paper we introduce a semi-supervised retinal vessel segmentation framework based on the idea of self-training and GAN. We adopt U-Net as our segmentation network given both labeled and unlabeled fundus image. For labeled data, the same method is adopted as traditional supervised learning. Inspired by self-training, the high confidence pixels of unlabeled data are selected by well-trained discriminator and then are marked as 0 or 1 to construct virtual label through the probability map generated from U-Net. Besides, PSO has been successfully applied to select the hyper-parameters of semi-supervised learning, which is beneficial for excavating maximum information from unlabeled dada. Under the collaboration of adversarial learning, self-training and PSO to select optimal hyper-parameters, we obtain the score of retinal vessel segmentation approximate to or even better than supervised learning using only 0.1 labeled data finally.

References

1. Abramoff, M.D., Garvin, M.K., Sonka, M.: Retinal imaging and image analysis. IEEE Rev. Biomed. Eng. **3**, 169–208 (2010)
2. Krause, M., Alles, R.M., Burgeth, B., Weickert, J.: Fast retinal vessel analysis. J. Real-Time Image Proc. **11**(2), 413–422 (2016)
3. Fraz, M.M., et al.: An approach to localize the retinal blood vessels using bit planes and centerline detection. Comput. Methods Programs Biomed. **108**(2), 600–616 (2012)
4. Wang, Y., Ji, G., Lin, P., Trucco, E.: Retinal vessel segmentation using multiwavelet kernels and multiscale hierarchical decomposition. Pattern Recogn. **46**(8), 2117–2133 (2013)
5. Mapayi, T., Viriri, S., Tapamo, J.-R.: Adaptive thresholding technique for retinal vessel segmentation based on GLCM-energy information. Comput. Math. Methods Med. **2015**, 11 (2015)
6. Becker, C., Rigamonti, R., Lepetit, V., Fua, P.: Supervised feature learning for curvilinear structure segmentation. In: Mori, K., Sakuma, I., Sato, Y., Barillot, C., Navab, N. (eds.) MICCAI 2013. LNCS, vol. 8149, pp. 526–533. Springer, Heidelberg (2013). https://doi.org/10.1007/978-3-642-40811-3_66
7. Liskowski, P., Krawiec, K.: Segmenting retinal blood vessels with deep neural networks. IEEE Trans. Med. Imaging **35**(11), 2369–2380 (2016)
8. Maninis, K.-K., Pont-Tuset, J., Arbeláez, P., Van Gool, L.: Deep retinal image understanding. In: Ourselin, S., Joskowicz, L., Sabuncu, Mert R., Unal, G., Wells, W. (eds.) MICCAI 2016. LNCS, vol. 9901, pp. 140–148. Springer, Cham (2016). https://doi.org/10.1007/978-3-319-46723-8_17
9. Souly, N., Spampinato, C., Shah, M.: Semi supervised semantic using generative adversarial network. In: IEEE International Conference Computer Vision (ICCV), pp. 5689–5697 (2017)
10. Goodfellow, I., et al.: Generative adversarial nets. In: Advances in Neural Information Processing Systems, pp. 2672–2680 (2014)
11. Esmin, A., Coelho, R., Matwin, S.: A review on particle swarm optimization algorithm and its variants to clustering high dimensional data. Artif. Intell. Rev. **44**(1), 23–45 (2015)
12. Lorenzo, P.R., et al.: Hyper-parameter selection in deep neural networks using parallel particle swarm optimization. In: Proceedings of the Genetic and Evolutionary Computation Conference Companion. ACM (2017)
13. Ronneberger, O., Fischer, P., Brox, T.: U-Net: convolutional networks for biomedical image segmentation. In: Navab, N., Hornegger, J., Wells, W.M., Frangi, A.F. (eds.) MICCAI 2015. LNCS, vol. 9351, pp. 234–241. Springer, Cham (2015). https://doi.org/10.1007/978-3-319-24574-4_28

14. Staal, J., et al.: Ridge-based vessel segmentation in color images of the retina. IEEE Trans. Med. Imaging **23**(4), 501–509 (2004)
15. Xie, S., Tu, Z.: Holistically-nested edge detection. In: Proceedings of the IEEE International Conference on Computer Vision, pp. 1395–1403 (2015)
16. Soares, J., Leandro, J.J., Cesar, R.M., Jelinek, H.F., Cree, M.J.: Retinal vessel segmentation using the 2-D Gabor wavelet and supervised classification. IEEE Trans. Med. Imaging **25**(9), 1214–1222 (2006)

Attention-Guided Decoder in Dilated Residual Network for Accurate Aortic Valve Segmentation in 3D CT Scans

Bowen Fan[1(✉)], Naoki Tomii[2], Hiroyuki Tsukihara[3], Eriko Maeda[3],
Haruo Yamauchi[3], Kan Nawata[3], Asuka Hatano[1], Shu Takagi[1],
Ichiro Sakuma[1], and Minoru Ono[3]

[1] Graduate School of Engineering, The University of Tokyo, Tokyo, Japan
percyfanbw@bmpe.t.u-tokyo.ac.jp
[2] Center for Disease Biology and Integrative Medicine,
The University of Tokyo, Tokyo, Japan
[3] The University of Tokyo Hospital, Tokyo, Japan

Abstract. Automatic aortic valve segmentation in cardiac CT scans is of high significance for surgeons' diagnosis on aortic valve disease and planning of aortic valve-sparing surgery. However, the very fast flapping speed, ambiguous shapes and extremely thin structures of the aortic valve lead to great difficulties in developing automatic segmentation algorithms. In this paper, we proposed an end-to-end deep learning method to address the problem of segmentation of the aortic valve from cardiac CT scans. Our method uses 3D voxel-wise dilated residual network (DRN) as backbone network and we equip it with novel attention-guided decoder modules to suppress non-valve artifacts and noise and pay attention on the fine leaflets in order to acquire accurate valve segmentation results. We conducted qualitative and quantitative analysis to compare with state-of-the-art (SOTA) 3D medical image segmentation models. Experiment results corroborate that the proposed method has very high competence.

Keywords: Aortic valve · 3D segmentation · Attention-guided decoder

1 Introduction

Aortic valve diseases like aortic insufficient are conditions in which the valve between the left ventricle and the ascending aorta doesn't work properly. For treatment of aortic valve diseases, valve-sparing surgeries like David operation are becoming more popular over valve-replacement surgeries for very favorable long-term results [1]. As surgical techniques in aortic valve repair surgeries continue to evolve, there is a growing need for understanding of patient-specific aortic valve anatomy since valve-sparing operations are being increasingly performed.

However, as valve-sparing surgeries are of much higher technical difficulties than valve replacement surgeries, 3D geometric modeling of the aortic valve could be used as a diagnostic tool to provide data on physiological parameters that are difficult to measure and provide help with surgeon's pre-operative planning. Such as how to determine the appropriately sized aorta graft or select proper suture points positions.

© Springer Nature Switzerland AG 2019
H. Liao et al. (Eds.): MLMECH 2019/CVII-STENT 2019, LNCS 11794, pp. 121–129, 2019.
https://doi.org/10.1007/978-3-030-33327-0_15

Cardiac CT is routinely used in the diagnosis of aortic valve diseases for the high spatial resolution it provides. Thus, geometric modeling of the aortic valve by segmentation from cardiac CT could be a robust strategy for delineation of the aortic valve's anatomy. However, accurate segmentation of aortic valve is highly challenging due to the weak and ambiguous boundaries of the leaflets in aortic valve caused by the high frequency motion (once per heart beat) and very thin structures (usually less than 1 mm), which shows in Fig. 1.

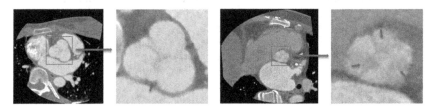

Fig. 1. Examples of two patients' CT images and corresponding subvolumes, the subvolumes are cropped centered around the aortic valve. Red arrows denote the missing or ambiguous boundaries of the aortic leaflets (Color figure online).

Recent deep learning methods for objects segmentation that based on fully convolutional networks (FCNs) [2] have shown overwhelming superiority over conventional segmentation methods. However, studies [3, 4] that apply deep learning on the aortic valve only focusing on the segmentation of the aorta or the aortic root and neglect the fine structures of the leaflets which provide the main sealing mechanism of the valve. While modeling of the whole aortic valve can help surgeons determine if a patient is a candidate for valve-sparing surgeries and provide indication of important feature points for pre-operative planning. Studies [5, 6] that attempted modeling the whole valve structures requires carefully designed handcrafted features, prior assumptions and constrains or manual tracing and identification and so on, while the aortic valve and surrounding structure is complex, especially with dynamic leaflets, these methods may result in time-consuming manipulations or suffer from inter/intra-observer variabilities as well as lack of robustness. To address this issue, we proposed to use end-to-end FCN for segmentation of the aortic valve. And to the best of our knowledge, this is the first work that apply deep learning method for segmentation of whole aortic valve structures.

Current design of FCN for image segmentation tasks mostly follows the 'encoder-decoder' structure, and the 'encoder-decoder' networks. Feature pyramid network (FPN) [7] is a typical 'encoder-decoder' structure that has been proved to be successful in many computer vision tasks including semantic segmentation. It has a pyramidal hierarchy that consisted of a bottom-up pathway for feature extraction, and a top-down pathway recovering spatial resolution from semantic encoded layers. Building on top of the idea of FPN, we chose extended 3D dilated residual network (DRN) [8] as decoder module and integrated it with concurrent channel & spatial excitation blocks [9] for performance promotion. And motivated by the recent success of attention mechanism, we devised an attention-guided decoder module that leverages multi-scale contextual information to better recover precise image details.

2   Method

2.1   Encoder

DRN. DRN [8] is a novel CNN architecture that incorporating residual connection and dilated convolutions. The idea of dilated convolutions is to enlarge the receptive field and conquer the extra information loss caused by downsampling steps. Such operations allow CNN models extract detailed information about less salient objects, like the leaflets in aortic valve. Yu et al. [8] first proposed to encapsulate dilated convolutions into the ResNet [10] architecture, and compared with vanilla ResNet, DRN removed the maxpooling layers and added 2 additional blocks at the end of the network without residual connections in order to suppress gridding artifacts caused by a series of dilated convolutions.

In this work, we replaced 2D convolutions in DRN with 3D ones, which is similar as the idea proposed in [11]. The design of the convolution blocks remains the same as in the original DRN that in each block there are 2 convolution operations followed by Batch normalization (BN) layers and rectified linear units (ReLU) layers. Before the last ReLU activation, the input and the transformed features are added altogether as the residual connection. We empirically reduce the size of the feature maps to one-eighth of the input volume by 3 strided convolutions. With such resolution, the network can preserve important details about less salient objects. The architecture is illustrated in detail in Fig. 2(a).

Squeeze and Excitation. The interdependencies between feature maps and channels recently were explicitly explored by Hu et al. [12], and they introduced a novel module called squeeze & excitation (SE) block that can recalibrate the channels of feature maps and capture the importance of each specific channel to emphasize on useful channels. In SE block, it first squeezes along channels and calculate per-channel importance then later expands these statistics as excitation on the channels-wise features. Such simple yet effective module can be seamlessly integrated into current popular CNN architectures and help to boost performance. But this module only excites the channel-level features, while for segmentation, the information in feature space can be more significant. To leverage the effect of SE block on spatial level, Roy et al. [9] referred the SE block as channel SE (cSE) and introduced another SE block called spatial SE (sSE) which excites the feature spatially and they incorporated them as concurrent spatial and channel SE blocks (scSE). Experiments in [9] shown that scSE block brought consistent performance promotion to different FCN architectures for segmentation and scSE outperformed either cSE block or sSE block.

For volumetric segmentation, we further extended scSE block into 3D level and inserted it into every basic blocks of 3D DRN. Consider a feature tensor $\mathbf{F} \in \mathbb{R}^{C \times H \times W \times D}$, where C is the channel number, and H, W and D is the height, width and Depth of the tensor respectively. In cSE block, the spatial squeezing is done by a 3D global average pooling operation P_{GA}, and two fully-connected layers $W_1 \in \mathbb{R}^{C \times \frac{C}{16}}$, $W_2 \in \mathbb{R}^{\frac{C}{16} \times C}$ and ReLU operator δ follows P_{GA}, where 16 is the reduction ratio. Then the feature maps are passed through a sigmoid layer σ for recalibration of channels; In sSE block, we applied a

3D convolution layer with weight as $W_3 \in \mathbb{R}^{1 \times 1 \times 1 \times C \times 1}$ on the feature maps to squeeze the channels and excite the spatial information by using another sigmoid layer σ rescaling the output. Finally, we obtained concurrent spatial and channel SE by element-wise addition. The scSE block is formulated as:

$$F_{cSE} = \sigma(W_1 \cdot \delta(W_2 \cdot P_{GA}(\mathbf{F}))) \tag{1}$$

$$F_{sSE} = \delta(W_3 \cdot F) \tag{2}$$

$$F_{scSE} = F_{cSE} \oplus F_{sSE} \tag{3}$$

The proposed encoder structure is detailed in Fig. 2(a).

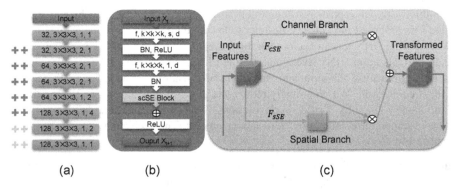

(a)   (b)   (c)

Fig. 2. The architecture of proposed encoder. (a) is the whole structure, the green block is a standard Conv-BN-ReLU block; the red block is the basic block with residual connection and scSE block implemented, (b) is the illustration of basic block with parameters (f, k × k × k, s, d), where f is the number of kernels, k is the kernel size, s is the stride and d is the dilation rate; '++' means there are two identical blocks stacked and only the first block has a strided convolution. (c) is the structure of scSE block (Color figure online).

2.2 Decoder

In the bottom-up pathway of FPN, as the spatial resolution decreases, more high-level structures are detected. Such high-level features can help enhance the spatial consistency of dense prediction since it is more semantic encoded. However, in the original design of FPN, the high-level features are propagated to low-level features only with element-wise addition after upsampling, that we think it is too simplistic for features mergence at different scales.

As a matter of fact, the scSE block works as a dual-branch module that leverage global context encoded in both feature channels and space so that it can learn 'what' and 'where' it should attend to in the feature maps, then it reweights the input feature itself for boosting representation ability. Inspired its structure, we devised an attention-guided decoder module to utilize the rich semantic information encoded in the high-level features to guide 'what' and 'where' to look for not in itself but in low-level features. The details of the module are described below:

First, the high-level $F_h \in \mathbb{R}^{C_h \times H_h \times W_h \times D_h}$ feature is upsampled as the same spatial dimension as low-level feature $F_l \in \mathbb{R}^{C_l \times H_l \times W_l \times D_l}$. Instead of using by interpolation or deconvolution to recover the feature maps to original input size, we assumed that using Dense Upsampling Convolution (DUC) of [13] can better recover fine-detailed information from coarse feature maps. As argued in [11], interpolation upsampling do not have learnable parameters while using deconvolution may leads to checkerboard artifacts. And DUC works as a learned interpolation process and has advantages to eliminate checkerboard artifacts. The DUC operation first transforms high-level features F_h to $F_h' \in \mathbb{R}^{C_l r^3 \times H_h \times W_h \times D_h}$ by 3D convolution $W_4 \in \mathbb{R}^{1 \times 1 \times 1 \times C_h \times C_h r^3}$, where r being the upsampling factor and we choose r as 2. And F_h' will be remapped as upsampled high-level features $F_h^{up} \in \mathbb{R}^{C_l \times r H_h \times r W_h \times r D_h}$, which is later merged with low-level feature F_l as $F_l' \in \mathbb{R}^{2C_l \times H_l \times W_l \times D_l}$. Then feature maps recalibrated by channels and space are calculated similarily as scSE block:

$$M_c = \sigma \left(W_5 \cdot \delta \left(W_6 \cdot P_{GA} \left(F_l' \right) \right) \right) \tag{4}$$

$$M_s = \sigma(W_8(\delta(W_7 \cdot F_l'))) \tag{5}$$

Where P_{GA}, σ, δ are 3D global average pooling, ReLU and sigmoid operation respectively. $W_5 \in \mathbb{R}^{2C_l \times \frac{2C_l}{16}}$, $W_6 \in \mathbb{R}^{\frac{2C_l}{16} \times C_l}$ are two fully connected layers. $W_7 \in \mathbb{R}^{1 \times 1 \times 1 \times 2C_l \times C_l}$ and $W_8 \in \mathbb{R}^{1 \times 1 \times 1 \times C_l \times 1}$ are two convolutional layers with kernel size as 1. Both feature maps are multiplied on the F_l then added up with F_h^{up} to $F_l'' \in \mathbb{R}^{C_l \times H_l \times W_l \times D_l}$. Finally, F_l'' is rectified it by another 3D convolution $W_9 \in \mathbb{R}^{3 \times 3 \times 3 \times C_l \times C_l}$ with , and it will be treated as high-level features F_h'' at finer scale.

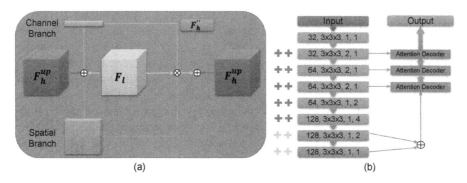

Fig. 3. (a) is the illustration of attention-guided decoder module proposed in this study and (b) is the full 'encoder-decoder' network we used for segmentation of the aortic valve. All variables are detailed in Sect. 2.2.

The proposed decoder module leverages the abundant context information in high-level features and help recover details of fine structures in low-level features. And this module will introduce very limited parameters to the model since most the operations are applied on squeezed features. The proposed module and whole network architecture are illustrated in Fig. 3.

3 Dataset and Implementation Details

Dataset and Pre-processing. We collected cardiac CT scans from 14 distinct patients and the scan of each patient contains 13 to 20 series of different cardiac phase that collected within one heartbeat. We selected several series at the end or beginning of diastole phase which have clearer leaflets structures. For each series there is a manual annotation delineated by an experienced radiologist, the annotation includes aortic root (AR), aortic leaflets (AL) and background. The 14 patients were randomly divided in to 5 groups for a 5-fold cross-validation. We cropped subvolumes that centered around the aortic valve from the original scans as shown in Fig. 1. The cropped subvolumes were resized to $48 \times 128 \times 128$ (D, H and W) and normalized as zero mean and unit variance. We performed volumetric data augmentation by random rotation, scaling and elastic deformation.

Training Environment and Parameters. The network was trained in PyTorch with a GTX 1080 Ti GPU. We used Adam optimizer with learning rate as 10^{-4}, the hyper-parameter $\beta 1$ was 0.9 and $\beta 2$ was 0.999, and weight decay as 10^{-4}. We chose cross-entropy error at each pixel over the categories as our objective function.

4 Experiments and Results

We carried out an ablation analysis to investigate the effectiveness of different components proposed in this study. The implanted variants of our method include: (1) 3D DRN + FPN; (2) 3D DRN (scSE) + FPN; (3) 3D DRN (scSE) + FPN (DUC). And finally, the proposed method. At the same time, we also implemented several advanced 3D segmentation models, including 3D U-Net [14] and V-Net [15], and two recently proposed FCNs that also integrated with different attention modules. One is the 3D U-Net with scSE modules in both encoder and decoder paths extended from [9]. The other is Attention U-Net [16], which leverages gated attention information.

We trained all these models with the same training strategy mentioned above till we observed an obvious plateau in validation loss for a fair comparison. The evaluation metrics employed includes Dice and Jaccard score for the AR, AL as well as whole aortic valve (AV). The quantitative comparison can be found in Table 1.

Table 1. Dice and Jaccard of different methods

	AR	AL	AV	AR	AL	AV
Networks	Dice			Jaccard		
3D U-net [14]	0.971(0.008)	0.618(0.068)	0.950(0.050)	0.940 (0.021)	0.453(0.051)	0.916(0.081)
V-net [15]	0.973(0.009)	0.615(0.035)	0.953(0.051)	0.943(0.019)	0.450(0.042)	0.918(0.088)
3D U-net + scSE [9]	0.978(0.008)	0.645(0.037)	0.961(0.048)	0.947(0.020)	0.479(0.040)	0.925(0.082)
Attention U-net [16]	0.977(0.006)	0.636(0.027)	0.959(0.048)	0.949(0.019)	0.474(0.031)	0.926(0.080)
Method (1)	0.975(0.008)	0.616(0.043)	0.956(0.049)	0.945(0.020)	0.451(0.039)	0.920(0.082)
Method (2)	0.977(0.007)	0.622(0.035)	0.957(0.047)	0.947(0.019)	0.462(0.034)	0.924(0.081)
Method (3)	0.976(0.008)	0.640(0.023)	0.959(0.047)	0.948(0.018)	0.478(0.024)	0.926(0.080)
Our method	0.979(0.007)	**0.667**(0.029)	0.960(0.048)	0.950(0.019)	**0.498**(0.028)	0.928(0.079)

As observed, the scores of AR in different methods are very close while for AL, which has thin structures and ambiguous boundaries, our method outperforms others by a large margin. Moreover, there is a consistent performance promotion with each proposed component added to the network. We also compared each method qualitatively in Fig. 4, where we visualized results of 2 slices in the middle of subvolumes of two patients. Finally, we visualized the reconstructed 3D model in Fig. 5.

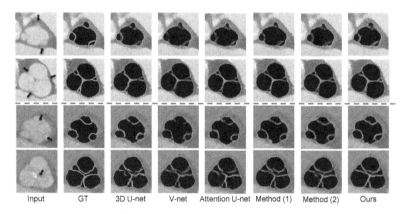

Input   GT   3D U-net   V-net   Attention U-net Method (1) Method (2) Ours

Fig. 4. Qualitative comparison between different methods. As shown in this figure, our method has the most similar segmentation results to the ground truth (GT). Furthermore, our method produced better inference of the blurring boundaries than others as indicated by red arrows (Color figure online).

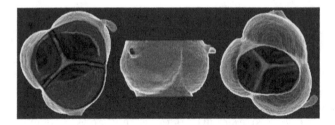

Fig. 5. Visualization of 3D aortic model of from top, side and bottom.

5   Conclusion

This paper presents the first deep learning method for aortic valve segmentation. The proposed method has achieved great performance segmenting the whole valve structures. The precise delineation of aortic valve morphology by segmentation can help surgeon with diagnosis of aortic diseases and planning of valve-sparing surgery. Furthermore, the reconstructed 3D model can be converted to surface models for computational fluid dynamics (CFD) simulation. Such simulation may also help us investigate the relation between thoracic aortic valve diseases and aortic flow patterns and offer us the possibility to improve the treatment of aortic valve diseases by optimizing the design of prosthetic heart valves in a controlled and specific way.

We proposed to use the 'encoder-decoder' structure to accurately segment the aortic valve. The encoder is built on 3D DRN with scSE blocks. And inspired by the scSE blocks, we devised a light-weight attention-guided decoder module that can be integrated into the FPN structure to recover the fine details of the feature maps. Our key idea is that high-level features contains useful information that can guide to refine the low-level features. Moreover, the proposed method is a general solution that has considerable potential to be extended to other medical image segmentation problems.

References

1. Beyersdorf, F., et al.: Current state of the reimplantation technique (DAVID Operation): surgical details and results. HSR Proc. Intensive Care Cardiovasc. Anesth. **4**(2), 73 (2012)
2. Long, J., et al.: Fully convolutional networks for semantic segmentation. In: CVPR, pp. 3431–3440 (2015)
3. Bai, W., et al.: Recurrent neural networks for aortic image sequence segmentation with sparse annotations. In: Frangi, A., Schnabel, J., Davatzikos, C., Alberola-López, C., Fichtinger, G. (eds.) MICCAI 2018. LNCS, vol. 11073, pp. 586–594. Springer, Cham (2018). https://doi.org/10.1007/978-3-030-00937-3_67
4. Lalys, F., et al.: Automatic aortic root segmentation and anatomical landmarks detection for TAVI procedure planning. Minim. Invasive Ther. Allied Technol. **28**(3), 1–8 (2018). https://doi.org/10.1080/13645706.2018.1488734
5. Pouch, A.M., et al.: Medially constrained deformable modeling for segmentation of branching medial structures: application to aortic valve segmentation and morphometry. Med. Image Anal. **26**(1), 217–231 (2015). https://doi.org/10.1016/j.media.2015.09.003

6. Khamooshian, A., et al.: Dynamic three-dimensional geometry of the aortic valve apparatus —a feasibility study. J. Cardiothorac. Vasc. Anesth. **31**(4), 1290–1300 (2017). https://doi.org/10.1053/j.jvca.2017.03.004

7. Lin, T.Y., et al.: Feature pyramid networks for object detection. In: CVPR, pp. 2117–2125 (2017)

8. Yu, F., et al.: Dilated residual networks. In: CVPR, pp. 636–644 (2017)

9. Roy, A.G., et al.: Concurrent spatial and channel 'squeeze & excitation' in fully convolutional networks. In: Frangi, A., Schnabel, J., Davatzikos, C., Alberola-López, C., Fichtinger, G. (eds.) Medical Image Computing and Computer Assisted Intervention – MICCAI 2018. LNCS, vol. 11070, pp. 421–429. Springer, Cham (2018). https://doi.org/10.1007/978-3-030-00928-1_48

10. He, K., et al.: Deep residual learning for image recognition. In: CVPR, pp. 770–778 (2016)

11. Shi, Z., et al.: Bayesian VoxDRN: a probabilistic deep voxelwise dilated residual network for whole heart segmentation from 3D MR images. In: Frangi, A.F., Schnabel, J.A., Davatzikos, C., Alberola-López, C., Fichtinger, G. (eds.) MICCAI 2018. LNCS, vol. 11073, pp. 569–577. Springer, Cham (2018). https://doi.org/10.1007/978-3-030-00937-3_65

12. Hu, J., et al.: Squeeze-and-excitation networks. In: CVPR, pp. 7132–7141 (2018)

13. Wang, P., et al.: Understanding convolution for semantic segmentation. In: WACV, pp. 1451–1460 (2018)

14. Çiçek, Ö., Abdulkadir, A., Lienkamp, Soeren S., Brox, T., Ronneberger, O.: 3D U-Net: learning dense volumetric segmentation from sparse annotation. In: Ourselin, S., Joskowicz, L., Sabuncu, M.R., Unal, G., Wells, W. (eds.) MICCAI 2016. LNCS, vol. 9901, pp. 424–432. Springer, Cham (2016). https://doi.org/10.1007/978-3-319-46723-8_49

15. Milletari, F., et al.: V-net: fully convolutional neural networks for volumetric medical image segmentation. In: 3DV, pp. 565–571 (2016)

16. Oktay, O., et al.: Attention U-Net: learning where to look for the pancreas. arXiv preprint (2018)

ARVBNet: Real-Time Detection of Anatomical Structures in Fetal Ultrasound Cardiac Four-Chamber Planes

Jinbao Dong, Shengfeng Liu$^{(\boxtimes)}$ (ID), and Tianfu Wang

School of Biomedical Engineering, Health Science Center, Shenzhen University,
Shenzhen 518060, China
liusf2009@163.com

Abstract. The quality assessment of ultrasound images is essential for prenatal diagnosis, in which detection of anatomical structures is the first and most important step in quality assessment. In clinical practice, it is usually done manually, which is experience-dependent, labor-extensive and time-consuming, as well as suffering from high inter- and intra-observer variability. In this paper, we propose a novel real-time detection model, named aggregated residual visual block network (ARVBNet), to accomplish automatic detection of anatomical structures in cardiac four-chamber plane (CFP) of fetal ultrasound images. Experiments on 1991 fetal ultrasound CFPs demonstrate the proposed network achieves state-of-the-art performance of 93.52% mean average precision (mAP) and a test speed of 101 frame-per-second (FPs). In addition, an extended experiment on the Pascal VOC dataset achieves state-of-the-art performance of 81.2% mAP as well, demonstrating the adaptability and generality of our proposed model.

Keywords: Anatomical structure detection · Aggregated residual visual block (ARVB) network · Ultrasound cardiac four-chamber plane · Deep learning

1 Introduction

Ultrasound (US) screening is widely used for obstetric diagnosis in routine clinical examination for the reason that US is low-cost and radiation-free [1]. The significance of quality control or assessment for fetal US images has been frequently emphasized. In [2], a guideline of quality assessment was proposed for the subjective assessment of the fetal US images. Quality control is essentially to judge whether it is a qualified (or standard) US plane, which is usually achieved by detecting whether the important anatomical structures can be clearly visible and well showed in the US view. Therefore, detection of anatomical structures is extremely essential for quality assessment of the US images especially the fetal CFPs with multiple anatomical structures. However, it is currently done by hand, suffering from some drawbacks, such as skilled experience and intensive labors, as well as high inter- and intra-observer variability.

To address these issues, it is imperative to develop an automatic detection framework of anatomical structures in clinical practice. Benefit from rapid development of

© Springer Nature Switzerland AG 2019
H. Liao et al. (Eds.): MLMECH 2019/CVII-STENT 2019, LNCS 11794, pp. 130–137, 2019.
https://doi.org/10.1007/978-3-030-33327-0_16

deep learning and artificial intelligence techniques, some related works have been presented for the topic. For example, Maraci et al. [3] presented an automated framework to detect the fetal breech presentation and heartbeat from US videos. To achieve automatic detection of anatomical structures (i.e., stomach bubble and umbilical vein) in fetal abdominal US images, Wu *et al.* [4] adopted a two-step strategy: (1) location of regions-of-interest (ROIs), and (2) detection of key anatomical structures. Experiments demonstrated a comparable result was obtained but it took approximately one minute for the detection of each image. This is not acceptable in the clinical practice. Therefore, a faster detection method for anatomical structures on the US images is desirable.

In this paper, we propose an automatic detection framework, in a one-stage manner, to detect anatomical structures in cardiac four-chamber plane (CFP) of fetal US images. Compared to other fetal US planes (e.g., abdominal, cranial), it is more difficult to detect anatomical structures for fetal cardiac US plane for high intra- and inter-variation, as shown in Fig. 1. To address these challenging issues, we firstly make the detailed criteria for all the structures in fetal US CFPs, according to the prenatal screening specification and experience from clinical radiologists, as summarized in Table 1. More importantly, a novel detection model, termed as Aggregated Residual Visual Block Network (ARVBNet), is proposed to detect the Left atrial pulmonary vein angle (PVA), Apex cordis and moderator band (ACMB) and irregular Multiple ribs (MRs) in the fetal cardiac US planes.

The contributions of this work are summarized as follows. First, to our knowledge, this is the first study to perform detection of key anatomical structures in a fully automated and fast manner for fetal US cardiac four-chamber views. Second, inspired

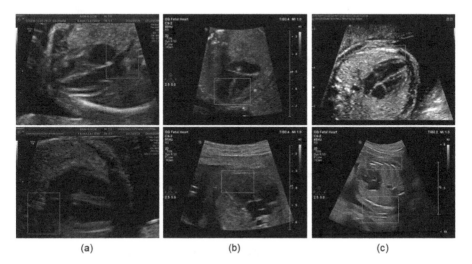

(a)   (b)   (c)

Fig. 1. Illustration of key anatomical structures in CFPs. Column (a) PVA, (b) ACMB, and (c) MRs. For (a) and (b), the upper row represents the structures are clear and visible, and the bottom indicates the structures are invisible. For (c), the upper row shows no more than one rib, and the bottom exhibits multiple ribs either on one side or both of sides in the image.

by human visual mechanism, we present the ARVBNet to imitate the relationship between the size and eccentricity of receptive fields, so as to largely strengthen the capability of feature representations of the networks. Finally, to validate the adaptability and generality of our ARVBNet, an extended experiment on the Pascal VOC dataset is performed and achieves state-of-the-art performance.

Table 1. Criteria of fetal CFP.

Structures	Criteria
PVA	PVA should be clearly visible between the left atrium and spine
ACMB	AC should be clearly visible, and MB should exhibit in hypo-echogenicity
MRs	MRs (more than or equal to two ribs) appear either on one side or both of sides

2 Methodology

2.1 Overview

Several studies in neuroscience showed that the size of human receptive field (HRF) is an eccentricity function in retinotopic maps in visual cortex and it increases with the eccentricity in each map [5]. Liu *et al.* [6] proposed receptive field blocks (RFBs) consisting of inception architecture and dilated convolution layers with different dilated rates, to simulate the relation between the size and eccentricity of HRF. Inspired by the mechanism, we propose a new module, namely ARVB, to enhance the capability of feature representations in the task of real-time detection. Specifically, the ARVB makes full use of grouped convolutions to perform feature extraction more comprehensively and dilated convolutions to simulate the human visual mechanism. In our model, the top two layers of single shot multibox detection (SSD) network are replaced with three ARVB modules (yellow cubic block in Fig. 2), so as to form the ARVBNet. The pipeline of the ARVBNet is shown in Fig. 2.

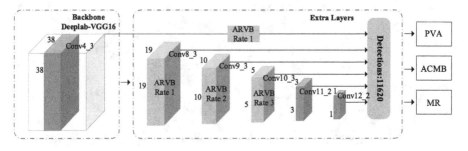

Fig. 2. Pipeline of the ARVBNet (Color figure online).

2.2 Aggregated Residual Visual Block

Each of the ARVB modules is composed of three layers. In the first layer, a 1×1 convolution layer is used to reduce the number of channels, which can not only decrease the number of the parameters for subsequent grouped and dilated convolutions, but also help to form a feature extraction hierarchy. The 3×3 grouped and dilated convolutions are adopted in the second layer, which can be easily realized through setting the grouped parameters and dilated rates simultaneously. Finally, a 1×1 convolution layer is followed to integrate feature information, reduce the number of the parameters and keep the input and output channel unchanged. Residual connection is used.

To mimic the relationship between the size and eccentricity of HRF, we explore the different rules (equidifferent, geometric and customized) to choose the dilated rates for the three ARVB modules. The tolerance of equidifferent rule is fixed as 2 (X, X + 2, X + 4 for three modules respectively); Common ratio of geometric rule is also set as 2 (X, 2 * X, 2^2 * X for three modules respectively). As to customized rule, we set the dilated rates for the three ARVB modules with X, X + 1, 2 * X + 1 respectively. Based on the experiment, X is set as 1. The detailed configurations for the three ARVB modules are shown in Table 2.

Table 2. Detailed configurations for the three ARVB modules.

Module	Output size	Parameters
ARVB_1	19×19	1×1, 1024
		3×3, 1024, C = 32, D = 1
		1×1, 1024
ARVB_2	10×10	1×1, 512
		3×3, 512, C = 32, D = 2
		1×1, 512
ARVB_3	5×5	1×1, 256
		3×3, 256, C = 32, D = 3
		1×1, 256

2.3 ARVBNet Detection Architecture

The ARVB modules are embedded into SSD to form the ARVBNet for real-time detection. Specifically, the top two convolutional layers of SSD are replaced with three ARVB modules, forming the top five convolution layers, each of which is tailed by classification and location regression. In addition, another ARVB module is utilized to scale the feature map after conv4_3.

Its two variants, namely ARVBNet-V2 and ARVBNet-V3, were also presented. The main difference is how to fuse the features at conv4_3. The ARVBNet only uses the raw feature of conv4_3 convolution layer (512 channels). In the ARVBNet-V2, a 1×1 convolution is first used to change the output channels of conv7 (fc7) from 1024 to 256, and then up-sampled to the same feature size as conv4_3. The output channel of the conv4_3 is also reduced to 256 and then concatenated with the features of the conv7 (fc7) to form a 512-channel fused features. On the basis of the ARVBNet-V2, we further concatenate the features of the conv3_3, to generate the ARVBNet-V3.

3　Experiments

3.1　Experimental Setup

For ARVBNet, we use data augmentation including rotation and flipping horizontally with five times augmentation for 1991 originally annotated fetal US CFP images. In our experiment, the whole dataset was randomly divided into three parts, of which 80%, 10%, 10% are used for training, validation and testing respectively. As usual, average precision (AP)/mean average precision (mAP) are used to evaluate the detection performance.

3.2　Determination of Dilated Rates

The default dilated rate of convolution layer is 1, namely default rule. For equidifferent and customized rule, three groups of the dilated rates were chosen respectively, and for geometric rule only two groups of the dilated rates were set. Note that three consecutive digits suffixes correspond the dilated rates of the three ARVB modules (e.g., ARVB-135 represents the dilated rates of the three ARVB modules are set 1, 3, 5 respectively). The evaluation results are shown in Table 3. The ARVB-123 obtain the best performance, which is therefore set as the final dilated rate.

Table 3. Evaluation results of different rules for ARVBNet (%).

Rule	Model	mAP	PVA	ACMB	MRs
Default	ARVB-111	93.40	90.72	99.86	89.62
Equidifferent	ARVB-135	93.43	90.60	99.86	89.82
	ARVB-246	90.51	90.67	90.91	89.95
	ARVB-357	93.46	90.70	99.93	89.74
Geometric	ARVB-124	93.51	90.75	99.97	89.82
	ARVB-248	90.24	90.38	90.77	89.58
Customized	ARVB-123	**93.52**	90.70	99.96	89.91
(X, X + 1, 2 * X + 1)	ARVB-235	93.45	90.65	99.96	89.73
	ARVB-347	90.46	90.66	90.89	89.84

3.3　Determination of Cardinality

Cardinality, the size of the set of transformations, is an extremely important element in addition to the dimensions of depth and width. Their experiments showed that it is a more efficient way to improve the performance to increase the cardinality. In our experiment, two ARVBNets (ARVB-111 and ARVB-123) were used to determine the cardinality. Experiments demonstrate that both of the two networks achieve the best performance with cardinality of 32, as shown in Table 4.

Table 4. Evaluation results of different cardinalities (%).

Model	Cardinality	mAP	PVA	ACMB	MRs
ARVB-111	16	90.37	90.72	90.91	89.47
	32	**93.40**	90.72	99.86	89.62
	64	93.39	90.72	99.86	89.61
ARVB-123	16	93.29	90.69	99.91	89.27
	32	**93.52**	90.70	99.96	89.91
	64	93.45	90.73	99.93	89.68

3.4 Effectiveness of More Anchors

Hu *et al.* [7] showed that low-level features may play an important role in detecting small objects. To validate the inference, Liu *et al.* [6] added more anchors (6 rather than 4 default prior anchors) at conv4_3 to achieve 0.2% performance improvement. Motivated by the improvement, we set 4 and 6 anchors at conv4_3 in our ARVBNet. Experiment results demonstrated 6 anchors improved 2.93% from 90.47% to 93.40% for ARVB-111 and 0.1% from 93.42% to 93.52% for ARVB-123, as shown in Table 5.

Table 5. Comparison of different anchors in the conv4_3 (%).

Net	Anchors	mAP	PVA	ACMB	MRs
ARVB-111	4	90.47	90.66	90.91	89.83
	6	**93.40**	90.72	99.86	89.62
ARVB-123	4	93.42	90.62	99.97	89.66
	6	**93.52**	90.70	99.96	89.91

3.5 Results on Fetal US CFP Images

For comparison, we also re-implement other excellent detection methods in the same environment, including Faster-RCNN in VGG [8] or ResNet-101 architecture [9], SSD [10], RFB Net [6] and FSSD [11]. In addition, we compare the input sizes, backbones

Table 6. Comparison of detection results on fetal US CFP images (%).

Method	Backbone	PVA	ACMB	MRs	mAP	FPs	Input size
Faster RCNN [8]	VGG	89.77	90.7	87.08	89.18	7	$\sim 600 \times 1000$
Faster RCNN [9]	ResNet	89.54	99.06	89.47	92.69	5	$\sim 600 \times 1000$
SSD300 [10]	VGG	89.91	90.86	88.21	89.66	109	300×300
FSSD300 [11]	VGG	90.55	99.95	90.01	93.50	83	300×300
RFB Net300 [6]	VGG	90.75	99.93	89.61	93.43	71	300×300
ARVB	VGG	90.7	99.96	89.91	**93.52**	101	300×300
ARVB-V2	VGG	90.54	99.97	89.44	93.32	98	300×300
ARVB-V3	VGG	90.65	99.96	89.86	93.49	94	300×300

and test speed of different methods. Note that, all the methods were implemented on the NVidia Geforce Titan Xp (Pascal architecture). For the results in detail, please refer to Table 6. The proposed ARVBNet achieves state-of-the-art mAP of 93.52% and keep a comparable testing speed of 101 FPs.

3.6   Extended Experiment

To validate the adaptability and generality of the ARVBNet, we also implement it on the PASCAL VOC dataset. For all the methods, the VOC 2007 *trainval* and VOC 2012 *trainval* are used as the training set and the VOC2007 *test* as testing set. As shown in Table 7, the ARVBNet-V2 achieves state-of-the-art mAP of 81.2% when taking as the input of the same or approximate size.

Table 7. Comparison with other detection architectures on PASCAL VOC 2007 test set.

Method	Backbone	Input size	mAP(%)
Faster RCNN [8]	VGG	$\sim 600 \times 1000$	73.2
Faster RCNN [9]	ResNet-101	$\sim 600 \times 1000$	76.4
R-FCN [12]	ResNet-101	$\sim 600 \times 1000$	79.5
YOLOv2 [13]	Darknet-19	352×352	73.7
SSD300 [10]	VGG	300×300	77.2
FSSD300 [11]	VGG	300×300	78.8
RFB Net300 [6]	VGG	300×300	80.5
RSSD300 [14]	VGG	300×300	78.5
DSSD321 [15]	ResNet-101	321×321	78.6
DSOD300 [16]	DS/64-192-48-1	300×300	77.7
ARVBNet	VGG	300×300	79.9
ARVBNet-V2	VGG	300×300	**81.2**
ARVBNet-V3	VGG	300×300	80.7

4   Conclusion

In the paper, we propose a novel ARVBNet to achieve the detection of anatomical structures in fetal US CFP images. The ARVB module can imitate the relationship between the size and eccentricity of receptive field similar to human visual system. Embedded into the SSD architecture to form the ARVBNet can not only improve the capability of feature representations, but also hold a fast test speed. Experiment results in a fetal US CFP dataset indicate our proposed method achieves state-of-the-art performance. In addition, an extended experiment on the PASCAL VOC dataset also achieves state-of-the-art performance, demonstrating the adaptability and generality of our proposed model.

Acknowledgements. This work is supported partly by National Natural Science Foundation of China (No. 61871274, 61801305 and 81571758), National Natural Science Foundation of Guangdong Province (No. 2017A030313377), Guangdong Pearl River Talents Plan (2016ZT0 6S220), Shenzhen Peacock Plan (No. KQTD2016053112051497 and KQTD2015033016104 926), and Shenzhen Key Basic Research Project (No. JCYJ20170413152804728, JCYJ20180 507184647636, JCYJ20170818142347251 and JCYJ20170818094109846).

References

1. Liu, S., Wang, Y., Yang, X., Lei, B., Liu, L., Li, S.X., et al.: Deep learning in medical ultrasound analysis: a review. Engineering **5**(2), 261–275 (2019)
2. Ville, Y.: 'Ceci n'est pas une échographie': a plea for quality assessment in prenatal ultrasound. Ultrasound Obstet. Gynecol. **31**(1), 1–5 (2008)
3. Maraci, M.A., Bridge, C.P., Napolitano, R., Papageorghiou, A., Noble, J.A.: A framework for analysis of linear ultrasound videos to detect fetal presentation and heartbeat. Med. Image Anal. **37**, 22–36 (2017)
4. Wu, L., Cheng, J.Z., Li, S., Lei, B., Wang, T., Ni, D.: FUIQA: fetal ultrasound image quality assessment with deep convolutional networks. IEEE Trans. Cybern. **47**(5), 1336–1349 (2017)
5. Wandell, B.A., Winawer, J.: Computational neuroimaging and population receptive fields. Trends Cogn. Sci. **19**(6), 349–357 (2015)
6. Liu, S., Huang, D., Wang, Y.: Receptive field block net for accurate and fast object detection. In: Ferrari, V., Hebert, M., Sminchisescu, C., Weiss, Y. (eds.) ECCV 2018. LNCS, vol. 11215, pp. 404–419. Springer, Cham (2018). https://doi.org/10.1007/978-3-030-01252-6_24
7. Hu, P., Ramanan, D.: Finding tiny faces. In: Proceedings of the IEEE conference on computer vision and pattern recognition, pp. 951–959 (2017)
8. Ren, S., He, K., Girshick, R., Sun, J.: Faster R-CNN: towards real-time object detection with region proposal networks. IEEE Trans. Pattern Anal. Mach. Intell. **39**(6), 1137–1149 (2017)
9. He, K.., Zhang, X., Ren, S., Sun, J.: Deep residual learning for image recognition. In: Proceedings of the IEEE Conference on Computer Vision and Pattern Recognition, pp. 770–778 (2016)
10. Liu, W., et al.: SSD: single shot multibox detector. In: Leibe, B., Matas, J., Sebe, N., Welling, M. (eds.) ECCV 2016. LNCS, vol. 9905, pp. 21–37. Springer, Cham (2016). https://doi.org/10.1007/978-3-319-46448-0_2
11. Li, Z., Zhou, F.: FSSD: feature fusion single shot multibox detector. arXiv preprint arXiv: 1712.00960 (2017)
12. Dai, J., Li, Y., He, K., Sun, J.: R-FCN: object detection via region-based fully convolutional networks. In: Advances in Neural Information Processing Systems, pp. 379–387 (2016)
13. Redmon, J., Farhadi, A.: YOLO9000: better, faster, stronger. In: Proceedings of the IEEE Conference on Computer Vision and Pattern Recognition, pp. 7263–7271 (2017)
14. Jeong, J., Park, H., Kwak, N.: Enhancement of SSD by concatenating feature maps for object detection. arXiv preprint arXiv:1705.09587 (2017)
15. Fu, C.-Y., Liu, W., Ranga, A, Tyagi, A, Berg, A.C.: DSSD: deconvolutional single shot detector. arXiv preprint arXiv:1701.06659 (2017)
16. Shen, Z., Liu, Z., Li, J., Jiang, Y., Chen, Y., Xue, X.: DSOD: learning deeply supervised object detectors from scratch. In: Proceedings of the IEEE International Conference on Computer Vision, pp. 1937–1945 (2017)

Proceedings of the Computing and Visualization for Intravascular Imaging and Computer Assisted Stenting

The Effect of Labeling Duration and Temporal Resolution on Arterial Transit Time Estimation Accuracy in 4D ASL MRA Datasets - A Flow Phantom Study

Renzo Phellan[1]([✉]), Thomas Lindner[2], Michael Helle[3], Alexandre X. Falcão[4], and Nils D. Forkert[1]

[1] Department of Radiology, Hotchkiss Brain Institute, and Biomedical Engineering Graduate Program, University of Calgary, Calgary, AB, Canada
{phellan.renzo,nils.forkert}@ucalgary.ca
[2] Clinic for Radiology and Neuroradiology, University Medical Center Schleswig-Holstein, Kiel, Germany
thomas.lindner@uksh.de
[3] Philips Technologie GmbH, Innovative Technologies, Hamburg, Germany
michael.helle@philips.com
[4] Laboratory of Image Data Science, Institute of Computing, University of Campinas, Campinas, SP, Brazil
afalcao@ic.unicamp.br

Abstract. Medical imaging modalities, such as four-dimensional arterial spin label magnetic resonance angiography (4D ASL MRA), can acquire blood flow data of the cerebrovascular system. These datasets are useful to determine criteria of normality and diagnose, study, and follow-up on the treatment progress of cerebrovascular diseases. In particular, variations in the arterial transit time (ATT) are related to hemodynamic impairment as a consequence of vascular diseases. In order to obtain accurate ATT estimations, the acquisition parameters of the applied image modality need to be properly tuned. In case of 4D ASL MRA, two important acquisition parameters are the blood labeling duration and the temporal resolution. This paper evaluates the effect of different settings for the two mentioned parameters on the accuracy of the ATT estimation in 4D ASL MRA datasets. Six 4D ASL MRA datasets of a pipe containing a mixture of glycerine and water, circulated with constant flow rate using a pump, are acquired with different labeling duration and temporal resolution. A mathematical model is then fitted to the observed signal in order to estimate the ATT. The results indicate that the lowest average absolute error between the ground-truth and estimated ATT is achieved when the longest labeling duration of 1000 ms and the highest temporal resolution of 60 ms are used. The insight obtained from the experiments using a flow phantom, under controlled conditions, can be extended to tune acquisition parameters of 4D ASL MRA datasets of human subjects.

Keywords: Hemodynamic analysis · Blood flow · Arterial transit time · Model fitting

© Springer Nature Switzerland AG 2019
H. Liao et al. (Eds.): MLMECH 2019/CVII-STENT 2019, LNCS 11794, pp. 141–148, 2019.
https://doi.org/10.1007/978-3-030-33327-0_17

1   Introduction

Hemodynamic information of the cerebrovascular system is useful to determine criteria of normality and diagnose, study, and follow-up on the treatment progress of cerebrovascular diseases, such as arteriovenous malformations, cerebral ischemia, and moyamoya disease [1]. In particular, variations in the arterial transit time (ATT) in the brain are related to hemodynamic impairment caused by cerebrovascular diseases [2].

Different imaging modalities are currently available to acquire blood flow data of the cerebrovascular system. For example, digital subtraction angiography [3], four-dimensional computed tomography angiography [4], four-dimensional arterial spin labeling magnetic resonance angiography (4D ASL MRA) [5], and others can be used for this purpose.

One common approach to analyze the blood flow data contained in the images is to estimate blood flow parameters using mathematical models, which need to be fitted to the observed signal for each voxel of the dataset containing the hemodynamic information. The model describes the expected behavior of the temporal signal of the selected imaging modality, considering the main modality-specific phenomena affected. The values of the required blood flow parameters can be calculated based on the continuous mathematical model fitted to the discrete temporal signal intensity curve.

The accuracy of the blood flow parameters estimation is usually limited by the temporal resolution of the acquired images and the amount of noise in the dataset [6]. Additionally, depending on the modality, other factors, such as labeling duration in case of 4D ASL MRA, can also affect the accuracy of the estimations. In this context, the present work focuses on the estimation of the ATT in six 4D ASL MRA datasets of a flow phantom, acquired with literature values of labeling duration and temporal resolution.

2   Four-Dimensional Arterial Spin Labeling Magnetic Resonance Angiography

4D ASL MRA is a medical imaging modality, which can simultaneously acquire blood flow and morphological data of the cerebrovascular system [5]. Instead of requiring the administration of an external contrast agent, 4D ASL MRA uses the water contained in blood as intrinsic contrast agent. During the acquisition, a radio-frequency (RF) pulse is applied to the base of the neck of the subject, parallel to the plane containing the main feeding arteries of the brain. The RF pulse inverts the magnetization of blood flow in the region where it is applied. The duration of the RF pulse (τ) determines if the cerebrovascular system will be imaged as it fills with labeled blood or as it flushes out. In particular, labeling durations of 300 ms [1] and 1000 ms [7] have been proposed in the literature.

Once the magnetically labeled blood flows into the imaging region, it is imaged at different time points, which depend on the temporal resolution (r) of the 4D ASL MRA dataset. Control images are also acquired when no labeled blood is present in the imaged region of the brain. As a result, a 4D ASL MRA dataset is comprised of a set of control and labeled pairs of images. The subtraction of corresponding control and labeled image pairs allows the removal of most signal originating from other non-vascular structures. Thus, the final result contains the signal of magnetically labeled blood flowing through the brain and some residual noise [1]. Figure 1 shows maximum intensity projections of 60 contiguous slices of the control, labeled, and subtracted images of three time-points of a 4D ASL MRA dataset of the brain of a human subject, acquired with a labeling time of 300 ms and temporal resolution of 120 ms.

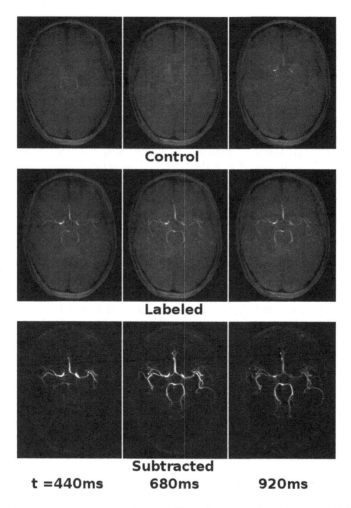

Fig. 1. Maximum intensity projections of 60 contiguous slices of control, labeled, and subtracted images of a 4D ASL MRA dataset of the brain of a human subject, acquired at three time-points: 440 ms, 680 ms, and 920 ms.

3   Blood Flow Parameter Estimation

The blood flow data contained in 4D ASL MRA datasets can be analyzed by fitting a mathematical hemodynamic model to the observed signal $S(v,t)$ of each vascular voxel v at time t. In particular, Okell et al. [7] designed a model for this specific image modality that takes into account the main acquisition phenomena of 4D ASL MRA datasets. The model is presented in Eq. 1.

$$S(v,t) = \int_{t-\delta_t-\tau}^{t-\delta_t} A(v)dt_d D(v,t_d)T(\delta_t,t_d)R(t) \tag{1}$$

$$D(v,t_d) = \begin{cases} s(\Gamma(1+ps))^{-1}\exp(-st_d)(st_d)^{ps} & \text{if } st_d > 0, ps > -1 \\ 0 & \text{otherwise} \end{cases} \tag{2}$$

$$T(\delta_t,t_d) = \exp(-(\delta_t + t_d)/T_{1b}) \tag{3}$$

$$R(t) = \cos(\alpha)^{(t-t_0)/TR}\sin(\alpha) \tag{4}$$

In Eq. 1, the signal $S(v,t)$ is expressed as a function of the relative volume of labeled blood $A(v)$ flowing through a voxel and the signal decay due to different factors, which include the dispersion of labeled blood before reaching the analyzed voxel $D(v,t_d)$, the T_1 relaxation of magnetically labeled blood $T(\delta_t,t_d)$, and the application of imaging pulses $R(t)$. The arterial transit time (ATT), represented by δ_t, is one of the most important blood flow parameters that can be estimated using this mathematical function, the labeling duration τ is an acquisition parameter set by the user, and the additional time delay t_d caused by the dispersion of labeled blood is the integration variable.

The signal decay due to dispersion of labeled blood is described in Eq. 2. It corresponds to a distribution that depends on the blood flow parameters sharpness s and time-to-peak p. The decay caused by T_1 relaxation of the labeled blood is shown in Eq. 3. It includes the longitudinal relaxation time of blood T_{1b}, which is approximately 1664 ms in a magnetic field of 3T [8]. Finally, Eq. 4 presents the formula of the signal decay due to imaging pulses applied to the labeled blood before it reaches voxel v, where α is the flip angle, TR is the repetition time, and t_0 corresponds to the time when the first imaging pulse is applied.

Optimization algorithms are commonly used to fit the described mathematical model to the signal contained in a 4D ASL MRA dataset. This work uses the multi-scale parameter search (MSPS) algorithm because it has been shown to yield good results in general benchmarks and medical applications [9].

4   Materials and Methods

4.1   Data Acquisition

Six 4D ASL MRA datasets of a flow phantom with a fluid delivered through a simple pipe at constant flow rate were acquired during the experiments. The pipe was filled with a fluid composed of 36% (vol.) glycerine in water, which is commonly used as a blood analog with similar viscosity [10]. The fluid was circulated at constant flow rate of 3.34 mL/s and average speed of 161.7 cm/s using a peristaltic pump (Sorin Group Deutschland GmbH, Munich, Germany). The pipe was fixated using sandbags and a bottle containing 1 L of demineralized water to represent other tissues, as suggested and used in previous studies [11].

The six 4D ASL MRA datasets were acquired on a Philips Achieva 3T MRI (Philips Healthcare, Best, The Netherlands). Each dataset contains pairs of volumetric control and labeled images, acquired using Look-Locker and Sensitivity Encoding (SENSE) to speed up the acquisition process. Each volumetric image contains 120 slices with 224×224 voxels. The voxel size is $0.94 \times 0.94 \times 1.0$ mm^3. Additional acquisition parameters include a T1-Turbo Field Echo (TFE) scan with a TFE factor of 16, SENSE factor of 3, TR/TE values of 7.7/3.7 ms, flip angle of 10°, and half scan factor of 0.7. Figure 2 shows maximum intensity projections of the images of a 4D ASL MRA dataset of the described flow phantom, acquired with labeling time (τ) of 300 ms and temporal resolution (r) of 120 ms.

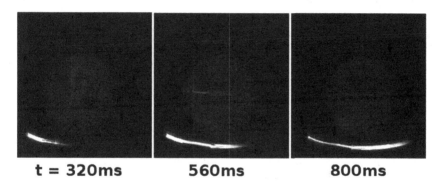

t = 320ms   **560ms**   **800ms**

Fig. 2. Maximum intensity projections of subtracted images of a 4D ASL MRA dataset of a flow phantom containing a mixture of glycerine and water at time points 320 ms, 560 ms, and 800 ms. This dataset was acquired using a labeling time (τ) of 300 ms and temporal resolution (r) of 120 ms.

The 4D ASL MRA datasets of the flow phantom were acquired in six scenarios, with different values for the labeling duration τ and temporal resolution r, in order to evaluate their effect on the estimation accuracy of the ATT. The values of τ and r were selected according to experiments reported in the literature [1,7], as detailed in Table 1. The time at which the first imaging pulse t_0 is applied is also indicated, together with the number of images in a dataset n.

4.2   Evaluation Method

Due to the variation of speed along the cross-sectional area of the pipe due to laminar flow, this work considers only the ATT values estimated at voxels of

Table 1. Labeling duration (τ), temporal resolution (r), first imaging pulse time (t_0), number of images in a dataset n, and average absolute error (AAE) when estimating the arterial transit time in each evaluated scenario. The acquisition parameters are selected according to experiments reported in [1] (scenarios 1 to 3) and [7] (scenarios 4 to 6). The lowest AAE is in bold.

Scenario	τ (ms)	r (ms)	t_0 (ms)	n	AAE (ms)	Acquisition time (min)
1	300	60	320	12	54.98 ± 22.85	10
2	300	90	320	8	89.49 ± 28.63	7
3	300	120	320	6	200.36 ± 42.42	5
4	1000	60	1020	12	**42.34 ± 21.69**	16
5	1000	90	1020	8	60.77 ± 24.76	11
6	1000	120	1020	6	136.17 ± 35.63	8

the centerline of the pipe, also referred to as skeleton. The pipe is segmented in the 4D ASL MRA datasets using a simple thresholding algorithm, followed by removal of small components that correspond to noise. The skeleton of the resulting segmentation is calculated using a skeletonization algorithm available in the Insight Toolkit framework (ITK) [12]. For each voxel contained in the skeleton, the ATT is estimated by fitting the blood flow model presented in Eq. 1 to the observed signal.

The ground-truth values for the ATT at each voxel v of the skeleton of the pipe are calculated by dividing the length of the centerline path from the extreme of the pipe to the voxel $L(v)$ by the average speed S of the water and glycerine mixture delivered by the pump, as it is presented in Eq. 5. The estimated and ground-truth values for the ATT along the skeleton are compared using the average absolute error (AAE). In order to enrich the comparison, the acquisition time of a dataset in each scenario is also recorded.

$$ATT(v) = L(v)/S \tag{5}$$

5   Results

The AAE between the ground-truth and estimated values for the arterial transit time (ATT) along the pipe skeleton and the acquisition time in each one of the six scenarios is presented on Table 1. It can be noticed that the AAE decreases when the labeling duration is increased for each pair of scenarios with the same temporal resolution: 1 vs. 4, 2 vs. 5, and 3 vs. 6. Additionally, the AAE increases when the temporal resolution is decreased in sets of scenarios with the same labeling duration: 1 vs. 2 vs. 3 or 4 vs. 5 vs. 6. The lowest AAE of 42.34 ± 21.69 ms is reached in Scenario 4, when the longest labeling time and highest temporal resolution are used. Nevertheless, Scenario 4 is also the case that requires the longest acquisition time of 16 min.

6 Discussion and Conclusion

The present paper evaluated the influence of the labeling duration (τ) and temporal resolution (r) on the arterial transit time (ATT) estimation accuracy. Labeling duration and temporal resolution are important acquisition parameters of 4D ASL MRA datasets and ATT is the most important blood flow parameter associated with hemodynamic impairment in the brain caused by cerebrovascular diseases.

The experiments were conducted in a controlled environment, using a flow phantom containing a mixture of glycerine and water, circulated at a constant flow rate. During the experiments, it was observed that the average absolute error (AAE) decreases when longer labeling times (τ) and higher temporal resolution (r) are used to acquire a 4D ASL MRA dataset. Consequently, the most accurate results, with the lowest AAE, are achieved when the longest τ of 1000 ms and the highest r of 60 ms are used.

Nevertheless, the scenario with the longest τ and the highest r is also the one leading to the longest acquisition time of 16 min. Depending on the specific application, long acquisition times are often associated with more motion artifacts or are simply clinically not feasible [13]. Thus, this trade-off between accuracy of the ATT parameter estimation and acquisition time has to be considered when designing the 4D ASL MRA datasets in research or clinical applications.

In terms of limitations, this work represents an initial evaluation of the estimation of blood flow parameters in 4D ASL MRA datasets in a real physical setting, under controlled conditions. Further analysis would be required to translate the obtained conclusion to human subjects. *In vivo* acquisitions would include additional challenges, such as motion artifacts, other sources of noise, additional acquisition parameters to be optimized, and more complex vascular geometries. Nevertheless, it is expected that this simplified scenario, using a pipe containing a fluid similar to blood, can support clinicians and physicists optimizing 4D ASL MRA sequences for clinical studies or routine diagnosis.

Acknowledgements. This work was supported by Natural Sciences and Engineering Research Council of Canada (NSERC), Hotchkiss Brain Institute (HBI), and Alberta Innovates. Dr. Nils D. Forkert is funded by Canada Research Chairs. Dr. Alexandre X. Falcão thanks CNPq 303808/2018-7 and FAPESP 2014/12236-1.

References

1. Phellan, R., Lindner, T., Helle, M., Falcão, A.X., Forkert, N.D.: Automatic temporal segmentation of vessels of the brain using 4D ASL MRA images. IEEE Trans. Biomed. Eng. **65**(7), 1486–1494 (2018)
2. Wang, J., et al.: Arterial transit time imaging with flow encoding arterial spin tagging (FEAST). Magn. Reson. Med. **50**(3), 599–607 (2003)
3. Ducos de Lahitte, M., Marc-Vergnes, J., Rascol, A., Guiraud, B., Manelfe, C.: Intravenous angiography of the extracranial cerebral arteries. Radiology **137**(3), 705–711 (1980)

4. Heinz, E., et al.: Examination of the extracranial carotid bifurcation by thin-section dynamicCT: direct visualization of intimal atheroma in man (Part 1). Am. J. Neuroradiol. **5**(4), 355–359 (1984)
5. Bi, X., Weale, P., Schmitt, P., Zuehlsdorff, S., Jerecic, R.: Non-contrast-enhanced four-dimensional (4D) intracranial MR angiography: a feasibility study. Magn. Reson. Med. **63**(3), 835–841 (2010)
6. Forkert, N.D., Fiehler, J., Illies, T., Möller, D.P., Handels, H., Säring, D.: 4D blood flow visualization fusing 3D and 4D MRA image sequences. J. Magn. Reson. Imaging **36**(2), 443–453 (2012)
7. Okell, T.W., Chappell, M.A., Schulz, U.G., Jezzard, P.: A kinetic model for vessel-encoded dynamic angiography with arterial spin labeling. Magn. Reson. Med. **68**(3), 969–979 (2012)
8. Hua, J., Qin, Q., Pekar, J.J., van Zijl, P.C.: Measurement of absolute arterial cerebral blood volume in human brain without using a contrast agent. Nucl. Magn. Reson. Biomed. **24**(10), 1313–1325 (2011)
9. Ruppert, G.C., et al.: Medical image registration based on watershed transform from greyscale marker and multi-scale parameter search. Comput. Methods Biomech. Biomed. Eng. Imaging Vis., 1–19 (2015)
10. Nguyen, T., Biadillah, Y., Mongrain, R., Brunette, J., Tardif, J.C., Bertrand, O.: A method for matching the refractive index and kinematic viscosity of a blood analog for flow visualization in hydraulic cardiovascular models. J. Biomech. Eng. **126**(4), 529–535 (2004)
11. Kim, S.J., et al.: Effects of MR parameter changes on the quantification of diffusion anisotropy and apparent diffusion coefficient in diffusion tensor imaging: evaluation using a diffusional anisotropic phantom. Korean J. Radiol. **16**(2), 297–303 (2015)
12. Yoo, T.S., et al.: Engineering and algorithm design for an image processing API: a technical report on ITK-the insight toolkit. Studies in Health Technology and Informatics, 586–592 (2002)
13. Saver, J.L.: Time is brain-quantified. Stroke **37**(1), 263–266 (2006)

Towards Quantifying Neurovascular Resilience

Stefano Moriconi[1]([✉]), Rafael Rehwald[2], Maria A. Zuluaga[3], H. Rolf Jäger[2], Parashkev Nachev[2], Sébastien Ourselin[1], and M. Jorge Cardoso[1]

[1] School of Biomedical Engineering and Imaging Sciences, King's College London, London, UK
`stefano.moriconi@kcl.ac.uk`
[2] Institute of Neurology, University College London, London, UK
[3] Universidad Nacional de Colombia, Bogotá, Colombia

Abstract. Whilst grading neurovascular abnormalities is critical for prompt surgical repair, no statistical markers are currently available for predicting the risk of adverse events, such as stroke, and the overall resilience of a network to vascular complications. The lack of compact, fast, and scalable simulations with network perturbations impedes the analysis of the vascular resilience to life-threatening conditions, surgical interventions and long-term follow-up. We introduce a graph-based approach for efficient simulations, which statistically estimates biomarkers from a series of perturbations on the patient-specific vascular network. Analog-equivalent circuits are derived from clinical angiographies. Vascular graphs embed mechanical attributes modelling the impedance of a tubular structure with stenosis, tortuosity and complete occlusions. We evaluate pressure and flow distributions, simulating healthy topologies and abnormal variants with perturbations in key pathological scenarios. These describe the intrinsic network resilience to pathology, and delineate the underlying cerebrovascular autoregulation mechanisms. Lastly, a putative graph sampling strategy is devised on the same formulation, to support the topological inference of uncertain neurovascular graphs.

1 Introduction

Cerebrovascular diseases, such as stroke, are the biggest source of long-term neurological disability in first world countries. In an acute setting, it is necessary to assess the risk of a neurovascular event, and to decide how best to intervene (i.e. thrombectomy vs thrombolysis). These decisions are currently ill-informed and would greatly benefit from supporting statistical and quantitative neurovascular measurements. In preventive care, vascular features and biomarkers could inform patient screening and allow for long-term stroke risk stratification. Despite the incidence and morbidity of cerebrovascular diseases [7], current studies are often limited to incidental findings in clinical trials. Group-based, quantitative, predictive analysis remains an unexplored research ground.

Previous hemodynamic case-studies [3,11–13] have provided localised predictive biomarkers of aneurysm formation and rupture, and indices of pathogenesis

© Springer Nature Switzerland AG 2019
H. Liao et al. (Eds.): MLMECH 2019/CVII-STENT 2019, LNCS 11794, pp. 149–157, 2019.
https://doi.org/10.1007/978-3-030-33327-0_18

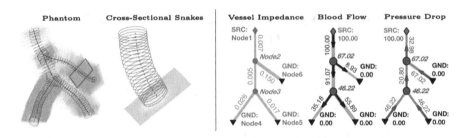

Fig. 1. Cross-sectional lumen segmentation of a vascular phantom using snakes [4]; hybrid vascular analog-equivalent of the phantom: impedance, flow and pressure drop.

for occlusive diseases on small portions of the cerebrovascular tree. These studies commonly rely on computationally-intensive fluid dynamics simulations to accurately quantify the blood-flow patterns and vessel wall characteristics, normally disregarding the natural compensation and redundancy mechanisms of the overall network. Recent work in hemodynamic computational fluid dynamics (CFD) have shown prohibitively long simulations for large and complex vascular networks, making the evaluation of how these networks react to perturbations an open challenge [13,14]. In [5,9,10], artificial physio-pathological equivalents were introduced as a computationally-efficient approximation of CFD analysis. These approximate models condense mechanical tubular features into simplified and compact lumped-parameters, modelling intrinsic whole-network autoregulation mechanisms. Even though these first-order approximations were found to correlate well with the fully-resolved CFD hemodynamic simulations in cardiac applications [6], neurovascular applications are still in their infancy. Ideally, these models should be fully data-driven, be able to specify phenotypical traits, and generalise to a number of perturbations.

Leveraging such efficient approximation and by integrating subject-specific vascular graphs from clinical angiographies, we introduce here a scalable and fast simulation framework that statistically estimates functional biomarkers by perturbing vascular topologies. In detail, we use a spatial graph of the neurovascular network to simulate steady-state blood flow using an analog-equivalent circuit approximation, thus modelling biomechanical lumped-parameters and topological connectivity directly from clinical scans. Assuming that a latent autoregulation mechanism underlies major brain arteries, we introduce multiple artificial perturbations (e.g. stenosis, tortuosity, occlusions) and simulate how the neurovascular network reacts to these changes. We then study how different perturbations lead to pressure/flow alterations, and result in downstream changes in vessel wall tension, providing a new metric of neurovascular resilience to different pathological scenarios. Beyond estimating biomarkers, a putative graph sampling strategy is lastly devised based on the same analog-equivalent formulation. This supports the topological inference of uncertain redundant vascular network by increasing the sparsity of a fully-connected neurovascular graph, yet preserving its most biologically-plausible set of realisations.

2   Methods

We build on prior work by automatically extracting a vascular graph of connected centerlines from angiographic images [1,2,8], and a active-contour-based lumen segmentation model [4], depicted in Fig. 1. Using this vascular representation, we first show how to create a mechanical vascular equivalent automatically from a geometrical segmentation of the neurovascular tree under the assumption of simplified hemodynamics. The extracted vascular lumped-parameter model is then converted into an analog closed-circuit configuration, enabling a computationally-efficient linear-approximation of blood flow and pressure drop. Lastly, we introduce geometrical and topological perturbations to the model to simulate how the vascular network would react to different events (e.g. embolism, stenosis) providing a measure of network resilience.

Hybrid Vascular Lumped-Parameters Model. Hemodynamic quantities are obtained from simplifying the Euler fluid equation, governing the fluid dynamics in the continuum. Here, we approximate non-linearities and the shock of an incompressible flow transient by assuming a cylindrical model of the underlying branch geometry, where a rigid pipe runs with fixed radius along the vascular elongated (i.e. z axial) direction. As demonstrated in [15], the axial motion of a fluid is derived from the Cauchy momentum of mass conservation to the differential Hagen-Poiseuille equation, i.e. $q_{\underline{z}}^{\max} = -\frac{1}{4\mu}\frac{\partial p}{\partial z} \cdot r^2$, under the assumption of a steady, fully-developed, and axisymmetric flow $\mathbf{q}$, showing non-turbulent motion, i.e. with null flow velocity for both radial and swirl components. The maximum flow occurs at the centre of the pipe of radius r, and the constant average axial flow $\overline{q}_{\underline{z}} = \frac{1}{2}q_{\underline{z}}^{\max}$ integrates its parabolic profile over the pipe's cross-section. Integrating also a linearly decreasing pressure drop ∂p along the entire length l of the pipe, a constant, average, axial flow $Q = \overline{q}_{\underline{z}}$ can be rewritten as

$$Q = \frac{\Delta P}{R}, \quad \text{with} \quad R = \frac{8\mu l}{\pi r^4} \quad \text{and} \quad r = \frac{1}{l}\int_l \sqrt{\frac{a(\sigma(\underline{z}))}{\pi}}\, d\underline{z}, \tag{1}$$

with ΔP the integral pressure gradient, R the average resistance of the rigid pipe of radius r, and μ the constant blood viscosity. In this work, the constant radius r is averaged along the pipe using the area of cross-sectional snakes $a(\sigma(\underline{z}))$.

Graph-Based Analog-Equivalent. Along with the hydraulic analogy of electric systems, we model analog-equivalent circuits as a set of connected lumped-parameters for the vascular network. A generic vascular graph $G = (N, E)$ is defined as a set of nodes $j = 1, ..., |N|$ (i.e. the branch-points), and the associated connecting edges $e_{(j_1,j_2)}$ (i.e. the vascular branches), encode in $E(j_1, j_2)$ the binary adjacency matrix. For each $e_{(j_1,j_2)}$, the tubular features are converted into electrical impedance for an analog equivalent, where purely dynamic components vanish for a steady-state flow. The impedances of the connected pipes

Input: R, P_{BC};   **Output:** $P, \Delta P, Q$
$C_{R^{-1}}(j_1, j_2) = -R(j_1, j_2)^{-1}$; $C_{P_{BC}} = \mathbf{0}_{|N| \times 1}$;   ▷ Initialisation
$C_{R^{-1}} = D_{R^{-1}} - A_{R^{-1}}$;   ▷ Circuit Admittance System
for all $P_{BC_j} \in \{SRC, GND\}$ **do**
  $C_{R^{-1}}(j_{1==}j, \forall j_2) = 0$; $C_{R^{-1}}(j_{1==}j, j_{2==}j) = 1$;
  $C_{P_{BC}}(j_{1==}j) = P_{BC_j}$;   ▷ Include Boundary Conditions
end
$P = C_{R^{-1}}^{-1} C_{PB}$;   ▷ Solve the Linear System
for all $E(j_1, j_2) == 1$ **do**
  $\Delta P(j_1, j_2) = P(j_1) - P(j_2)$;   ▷ Assign Potential Difference
  $Q(j_1, j_2) = \Delta P(j_1, j_2) \cdot R(j_1, j_2)^{-1}$;   ▷ Assign Current (Ohm's law)
end

Algorithm 1. Graph-based analog-equivalent system: definition and solver.

simplifies to real-valued resistances $R = f(l, r)$ as in Eq. 1. These are embedded in the associated resistance-weighted adjacency matrix $R(j_1, j_2) = R_{e_{(j_1, j_2)}}$. In a similar form, the flow $Q(j_1, j_2)$ and the pressure drop $\Delta P(j_1, j_2)$ are translated into current and potential difference for each vascular branch, respectively. Simulating a closed-loop analog circuit, voltage generators (SRC_j) and potential grounds (GND_j) are introduced in the system. These model the pressure at the inlets or outlets of the network as node-wise potential boundary conditions (P_{BC}). By coupling linear lumped-parameters and the set of boundary conditions, the analog-equivalent circuit is solved using Kirchhoff's laws as a linear system of equations. As described in Algorithm 1, $C_{R^{-1}}$ is the circuit admittance matrix. $C_{R^{-1}}$ is initialised with negative and inverse resistance values and subsequently integrates the equivalent topological system where $D_{R^{-1}}$ and $A_{R^{-1}}$ represent the associated diagonal degree and the adjacency matrix respectively, as in a canonical graph Laplacian. $C_{P_{BC}}$ is the node-wise potential vector of boundary conditions, and P is the node-wise potential solution of the linear system of equations. The canonical passive sign convention is enforced (Fig. 1).

Modelling Perturbations on Vascular Topologies. We introduce two types of perturbations to account for changes in structural connectivity and flow resistance modulation $\mathcal{M}$. The structural connectivity perturbation is achieved by

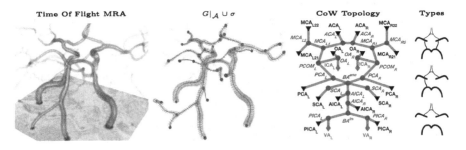

Fig. 2. Circle of Willis: MR angio, snake segmentation, manual landmarks and graph equivalent for an exact network ($\mathcal{A}$). SRC ($\lozenge$) and GND ($\blacktriangledown$) are shown for in/outlets.

altering $\tilde{G}(N, \tilde{E})$ with a mask E as $\tilde{E} = \mathcal{E} \circ (E \circ \mathcal{A})$, where $\mathcal{E}(j_1, j_2) \sim \mathcal{B}(\lambda)$. Here, $\mathcal{E}$ follows a Bernoulli distribution $\mathcal{B}$ of probability λ. These model random occlusions, which disrupt the connectivity by a factor $\varepsilon = (1 - \lambda)$, on average. $\mathcal{A}$ is an anatomical prior where non-zero edges $\mathcal{A}(j_1, j_2)$ weight the likelihood of certain cerebrovascular connections. In general $\mathcal{A}$ is *unknown* for non-annotated graphs, meaning that $\mathcal{A} = \mathbf{1}_{|N| \times |N|}$, therefore vanishing in $\tilde{E}$. Prior knowledge can be embedded in $\mathcal{A}$ if available. The second type of perturbation, namely vascular stenoses and vessel tortuosity, are modelled for both reduced radii r and longer pipes' lengths l, respectively. These are element-wise integrated in $\tilde{R}_{\tilde{E}} = \mathcal{M} \circ R_{\tilde{E}}$, with $\mathcal{M}(j_1, j_2) \sim 1 - U(0, m)$, following a uniform distribution with $m < 1$. Note that these perturbations are computationally very efficient, as they are defined as simple matrix-to-matrix element-wise transformations.

3 Experiments and Results

Datasets: We use six MR time-of-flight angiographies of the Circle of Willis (CoW), with each subject is classified into 3 different CoW phenotypes and manually labelled as in Fig. 2, and vascular graphs are extracted following [8].

Controlled Simulations on *Exact* Topologies (CoW). Pressure potentials are initialised at the anatomical inlets, whereas potential grounds are set at the terminal branches of the CoW (Fig. 2). Given an anatomical prior $\mathcal{A}$ from the annotated graph, we first evaluate the autoregulation mechanisms by simulating a stenotic Internal Carotid Artery (ICA) and an occlusion of the Posterior Communicating Artery (PCOM), as sanity test in a simple, yet realistic, scenario. In

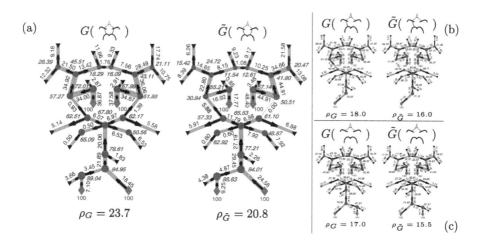

Fig. 3. Autoregulation mechanisms: blood flow, pressure and network resilience ρ for unperturbed graphs, and for the simulated stenotic ICA and occluded PCOM. (Color figure online)

Fig. 3 biologically compatible autoregulation mechanisms are observed for different types of the Circle of Willis. On average, reduced flow and pressure values are found in the perturbed ipsi-lateral branch of the network, whereas minimally affected quantities are observed for the contra-lateral part. While flow is marginal in the PCOMs for the unperturbed network Fig. 3(a), it increases (highlight) after the simulated stenosis and occlusion (purple edges), where the flow overdraft is compensated by the posterior circulation. Similar autoregulation mechanisms are observed for the other phenotypes Fig. 3(b) and (c), where major compensations are given by the anterior left-right circulatory contribution at the Anterior Communicating Artery (ACA) level. Flow readjustment were intrinsically different for different CoW phenotypes. Despite the relatively small ACA size, increased flow is observed (highlighted) contro-lateral to the simulated perturbation. Lastly, resilience indices ρ show a decreasing trend for the *same* perturbation on the different networks.

Random Perturbations on *Exact* Topologies (CoW). Simulations are computed by perturbing *only* the resistance-equivalents, where fluctuations in $\mathcal{M}$ modulate both radius and length of the pipes. Perturbations account for 3 classes with maximal resistance increment $m^{\mathrm{max}} = 50\%$, and a total $n = 1000$ instances per class. Flow and pressure are evaluated also on unperturbed equivalents for comparison. The n simulated quantities are then averaged for the same phenotype. A global network resilience metric is defined as $\rho_G = \frac{1}{|E|}\sum_{|\tilde{E}d|}\rho$, with $\rho = \frac{(\Delta P \cdot Q)}{\pi r^2 l}$, where $|\tilde{E}|$ is the total number of vascular branches *after* the topological perturbation (here $\mathcal{E} = \mathbf{1}_{|N| \times |N|}$), being $|\tilde{E}d|$ the diffused ones, i.e. those having non-zero Q and ΔP. The scalar ρ_G is an integral surrogate for the branch functionality given the network perturbation. In order words, it is a scalar describing how resilient, or how affected, a branch is by a random perturbation anywhere in the neurovascular tree. Assuming healthy networks being

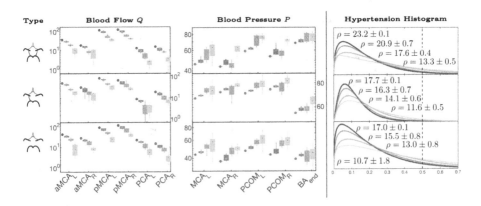

Fig. 4. Flow, pressure and hypertension histogram for unperturbed anatomically exact topologies and for 3 perturbation classes of increasing stenoses and tortuosity.

well diffused, ρ_G is maximal for unperturbed equivalents, whereas it decreases for impairing modulations. In Fig. 4, flow and pressure distributions are depicted for a representative set of CoW edges and nodes. For each perturbation class (i.e $0 < m_1 < 0.2, 0.2 < m_2 < 0.3$, and $0.3 < m_3 < 0.5$), the hemodynamic quantities are compared against the unperturbed values. On average, flow is decreased, in line with the overall increased impedance of the vascular network. Conversely, the distributed pressure increases progressively as the degree of perturbation, with relatively smaller ratio of increase at the Basilar Artery terminal point (BA^{end}).

As a second tier analysis, a hypertension histogram is fitted in Fig. 4 with a gamma distribution. Here, hypertension is defined as the pressure normalised by the mean cross-sectional area of the vessel. An unperturbed CoW shows a hypertension profile skewed towards low values; histograms shows a broader profile for increasing perturbations, with more small vessels reporting relatively high pressure. This suggests that increased hypertension tends to affect the whole CoW even for localised stenoses (leftwards shift of the histogram), and increased risk of vascular rupture (larger area above a certain threshold, e.g. the dashed line in Fig. 4). A higher prevalence of zero-force is also observed in the simulated stenotic regions, suggesting higher risk of ischemia. Resilience ρ was also found to decrease for all topologies at increasing levels of perturbation.

Perturbations on Redundant Uncertain Topologies (CoW). So far, analyses assumed a specific realisation of a vascular graph. However, robustly extracting the vascular topology is a challenging task due to poor image resolution. In our validation, we observed that erroneously extracted vascular graphs, i.e. those with the wrong connections, exhibited abnormal biomechanical properties. We thus hypothesise that the proposed simulation framework can assess the plausibility of putative vascular graphs. Relaxing the assumption of a known anatomical prior (i.e. vanishing $\mathcal{A}$), occlusive perturbations $\mathcal{E}$ are introduced for an over-connected graph G, which embeds uncertainty among vascular junctions. Similar boundary conditions are initialised for those nodes closest to the annotated in/outlets; however, no resistance modulation is performed. Note that simulating complete occlusions on a redundant vascular network is equivalent to re-sample G with subnets and evaluate their biological compatibility. Here, three classes of randomly occluded topologies $\tilde{G}$ are generated for $\varepsilon = 0.2, 0.3, 0.5$, each with a total of $n = 1000$ instances. For each class, an inverse resilience adjacency matrix $\hat{\rho}$, of the same size as $\tilde{E}$, is determined as $\hat{\rho}(j_1, j_2) = \rho(j_1, j_2)^{-1}$, and an associated likelihood matrix $\mathcal{L}$ is integrated for all simulations in each class. Specifically, $\mathcal{L} = \sum_n \rho_n \cdot \mathrm{MST}(\hat{\rho}_n)$, where MST is the minimum spanning tree maximising the resilience of each perturbed instance.

From our experiments we obtain putative re-sampled graphs $\tilde{G}$ resulting in subsets of most hemodynamically-compatible branches from an initial fully-connected topology. Major sparsity in the associated adjacency matrix is found for $\varepsilon = 0.5$ and by thresholding the likelihood $\mathcal{L}$ above the median. Although the supra-threshold $\tilde{G}$ shows a reduced redundancy in the connectivity pattern, the correct CoW phenotype is kept *intact*. Also, similar patterns are found for

$\varepsilon = 0.2, 0.3$. This suggests that for $n \underset{\longrightarrow}{\infty}$ simulations and for different degrees of perturbations, a family of hemodynamically-compatible graphs statistically emerges from an uncertain and redundant graph, by jointly maximising the subnet resilience and by integrating overlapping minimal acyclic realisations.

4   Discussion and Conclusions

We present a simplified graph-based simulation framework, which statistically estimates biomarkers from a series of perturbations on the neurovascular network. Asymptotic flow and pressure are determined from data-driven, subject-specific lumped equivalents from clinical angiographies, leveraging an analog configuration and modelling pathological conditions. The adopted approximation cannot model vascular fluid-structure interactions, nor the effect of a pulsating flow as in fully-resolved CFD simulations. However, the high-throughput (0.4 ± 0.2 ms per simulation), the arbitrary graph scalability, and the flexibility for network perturbation allow an early evaluation of the steady-state mechanisms underlying the cerebral autoregulation in a compact and reproducible way. For three healthy CoW phenotypes autoregulation mechanisms and functional distributions are first evaluated with a controlled perturbation, then with a series of random morphological modulations spanning over all the vascular network. Data-driven results on exact topologies are in line with the literature, where similar compensation strategies and distributions were observed in case-studies and on artificial physio-pathological models [5,9,10]. A putative graph sampling is formulated for uncertain redundant topologies, where a family of compatible graphs statistically emerge from jointly maximising the subnet resilience and integrating overlapping minimal spanning trees. Notwithstanding the novelty of presented results, which are the first for image-based simulations of clinically relevant neurovascular networks with perturbations, a more extensive validation is still required. Developments will address more phenotypes, together with a longitudinal cohort of patients to evaluate the predictors vs. the clinical outcomes. Also, by relaxing the steady-flow, time-resolved analyses will account for coupling dynamic modalities (e.g. arterial spin labelling) and pulsating simulations.

References

1. Antiga, L., Steinman, D.: The vascular modeling toolkit (2008)
2. Aylward, S., et al.: TubeTK, Segmentation, Registration, and Analysis of Tubular Structures in Images. Kitware Inc., New York (2012)
3. Cebral, J.R., et al.: Characterization of cerebral aneurysms for assessing risk of rupture by using patient-specific computational hemodynamics models. Am. J. Neuroradiol. **26**(1), 2550–2559 (2005)
4. Cheng, Y., et al.: Accurate vessel segmentation with constrained B-snake. IEEE Trans. Image Process. **24**(8), 2440–2455 (2015)

5. Chnafa, C., et al.: Improved reduced-order modelling of cerebrovascular flow distribution by accounting for arterial bifurcation pressure drops. J. Biomech. **51**, 83–88 (2017)
6. Fossan, F.E., et al.: Optimization of topological complexity for one-dimensional arterial blood flow models. J. Royal Soc. Interface **15**(149), 20180546 (2018)
7. Mathers, C., et al.: The global burden of disease: 2004 Update. World Health Organization (2008)
8. Moriconi, S., et al.: Inference of cerebrovascular topology with geodesic minimum spanning trees. IEEE TMI **38**(1), 225–239 (2018)
9. Onaizah, O., et al.: A model of blood supply to the brain via the carotid arteries: effects of obstructive vs. sclerotic changes. Med. Eng. Phys. **49**, 121–130 (2017)
10. Ryu, J., et al.: A coupled lumped-parameter and distributed network model for cerebral pulse-wave hemodynamics. J. Biomech. Eng. **137**(10), 101009 (2015)
11. Shojima, M., et al.: Magnitude and role of wall shear stress on cerebral aneurysm: computational fluid dynamic study of 20 MCA aneurysms. Stroke **35**(11), 2500–2505 (2004)
12. Steinman, D., et al.: Computational modeling of arterial biomechanics: insights into pathogenesis and treatment of vascular disease. J. Vasc. Surg. **37**(5), 1118–1128 (2003)
13. Taylor, C., Humphrey, J.: Open problems in computational vascular biomechanics: hemodynamics and arterial wall mechanics. CMAME **198**, 3514–3523 (2009)
14. Urick, B., et al.: Review of patient-specific vascular modeling: template-based isogeometric framework and the case for CAD. Arch. Comput. Methods Eng. **26**(2), 381–404 (2017)
15. Vitturi, M.D.: Navier-stokes equations in cylindrical coordinates (2016)

Random 2.5D U-net for Fully 3D Segmentation

Christoph Angermann$^{(\boxtimes)}$ and Markus Haltmeier

Department of Mathematics, University of Innsbruck,
Technikerstraße 13, 6020 Innsbruck, Austria
{christoph.angermann,markus.haltmeier}@uibk.ac.at
http://applied-math.uibk.ac.at

Abstract. Convolutional neural networks are state-of-the-art for various segmentation tasks. While for 2D images these networks are also computationally efficient, 3D convolutions have huge storage requirements and therefore, end-to-end training is limited by GPU memory and data size. To overcome this issue, we introduce a network structure for volumetric data without 3D convolution layers. The main idea is to include projections from different directions to transform the volumetric data to a sequence of images, where each image contains information of the full data. We then apply 2D convolutions to these projection images and lift them again to volumetric data using a trainable reconstruction algorithm. The proposed architecture can be applied end-to-end to very large data volumes without cropping or sliding-window techniques. For a tested sparse binary segmentation task, it outperforms already known standard approaches and is more resistant to generation of artefacts.

Keywords: Deep learning · U-net · Volumetric segmentation ·
Biomedical imaging · Magnetic resonance angiography

1   Introduction

Deep convolution neural networks have become a powerful method for image recognition [4,9]. In the last few years they also exceeded the state-of-the-art in providing segmentation masks for 2D images. Long et al. [6] proposed the idea to transform VGG-nets [9] to deep convolution filters for obtaining semantic segmentations of 2D data. Based on these deep convolution filters, Ronneberger et al. [8] introduced a novel network architecture, the so-called U-net. With this architecture they redefined the state-of-the-art in image annotation till today. The U-net provides a powerful 2D segmentation tool for biomedical applications, since it has been demonstrated to learn highly accurate segmentation masks from only very few training samples.

Among others, the fully automated generation of volumetric segmentation masks is becoming more and more important for biomedical applications. This task is still challenging. One idea is to extend the U-net structure to volumetric data by using 3D convolutions, as has been proposed in [1,3,7]. Some special

© Springer Nature Switzerland AG 2019
H. Liao et al. (Eds.): MLMECH 2019/CVII-STENT 2019, LNCS 11794, pp. 158–166, 2019.
https://doi.org/10.1007/978-3-030-33327-0_19

applications require end-to-end segmentation, where it is disadvantageous to use sliding-window approaches or to work with smaller patches. For such end-to-end tasks, significant drawbacks of 3D convolution models are the huge memory requirements and the resulting restrictions to the model's complexity. Deep learning segmentation methods are therefore often applied to 2D slice images [1]. However, these slice images do not contain information of the full 3D data, which makes the segmentation task much more challenging.

To address the drawbacks of existing approaches, we introduce a network structure which is able to generate accurate 3D segmentation masks of very large volumes. The main idea is to include projection layers from different directions which transform the data to 2D images containing information of the full 3D data. The projection method mainly depends on the application. Common used methods are the maximum intensity projection or the Radon-transform [2]. We then apply the 2D U-net to these projection images and propose a learnable reconstruction algorithm to lift them again to volumetric data.

As one targeted application, we test the proposed model for segmenting blood vessels in 3D magnetic resonance angiography (MRA) scans (Fig. 1). We are given volumetric MRA scans of 119 patients, which face the arteries and veins between the brain and the chest. Also the 3D ground truths of these 119 patients have been provided. These segmentation masks have been generated by hand which takes hours for each patient. Our goal is the fully automated generation of sparse 3D segmentation masks of those vessels. For that purpose we use deep learning and neural networks. At the first glance, this problem may seem to be quite easy because we only have two labels (background and blood vessel), where thresholding could be applied. However, we are not interested into segmentation of those vessels with highest intensity, but in those which assist the doctor to detect dangerous to health abnormalities. This is the reason why we can not use sliding-window techniques, since the model is not able to determine out of a small patch if the seen vessel is "important" for the segmentation. Other challenges are caused by the big size of the volumes ($96 \times 288 \times 224$ voxels) and by the very unbalanced distribution (in average, 99.76 % of all voxels indicate background).

In the following Section, we give a outline of some already existing methodologies and then propose the projection-based 2.5D U-net architecture in Sect. 3. In Sect. 4, we discuss some numerical results on our targeted application.

 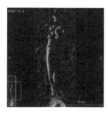  

(a) Transversal.   (b) Sagittal.   (c) Coronal.   (d) 3D annotation.

Fig. 1. In every plane (a)–(c) the blood vessels of interest are marked in red. In (d) we see the corresponding 3D segmentation mask. The segmentation was conducted with the freeware ITK-SNAP [11]. (Color figure online)

2 Background

2.1 3D U-net

The U-net used for binary 3D segmentation is a mapping $\mathcal{U}\colon \mathbb{R}^{a\times b\times c} \to [0,1]^{a\times b\times c}$ which takes 3D data scans as input and outputs for each voxel the probability of being a foreground voxel (e.g. denoting a blood vessel). The 3D U-net used in this paper has exactly the same structure as in [8] with the use of 3D convolution and 3D pooling layers. Due to the huge size of the training samples ($96 \times 288 \times 224$ voxels), we have to take special care of memory space if we want to conduct end-to-end segmentation. This causes restrictions to the amount of downsampling steps and channel sizes in the model. Therefore, we are able to conduct only 4 downsampling steps with channel size 128 in the deepest convolution block to ensure, end-to-end training is still manageable by our *NVIDIA GeForce RTX 2080* GPU. This results into a model consisting of 1.6×10^6 trainable parameters, which are updated for every training sample (minibatch size 1). The model is trained with the Dice-loss function [7]

$$\ell(y, \hat{y}) = 1 - \frac{2\sum_k (y \odot \hat{y})_k}{\sum_k \hat{y}_k + \sum_k y_k}, \tag{1}$$

where $\odot$ denotes pointwise multiplication, the sums are taken over all voxel locations, $\hat{y} = \hat{f}(x)$ are the probabilities predicted by the U-net, and y is the corresponding ground truth.

2.2 Slice-by-Slice 2D U-net

The naive approach for reducing memory requirements of 3D segmentation is to process each of the slice images independently through a 2D segmentation network (compare [1]).

For application, we take our MRA scans and extract their slices to a dataset, which now consists of over 10000 slice-images of size 288×224. The next step is to train a 2D segmentation model like the 2D U-net [8, Fig. 1] with approximately 8.6×10^6 parameters. Here we also make use of the Dice-loss function in Eq. (1). Stacking these segmented slices to 3D volumes again after propagating them through the 2D network yields the 3D segmentation masks.

3 Projection-Based 2.5D U-net

3.1 Proposed 2.5D U-net Architecture

As mentioned in the introduction, the main idea is to include projection layers from different directions. Due to the high sparsity and the orientation of the vessels in our application, maximum intensity projection (MIP) as projection technique seems to be an appropriate choice (Fig. 2).

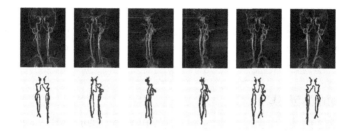

Fig. 2. MIP images of a 3D MRA scan with directions $\theta \in \{k \times 36° \mid k = 0, \ldots, 5\}$.

The proposed 2.5D U-net takes the form

$$\mathcal{N}(x) = \mathcal{T} \circ \mathcal{R}_{p,\Theta} \circ \mathcal{F}_p \circ \begin{bmatrix} \mathcal{U} \circ \mathcal{M}_{\theta_1}(x) \\ \vdots \\ \mathcal{U} \circ \mathcal{M}_{\theta_p}(x) \end{bmatrix}, \tag{2}$$

where

- $\mathcal{M}_{\theta_i} : \mathbb{R}^{a \times b \times c} \to \mathbb{R}^{b \times c}$ are MIP images for different directions $\theta_1, \ldots, \theta_p$,
- $\mathcal{U} : \mathbb{R}^{b \times c} \to [0, 1]^{b \times c}$ is exactly the same 2D U-net structure as in [8, Fig. 1],
- $\mathcal{F}_p : ([0, 1]^{b \times c})^p \to (\mathbb{R}^{b \times c})^p$ is a learnable filtration,
- $\mathcal{R}_{p,\Theta} : (\mathbb{R}^{b \times c})^p \to \mathbb{R}^{a \times b \times c}$ is a reconstruction operator using p *linear back-projections* for directions $\theta_1, \ldots, \theta_p \in \Theta$ as illustrated in Fig. 3a,
- $\mathcal{T} : \mathbb{R}^{a \times b \times c} \to [0, 1]^{a \times b \times c}$ is a fine-tuning operator (average pooling followed by a learnable normalization followed by the sigmoid activation).

(a)   **(b)**

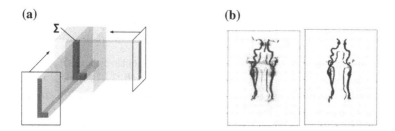

Fig. 3. (a): Reconstruction operator $\mathcal{R}_{2,\{0,90\}}$: Voxel value is defined as the sum over the corresponding 2D values. (b): Network's output without filtration (left) and with filtration (right).

The backprojection operator $\mathcal{R}_{p,\Theta}$ causes a shadow (Fig. 3b, left), which suggests the usage of filtrated backprojection. Therefore, we apply a convolution layer $\mathcal{F}_p$ before linear backprojection. Using 1×2 filters, which get adapted during training for each projection direction $\theta \in \Theta$ individually, solves the problem

(Fig. 3, right). For the fine-tuning operator $\mathcal{T}$ we use average pooling with pool-size (2, 2, 2). This is followed by a learnable normalization, that additionally shifts the pooled data by an adjusted parameter since the decision boundaries have been changed by the operator $\cdot \mathcal{R}_{p,\Theta}$.

3.2 Random 2.5D U-net

We set $\Theta = \{k \times \frac{180}{m} \mid k = 0, \ldots, m - 1\}$ and construct MIP images for all $\theta \in \Theta$, where m denotes the number of projections we want to use for the volumetric reconstruction. Again considering end-to-end training, it is not possible to update the model $\mathcal{N}$ using all $|\Theta| = m$ projection images if m is large due to memory issues. Therefore, we propose a random training strategy with two paths:

1. **Path 1:** We consider for $k = 0, \ldots, p - 1$, $p \ll m$, the set $\Theta_k \triangleq \{k, k+1, \ldots, k + \frac{180}{p} - 1\}$ and choose for each epoch one angle $\hat{\theta}_k \in \Theta_k$ uniformly at random. For that p projection directions, we generate the corresponding MIP images out of the 3D input x and process them through the network $\mathcal{N}$, that has the same structure as in Eq. (2). The first output $\hat{y}_{\text{aux}}$ is then the learned reconstruction of the p randomly chosen MIP segmentations. Note, that the 2D convolution part $\mathcal{U}$ in Eq. (2) is also trained with these random projections.

2. **Path 2:** Here we generate for all m projection directions in Θ the corresponding MIP images out of the same 3D input x. We take the 2D convolution network $\mathcal{U}$ out of the first part and apply it to the m projection images. Note, that $\mathcal{U}$ is only needed for application and we do not update parameters of $\mathcal{U}$ in this path (Fig. 4). Given the m predictions $\mathcal{U}(M_{\theta_1}(x)), \ldots, \mathcal{U}(M_{\theta_m}(x))$, we are able to train a filtration layer $\tilde{\mathcal{F}}_m$ and a new fine-tuning operator $\tilde{\mathcal{T}}$. These are the only layers which get updated in this path. The final output of the second path is then computed by $\hat{y} = \tilde{\mathcal{T}} \circ \mathcal{R}_{m,\Theta} \circ \tilde{\mathcal{F}}_m \circ [\mathcal{U}(M_{\theta_1}(x)), \ldots, \mathcal{U}(M_{\theta_m}(x))]$. Note that this output contains information of all m projection directions. The final segmentation is generated by applying a threshold of 0.5 to $\hat{y}$.

In conclusion, although we only use p random directions for adjustment of the 2D convolution part in $\mathcal{N}$ (first path), we are able with the help of $\mathcal{U}$ to construct simultaneously volumetric segmentation masks using available information from all m projection directions $\theta \in \Theta$ (second path) with $m \gg p$. Experiments show, that $p = 12$ in path 1 and $m = 60$ in path 2 are appropriate choices for our task, since for higher values only computational costs increase but not the accuracy.

We make use of the following joint Dice-loss function:

$$\tilde{\ell}_c(y, \hat{y}, \hat{y}_{\text{aux}}) = c \cdot \ell(y, \hat{y}_{\text{aux}}) + (1 - c) \cdot \ell(y, \hat{y}),$$

where y is the ground truth related to input tensor x, $\hat{y}_{\text{aux}}$ is the model's first output (path 1), $\hat{y}$ is the model's second output (path 2) and therefore the final segmentation prediction, and ℓ is the Dice-loss function in Eq. (1). We choose the regularization $c(n_{\text{epoch}} + 1) = c(n_{\text{epoch}}) \cdot 0.99^{n_{\text{epoch}}}$ for balance parameter c, where c gets initialized with $c(1) = 0.99$.

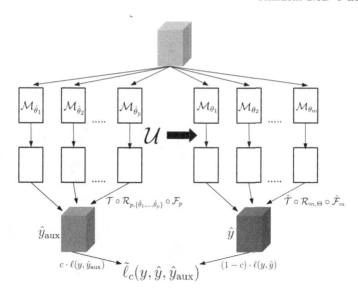

Fig. 4. Architecture of the random 2.5D U-net.

4   Numerical Results

We evaluate the following metrics during training:

- *mean accuracy* [6]: $\mathbf{MA} \triangleq \frac{1}{2}\left(\frac{\text{TN}}{\text{TN}+\text{FP}} + \frac{\text{TP}}{\text{TP}+\text{FN}}\right)$
- *mean intersection over union* [6]: $\mathbf{IU} \triangleq \frac{1}{2}\left(\frac{\text{TN}}{\text{TN}+\text{FP}+\text{FN}} + \frac{\text{TP}}{\text{TP}+\text{FN}+\text{FP}}\right)$
- *Dice-coefficient* [3,7]: $\mathbf{DC} \triangleq \frac{2\cdot\text{TP}}{2\cdot\text{TP}+\text{FN}+\text{FP}}$

For training, Adam-optimizer [5] is used with learning rate 0.001 in combination with learning-rate-scheduling, i.e. if validation loss does not decrease within 3 epochs the learning rate gets halved. If the network shows no improvement for 5 epochs, the training process gets stopped (early stopping) and the weights of the best epoch in terms of validation loss get restored. For every model we conduct 7 training-runs using cross-validation:

- **3D U-net:** Dice-loss of **0.195 ± 0.088**, MA of 91.1% ±2.82%, IU of 86.3% ± 3.57% and DC of **82% ± 6.07%**. Average total training time is 31.8 min on *NVIDIA GeForce RTX 2080* GPU and a memory space of 6.15 gigabyte is allocated during training. Application time to a test sample is 235 ms.
- **slice-by-slice 2D U-net:** Dice-loss of **0.154 ± 0.095**, MA of 91.8% ±6.77%, IU of 87.1% ±5.86% and DC of **84.6% ±9.56%**. Total training time is 16.8 min on GPU and a memory space of 1.83 gigabyte is allocated. Application time is 473 ms.

(a)

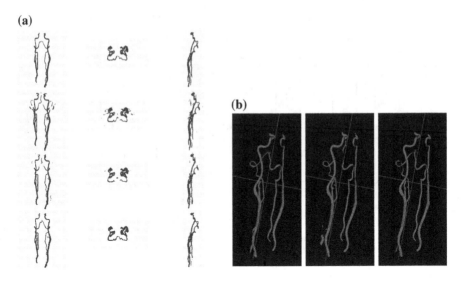

Fig. 5. (a): Ground truth (first), segmentation generated by slice-by-slice 2D U-net approach (second), the 3D U-net (third) and the random 2.5D U-net (fourth). (b): Ground truth (left), 3D segmentation mask generated by the 3D U-net (middle) and by the random 2.5D U-net (right).

- **random 2.5D U-net:** Dice-loss of **0.148 ± 0.019**, MA of 92.7% ± 1.21%, IU of 87.6% ± 1.34% and DC of **85.6% ± 1.91%**. Total training time is 58.7 min on GPU and a memory space of 6.69 gigabyte is allocated. Application time is 349 ms.

Although the 3D U-net demonstrates high precision in our sparse application (Fig. 5a and b), it produces too much artefacts, which constitutes an essential drawback. Additionally, we are very limited in the choice of convolution layers and corresponding channel sizes due to the huge size of the input data. So with this model it is hardly possible to conduct end-to-end segmentation for even larger biomedical scans with more channels on our GPU.

As we observe in Fig. 5a, the slice-by-slice approach even generates more artefacts. Also the high standard deviation of the metrics between different test samples shows, that this approach does not generate segmentations with consistent reliability, which is a huge drawback.

Considering evaluation metrics, the random approach outperforms all prior discussed models and the problem of artefacts vanishes (Fig. 5a and b). Furthermore, it uses nearly the same memory space as the 3D convolution model during training, but is also applicable to bigger input scans without memory concern due to the 2D convolution part. This is not possible for the 3D U-net.

5 Conclusion

Although the construction of 3D segmentation masks with the help of 3D U-net [1,3,7] delivers very satisfying results for vessel segmentation, generation of artefacts and the restrictions to model's complexity due to memory issues are hardly sustainable. Therefore, we proposed the random 2.5D U-net structure, that is able to conduct volumetric segmentation of very big biomedical 3D scans so we can train a network without any concern about memory space and input size. For the targeted application, the random 2.5D U-net even outperformed the standard slice-by-slice and 3D convolution approaches and showed more consistent accuracy for test application.

Note that the proposed network structure can be used for different projection techniques. For blood vessel segmentation, maximum intensity projection seemed to be the most fitting projection method due the high sparsity and orientation of the vessels. For volumetric end-to-end segmentation of different types of biomedical scans, other projection types can be used, e.g. the Radon-transform for kidney segmentation using the corresponding inversion formula [2].

There already exist approaches for saving memory and time in 3D convolution models using convolution with cross-hair filters [10]. In future work, we will compare our methodology to this technique. We will also investigate the use of the random 2.5D U-net architecture for other projection types and applications, e.g. for 3D multilabel segmentation of spines or volumetric image reconstruction.

References

1. Çiçek, Ö., Abdulkadir, A., Lienkamp, S.S., Brox, T., Ronneberger, O.: 3D U-Net: learning dense volumetric segmentation from sparse annotation. In: Ourselin, S., Joskowicz, L., Sabuncu, M.R., Unal, G., Wells, W. (eds.) MICCAI 2016. LNCS, vol. 9901, pp. 424–432. Springer, Cham (2016). https://doi.org/10.1007/978-3-319-46723-8_49
2. Deans, S.R.: The Radon Transform and Some of its Applications. Courier Corporation, Chelmsford (2007)
3. Erden, B., Gamboa, N., Wood, S.: 3D convolutional neural network for brain tumor segmentation (2018)
4. He, K., Zhang, X., Ren, S., Sun, J.: Deep residual learning for image recognition. In: Proceedings of the IEEE conference on computer vision and pattern recognition, pp. 770–778 (2016)
5. Kingma, D.P., Ba, J.: Adam: a method for stochastic optimization (2014)
6. Long, J., Shelhamer, E., Darrell, T.: Fully convolutional networks for semantic segmentation. In: Proceedings of the IEEE Conference on Computer Vision and Pattern Recognition, pp. 3431–3440 (2015)
7. Milletari, F., Navab, N., Ahmadi, S.A.: V-net: fully convolutional neural networks for volumetric medical image segmentation. In: 2016 Fourth International Conference on 3D Vision (3DV), pp. 565–571. IEEE (2016)
8. Ronneberger, O., Fischer, P., Brox, T.: U-Net: convolutional networks for biomedical image segmentation. In: Navab, N., Hornegger, J., Wells, W.M., Frangi, A.F. (eds.) MICCAI 2015. LNCS, vol. 9351, pp. 234–241. Springer, Cham (2015). https://doi.org/10.1007/978-3-319-24574-4_28

9. Simonyan, K., Zisserman, A.: Very deep convolutional networks for large-scale image recognition. arXiv preprint arXiv:1409.1556 (2014)
10. Tetteh, G., et al.: Deepvesselnet: Vessel segmentation, centerline prediction, and bifurcation detection in 3-d angiographic volumes. arXiv preprint arXiv:1803.09340 (2018)
11. Yushkevich, P.A., et al.: User-guided 3D active contour segmentation of anatomical structures: significantly improved efficiency and reliability. Neuroimage **31**(3), 1116–1128 (2006)

Abdominal Aortic Aneurysm Segmentation Using Convolutional Neural Networks Trained with Images Generated with a Synthetic Shape Model

Karen López-Linares[1,2,3]([✉]), Maialen Stephens[1], Inmaculada García[1,2],
Iván Macía[1,2], Miguel Ángel González Ballester[3,4], and Raúl San José Estepar[5]

[1] Vicomtech Foundation, San Sebastián, Spain
klopez@vicomtech.org
[2] Biodonostia Health Research Institute, San Sebastián, Spain
[3] BCN Medtech, Department of Information and Communication Technologies,
Universitat Pompeu Fabra, Barcelona, Spain
[4] ICREA, Barcelona, Spain
[5] Applied Chest Imaging Laboratory, Brigham and Women's Hospital,
Harvard medical school, Boston, USA

Abstract. An abdominal aortic aneurysm (AAA) is a ballooning of the abdominal aorta, that if not treated tends to grow and rupture. Computed Tomography Angiography (CTA) is the main imaging modality for the management of AAAs, and segmenting them is essential for AAA rupture risk and disease progression assessment. Previous works have shown that Convolutional Neural Networks (CNNs) can accurately segment AAAs, but have the limitation of requiring large amounts of annotated data to train the networks. Thus, in this work we propose a methodology to train a CNN only with images generated with a synthetic shape model, and test its generalization and ability to segment AAAs from new original CTA scans. The synthetic images are created from realistic deformations generated by applying principal component analysis to the deformation fields obtained from the registration of few datasets. The results show that the performance of a CNN trained with synthetic data to segment AAAs from new scans is comparable to the one of a network trained with real images. This suggests that the proposed methodology may be applied to generate images and train a CNN to segment other types of aneurysms, reducing the burden of obtaining large annotated image databases.

Keywords: Abdominal aortic aneurysm · Segmentation · Convolutional Neural Network · Synthetic images · Principal component analysis

K. López-Linares and M. Stephens—Equally contributing authors.

© Springer Nature Switzerland AG 2019
H. Liao et al. (Eds.): MLMECH 2019/CVII-STENT 2019, LNCS 11794, pp. 167–174, 2019.
https://doi.org/10.1007/978-3-030-33327-0_20

1   Introduction

An abdominal aortic aneurysm (AAA) is a focal dilation of the aorta, which in most of the cases requires surgical treatment to prevent its rupture. Computed Tomography Angiography (CTA) is the preferred imaging modality for the management of AAAs, from the diagnosis to the pre-operative planning of the intervention and the post-operative follow-up. Specifically, the diagnosis consists in evaluating the rupture risk by measuring the size of the AAA from a CTA scan. The follow-up aims at evaluating the progression of the AAA, i.e. the post-operative shrinkage of the AAA or its expansion if the intervention is unsuccessful. Hence, automatic AAA segmentation tools are essential to aid the clinicians in these tasks and they open up the opportunity to perform complex analyses of AAA morphology and biomechanics.

Convolutional Neural Networks (CNNs) have shown the ability to automatically and accurately segment infra-renal AAAs from pre-operative and post-operative CTA scans [1,2]. CNNs efficiently learn implicit object representations at different scales from input annotated data. However, the need for such annotations is one of the main limitations of CNN-based segmentation approaches, since obtaining them is time-consuming and requires expert knowledge. Here is where synthetic image generation and data augmentation play an important role in order to train a network from few annotated input data.

Thus, the aim of this study is to evaluate the ability of a 3D CNN trained only with images generated with a synthetic shape model to segment aneurysms from real CTA scans. The employed synthetic image generation approach [3] is based on realistic deformations computed from the Principal Component Analysis (PCA) of deformation fields extracted from the registration of few real CTA scans. Furthermore, we run several experiments to evaluate the performance and generalization of the network when gradually reducing the amount of input real CTA images used for synthetic image generation.

2   State-of-the-art

Segmentation of the AAA thrombus from CTA images is challenging since it appears as a non-contrasted structure with fuzzy borders, and its shape varies among patients, which makes it difficult to develop robust automatic segmentation approaches. Traditionally proposed methods combine intensity information with shape constraints to minimize a certain energy function using level-sets [9], graph-cuts [4,5,8] or deformable models [6,7]. However, these algorithms require user interaction and/or prior lumen segmentation along with centerline extraction and their performance highly depends on multiple parameter tuning, affecting their robustness and clinical applicability.

More recently, CNNs have gained attention in the scientific community for solving complex segmentation tasks, surpassing the previous state-of-the-art performance in many problems. CNN-based approaches have shown state-of-the-art results in infra-renal AAA segmentation from both pre-operative and post-operative CTA scans in a fully automatic manner and without the need of any additional prior segmentation from the scans [1, 2]. The main limitation of these approaches is the need of large amounts of annotated datasets to improve the network generalization when having different types of aneurysms.

Obtaining annotated images to train CNNs is a time-consuming task and requires expert knowledge. Hence, researchers try to alleviate the burden by using data augmentation techniques. Applying rotation, translation, scaling, reflection and other random elastic deformations is the most common approach to increase the number of annotated images [10]. Realistic deformations to increase the image database have also been proposed [3, 11], as well as generative adversarial networks [12]. In this work, we leverage realistic elastic deformations to generate a synthetic shape model in order to train a CNN only with data created with this model, and to test its ability to segment aneurysms from new, real CTA scans. The proposed approach could be used in the future to extend the segmentation to aneurysms at other sites of the aorta, such as thoracic aneurysms, or cerebral aneurysms without the need of large annotated databases.

3 Methods

Hereby, we aim at evaluating the generalization ability of a 3D CNN trained on data generated with a synthetic shape model to segment infra-renal AAAs from real CTA scans. The followed procedure consists in 3 main steps: synthetic image generation, CNN training with synthetic data, and validation using real data. Synthetic images are created using a method based on the principal component analysis (PCA) of deformation fields extracted from the registration of real CTA scans to a reference real CTA scan, as explained in Sect. 3.2. In a second step, we train the 3D CNN designed in [2] with the generated synthetic data. Finally, we evaluate the performance of the network to segment AAAs from real CTA scans and compare the results with the baseline model presented in [2] for the same testing datasets. This baseline network was trained with more than double real input scans, plus rotations and translations.

3.1 Abdominal Aortic Aneurysm Datasets

The employed CTA volumes have been provided by Donostia University Hospital. They have been obtained with scanners of different manufacturers with an in-plane spatial resolution in the range of 0.725 mm to 0.977 mm in x and y, and a slice thickness of 0.625 mm to 1 mm in the z direction. We work with 28 postoperative CTA datasets of patients with an infra-renal AAA and that have been treated with EVAR. We use a maximum of 12 CTAs to generate synthetic images, and the remaining 16 are saved for testing the CNN model. Ground truth annotations have been obtained semi-automatically using the segmentation method developed in [1] and manually correcting the results.

3.2 Synthetic Shape Model Generation Using Realistic Deformations

Elastic deformation-based data augmentation has been widely applied in medical imaging to increase the amount of input data to train a network. In [3], a novel approach to obtain synthetic images from realistic deformations was proposed to aid the segmentation of the pulmonary artery from CT scans. We aim at applying this method to generate synthetic AAA CTA scans, following the procedure shown in Fig. 1. The next steps are performed:

1. Register real AAA ground truths to a reference mask using the BSpline registration method implemented in 3D Slicer and extract the 3D deformation fields corresponding only to the elastic transform. The registration is done using the ground truth aneurysm masks.
2. Run the PCA from the fields and extract the eigenvectors and eigenvalues. The PCA components, together with the mean deformation extracted from the input fields, characterize the main AAA deformation directions.
3. Generate new deformation fields by weighting the eigenvectors with random values between 0 to $\pm$ the square root of the corresponding eigenvalue.
4. Generate synthetic volumes by applying these deformation fields to each original CTA volume, following Eq. 1.

$$\tilde{I}_j : \sum_{i=1}^{n} < w_i * B_i > +\mu \tag{1}$$

where $\tilde{I}_j$ is the new synthetic image, n is the number of eigenvectors, w_i are the weights generated from the eigenvalues, B_i are the eigenvectors, and μ is the mean deformation extracted from the original deformation fields.

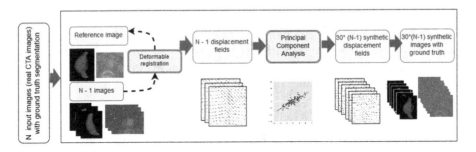

Fig. 1. Synthetic image generation using realistic deformations.

With this procedure, we create 6 different datasets to run 6 experiments, consisting in training the CNN using a different amount of input real CTA and reference scans. Table 1 summarizes the number of images used in each experiment. The amount of applied translations and rotations are selected to approximate the total number of images used to train the baseline model in [2]. From experiment 1 to 3, we use a single CTA scan as reference and gradually reduce the amount of additional scans to register and create the shape model. In experiments 4 to 6, 2 reference scans are used. Figure 2 shows some created synthetic images and segmentations.

Table 1. Summary of the employed data used to train the network in each experiment.

Experiment	1	2	3	4	5	6
Total number of scans	12	8	4	12	8	4
Number of scans used as reference	1	1	1	2	2	2
Number of scans registered to each reference	11	7	3	11	7	3
Number of synthetic images	330	210	90	660	420	180
Applied translations	2	4	9	2	2	4
Applied rotations	3	4	9	3	2	5
Total number of images to train the network	1650	1680	1620	1650	1680	1620

3.3   3D Convolutional Neural Network for AAA Segmentation

Once the images generated with the synthetic shape model are created, we proceed to train the 3D CNN proposed in [2], specifically designed to segment AAAs from CTA scans. The net combines fine edge detection with global information about the shape and location of the aneurysm thanks to the fusion of features maps at different scales. Figure 3 shows the architecture of the CNN, for which more details can be found in [2].

Original image   Synthetic CTA image 1   Synthetic CTA image 2

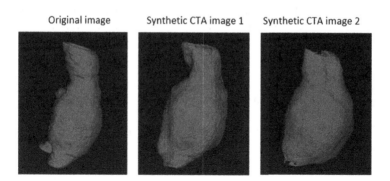

Fig. 2. Examples of generated synthetic images.

The network is trained using the aforementioned datasets, and to reduce the impact of the amount of images used to train the network in each experiment and to better evaluate the influence of the amount of input real CTA scans and number of reference scans, we apply a different number of rotations and translations in each case. Table 1 shows a summary of the total number of images employed to train the network, and how they have been created.

We set the initial learning rate to 1e-4, a batch size of 2 and Adam optimization are employed. A weighted Dice loss function is minimized [2]. The network is trained on a TITAN X Pascal (NVIDIA) GPU card with 11.91GB memory.

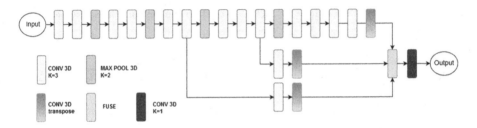

Fig. 3. Proposed 3D convolutional neural network for aneurysm segmentation.

4 Results

The created CNN models are tested with the same 16 CTA scans used during the inference step in the baseline model from [2], which allows to study the generalization of the network when trained on synthetic data as compared to the network trained on real CTA scans. Furthermore, this baseline model is created from 28 real CTA scans, whereas our proposed approach requires a maximum of 12 annotated scans to generate the shape model. The total number of images after augmentation used in our experiments and to train the model in [2] is very similar, to minimize the impact of the amount of images used for training.

We compute the Dice and Jaccard scores between the ground truth annotations and the automatic segmentations as in [2]. Table 2 shows the obtained results for each of the experiments and the baseline values presented in [2].

Table 2. Mean Dice and Jaccard scores for the testing datasets, for the networks trained on synthetic data and the baseline model trained on real CTA scans

	Baseline [2]	Exp 1	Exp 2	Exp 3	Exp 4	Exp 5	Exp 6
Dice	0.88 ± 0.05	0.84 ± 0.01	0.75 ± 0.05	0.57 ± 0.08	0.85 ± 0.01	0.76 ± 0.06	0.71 ± 0.06
Jaccard	0.78 ± 0.08	0.73 ± 0.01	0.64 ± 0.05	0.44 ± 0.06	0.75 ± 0.01	0.65 ± 0.05	0.59 ± 0.05

The obtained Dice and Jaccard scores for the testing datasets when training the network with synthetic data created from 12 original CTA scans (experiment 1 and 4) are close to the values achieved in [2], in which the network was trained with 28 real CTA scans. This concludes that our proposed synthetic image generation approach allows to create realistic images that can be used to effectively train a CNN with a reduced amount of input annotated data.

Furthermore, when comparing the performance of the network when using more datasets as reference (experiments 4,5 and 6), an improvement in the Dice and Jaccard scores is achieved. This improvement is more notable when comparing experiment 3 and experiment 6, in which only 4 datasets are used to train the network. For example, if a t-test between the Jaccard coefficients of experiments 1 and 4 is computed, a p-value of 3.65e-6 is achieved, meaning that the difference is significant. Having more reference datasets to extract deformation fields and create the synthetic shape model allows to account for a larger variability of the input data, which improves the generalization of the CNN. This result suggests that even having less input data, using the proposed technique with multiple reference scans can help creating a representative image database to train an AAA segmentation network that can be used to segment real CTA scans.

Finally, to further evaluate the value of the proposed augmentation method, we run a test in which we compare the performance of the network when trained (1) only with the original 12 CTA scans, (2) only applying augmentation via rotations and translations, and (3) including the synthetically generated images from experiment 1. Table 3 shows the results, which indeed confirm that using the images generated with our approach boosts the performance of the CNN.

Table 3. Influence of adding the synthetic images in the performance of the network. T: translations, R: rotations.

Training data	(I) 12 real CTA	(II) I + 2 T + 3 R	(III) II + 330 synthetic images
Dice	0.22 ± 0.07	0.42 ± 0.02	0.84 ± 0.01
Jaccard	0.13 ± 0.00	0.27 ± 0.01	0.73 ± 0.01

5   Conclusions

This work aimed at evaluating the ability of a CNN trained only with images generated with a synthetic shape model to segment infra-renal aneurysms from real CTA scans. Having large annotated image databases to train a network is one of the main limitations of deep learning-based approaches, and thus, applying a proper methodology to generate synthetic images that account for a large variability of the input data is essential. Obtaining these images with the proposed synthetic shape model allows to generate plausible, realistic scans, controlling the final shape of the generated AAA scan, contrarily to using a fully random elastic deformation.

Our experiments have shown that the described synthetic image generation approach allows to create a wide variety of CTA images to train a CNN. Using less than a half of the original CTA scans employed in [2], the 3D CNN trained with synthetic data is able to accurately segment real aneurysm with comparable Dice and Jaccard coefficients as when the network is trained with real scans. Additionally, we have proved that using more reference datasets to extract deformation fields can further improve the segmentation results.

Hence, the obtained results suggest that the proposed methodology may be applied to generate images and train a CNN to segment other arterial or cerebral aneurysms, without the need of large annotated image databases. This is the aim of our future work, as well as including other synthetic image generation methods, such as generative adversarial networks.

References

1. López-Linares, K., et al.: Fully automatic detection and segmentation of abdominal aortic thrombus in post-operative CTA images using deep convolutional neural networks. Med. Image Anal. **46**, 202–214 (2018)
2. López-Linares, K., García, I., García-Familiar, A., Macía, I., González Ballester, M.A.: 3D convolutional neural network for abdominal aortic aneurysm segmentation. arXiv preprint arXiv:1903.00879 (2019)
3. López-Linares, K., et al.: 3D pulmonary artery segmentation from CTA scans using deep learning with realistic data augmentation. In: Image Analysis for Moving Organ, Breast, and Thoracic Images, pp. 225–237 (2018)
4. Duquette, A.A., Jodoin, P.M., Bouchot, O., Lalande, A.: 3D segmentation of abdominal aorta from CT-scan and MR images. Comput. Med. Imaging Graph. **36**(4), 294–303 (2012)
5. Freiman, M., Esses, S.J., Joskowicz, L., Sosna, J.: An iterative model-constrained graph-cut algorithm for abdominal aortic aneurysm thrombus segmentation. In: IEEE International Symposium on Biomedical Imaging: From Nano to Macro, pp. 672–675(2010)
6. Demirci, S., Lejeune, G., Navab, N.: Hybrid deformable model for aneurysm segmentation. In: IEEE International Symposium on Biomedical Imaging: From Nano to Macro, pp. 33–36 (2009)
7. Lalys, F., Yan, V., Kaladji, A., Lucas, A., Esneault, S.: Generic thrombus segmentation from pre and postoperative CTA. Int. J. Comput. Assist. Radiol. Surg. **12**(9), 1–10 (2017)
8. Siriapisith, T., Kusakunniran, W., Haddawy, P.: Outer wall segmentation of abdominal aortic aneurysm by variable neighborhood search through intensity and gradient spaces. J. Digital Imaging **31**(4), 490–504 (2018)
9. Zohios, C., Kossioris, G., Papaharilaou, Y.: Geometrical methods for level set based abdominal aortic aneurysm thrombus and outer wall 2D image segmentation. Comput. Methods. Program. Biomed. **107**(2), 202–217 (2012)
10. Çiçek, Ö., Abdulkadir, A., Lienkamp, S.S., Brox, T., Ronneberger, O.: 3D U-Net: Learning Dense Volumetric Segmentation from Sparse Annotation. In: Ourselin, S., Joskowicz, L., Sabuncu, M.R., Unal, G., Wells, W. (eds.) MICCAI 2016. LNCS, vol. 9901, pp. 424–432. Springer, Cham (2016). https://doi.org/10.1007/978-3-319-46723-8_49
11. Roth, H.R., et al.: DeepOrgan: multi-level deep convolutional networks for automated pancreas segmentation. In: Navab, N., Hornegger, J., Wells, W.M., Frangi, A.F. (eds.) MICCAI 2015. LNCS, vol. 9349, pp. 556–564. Springer, Cham (2015). https://doi.org/10.1007/978-3-319-24553-9_68
12. Kazeminia, S., et al.: GANs for medical image analysis. arXiv preprint arXiv:1809.06222 (2018)

Tracking of Intracavitary Instrument Markers in Coronary Angiography Images

Yihe Zhang[1], Xiuxiu Bai[1], Qinhua Jin[2], Jing Jing[2], Yundai Chen[2(✉)],
Qiang Liu[3], Wenhui Tang[3], Quanmao Lu[4], Yanan Mi[4], Rui Zhu[5],
and Yihui Cao[4]

[1] School of Software Engineering, Xi'an Jiaotong University,
Xi'an, People's Republic of China
[2] Department of Cardiology, Chinese PLA General Hospital,
Beijing, People's Republic of China
cyundai@vip.163.com
[3] Fuwai Hospital Chinese Academy of Medical Sciences,
Beijing, People's Republic of China
[4] Shenzhen Vivolight Medical Device & Technolog Co., Ltd.,
Shenzhen, People's Republic of China
[5] Xi'an Institute of Optics and Precision Mechanics,
Chinese Academy of Sciences, Xi'an, People's Republic of China

Abstract. In order to quickly and accurately obtain the marker points in coronary angiography images in interventional surgery for cardiovascular diseases, this paper proposes a method for tracking the marker points in coronary angiography images. Firstly, it is necessary for the operator to manually mark a small number of vascular center points to find the position of the guide line and the labeled points on the guide wire. So the vascular center line can be obtained by using the vascular center point of artificial labeling with Hessian matrix eigenvector. Then we design a filter to detect the guide wire by combining the characteristics of the guide wire and the center line of the vessel. Finally, the marker point is detected by filtering along the guide wire. In the following images, all the vascular center points in the image are obtained by the automatic vascular centerline acquisition algorithm, and the vascular centerline of the frame is obtained by Iterative Closest Point (ICP) registration of the point set with the adjacent frame centerline. Then the guide wire acquisition method of this frame image is consistent with the above algorithm. Finally, the marker of the frame is obtained by combining the positions of the adjacent frame marker and frame guide wire. The experimental results show that our method can quickly and accurately detect the location of marker points in coronary angiography image sequence with a small amount of manual assistance, and can be applied to the computer-aided diagnosis and treatment of cardiovascular diseases.

Keywords: Angiography · Cardiovascular · Object tracking · Coronary angiography image

© Springer Nature Switzerland AG 2019
H. Liao et al. (Eds.): MLMECH 2019/CVII-STENT 2019, LNCS 11794, pp. 175–183, 2019.
https://doi.org/10.1007/978-3-030-33327-0_21

1   Introduction

In cardiovascular interventional surgery, coronary angiography images and intra-cavitary images can directly display the information in coronary vessels for a doctor who needs to combine these two kinds of images for comprehensive diagnosis and treatment. However, these two kinds of images are independent acquisition with little correlation. In order to establish a connection between them, a marking is typically provided on the intracavity video instrument and will show on the coronary angiography image. During operation, an operator needs to manually obtain the position of each frame marker in the coronary angiography image to match the intracavitary image. However, the way to acquire a marker is both time-consuming and laborious, and a manual marker error might exist and disturb diagnosis. Therefore, we propose a detection and tracking method for the marker.

Research on tracking tag detection is rarely found. This paper proposes a detection method based on centerline-guide-marker. For the first frame, the operator needs to manually mark a small number of vascular center points to determine the position of the guidewire and the marker on the guidewire in the vessel. The vascular centerline is obtained by using Hessian matrix eigenvector and artificial marker [7,8]. Then the corresponding filter is designed according to the image characteristics of the guidewire and the vessel centerline is combined to detect the guidewire [9]. Finally, the marker points are detected through the guidewire. In the next image, all the centerpoints of vessels in the image are obtained by using the automatic automatic vascular centerline algorithm [11], and the Iterative Closest Point (ICP) algorithm [5] is used to register the centerline of the points and the adjacent frame. The guidewire of the frame is acquired by the first frame acquisition of the guidewire algorithm. Finally, the marker of the frame is obtained by combining the position of the adjacent frame marker and the position of the guide wire of the frame.

In summary, our contributions are: (1) We propose a Hessian matrix-based eigenvector centerline detection method to obtain the centerline of the first frame. (2) A detection method of vascular centerline and marker based on adjacent frames is proposed to track the position of blood vessels in coronary angiography images. (3) According to the image characteristics of the guide wire, a corresponding filter is designed to detect the guide wire and obtain the guide wire in the coronary angiography image. Finally, the detection and tracking of markers in coronary angiography images are realized.

2   Method

In this section, it introduces the method of automatic detection and tracking of marker in details. Figure 1 describes the framework of the method. The methods in this paper are described below.

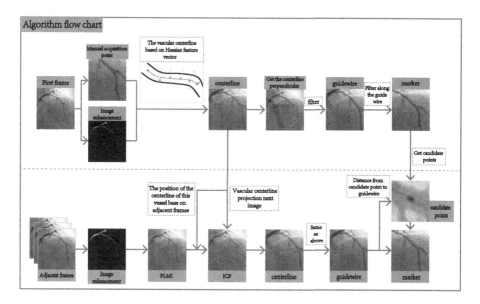

Fig. 1. The framework shows the overall algorithm flow of this paper.

2.1 Centerline Extraction

Before obtaining the vascular centerline, the image needs to be enhanced by the multi-scale vascular enhancement method (MVEF) [7]. Then, according to the different input, the obtained vascular centerline is divided into two parts: the first frame and the adjacent frame. For the first frame vascular centerline requires human get a small amount of starting point, while the adjacent frames should refer to the known vascular centerline of the adjacent images. This will be detailed in two sections.

Based on Hessian Matrix Eigenvectors. Angiographic images are enhanced by multi-scale vascular enhancement [11], the points on the central line of vessels in the enhanced image show the brightest local area. According to the characteristics of Hessian matrix [10], the feature vector of the middle point of the tubular structure presents the following characteristics:

$$\|\lambda_1\| \leqslant 0, \|\lambda_1\| \ll \|\lambda_2\|, \tag{1}$$

where the eigenvector of λ_1 of this point is along the direction of the vessel, and the eigenvector of λ_2 is orthogonal to the vessel.

According to the above characteristics [1,4], this paper proposes a method to obtain the vascular centerline based on Hessian feature vector. The overall process of obtaining the centerline is shown in Fig. 2.

The starting and ending points are P and U by manual. First obtain the point P Hessian matrix eigenvector $\lambda_{1(P)}$ of and $\lambda_{2(P)}$, combined with the point

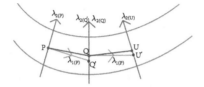

Fig. 2. The orange color shows the blood vessel wall. P and U respectively represent the starting and ending points of the manually labeled vascular centerline, where $\lambda_{1(m)}$ and $\lambda_{2(m)}$ are the eigenvectors of Hessian at point m (where m represents P, Q', Q and U). And the red line in the figure is the vascular centerline obtained by the algorithm. (Color figure online)

P as the starting point and the $\lambda_{1(P)}$ vector direction, in a certain step length to extract candidate Q', and step size threshold is not easy to be too long, otherwise the point might be outside the vessel. And then obtain the Q' point Hessian matrix eigenvector $\lambda_{2(Q')}$, centered on Q' points combined with $\lambda_{2(Q')}$ vector direction, in the vessels within the scope of searching for pixel values the brightest point Q, is that point for the center of the vessels. Finally, Q is used as the starting point to obtain the vascular central point U in the same steps. The central point of the vessel is obtained through cyclic iteration until the last point is the end point of the input. The obtained point set is connected into a line, that is, the central line of vessel (red line).

Adjacent Frames. In the whole angiographic sequence, first, the centerline of the first frame is obtained by the method based on Hessian matrix eigenvectors. Then by the automatic vessels centerline extraction method [11] get the all vascular center points in the adjacent frames. These points are used as candidate points to obtain the vascular centerline of the frame image. In the method of screening candidate points, this paper uses the feature that the vessels in the two adjacent frames in the coronary angiography images have no obvious difference in the degree of curvature [2,6], but only change in position. Based on the Iterative Closest Point (ICP) algorithm [5], we registered the candidate points and the known vascular centerline of the adjacent frame, removed the corresponding noise points, and screened out the vascular centerpoint of the frame. Then the same method is used to iteratively obtain the centerline of the vessel segment at the same position in each frame of the sequence, so as to realize the tracking of the vessel segment.

2.2   Guidewire Detection

In coronary angiography images, since the position of the guidewire does not coincide with the centerline, and the gray value of the guidewire is usually smaller than the background value, and the image shows a darker curve. In the detection guidewire, first, there need to get the Hessian matrix eigenvectors at all center

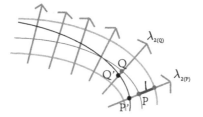

Fig. 3. The orange color shows the vessel wall. The red line is the centerline of the vessel and the black line is the guidewire. P and Q are the points on the centerline, $\lambda_{2(P)}$ and $\lambda_{2(Q)}$ are their orthogonal vectors to vessels. l is the step size (10 pixels). P' and Q' are the points on the guidewire corresponding to the detected vascular centerline. (Color figure online)

points, as shown in Fig. 3. It takes that center point P of the vessel as the centerline, and then obtains the pixel point in the range of length $l(l = 10)$ along the vector direction $\lambda_{2(p)}$ orthogonal to the vessel. Thereby obtaining $2l + 1$ pixel points for the center. According to the characteristics of the guidewire in the vessel, the corresponding filter is designed to filter the obtained pixel points, and its purpose is to enhance the gradient between adjacent pixels. Compared with the background, the guidewire is slightly dimmer in the vessel, so the position of the pixel with the smallest intensity value is obtained and the point is taken as the candidate point of the guidewire at this position. However, due to the uneven distribution of contrast agent, it is possible that the position of the smallest pixel point is not the position of the guidewire. Therefore, this paper screens candidate points by combining the gradient between pixels. When the gradient of the candidate point and the pixel at the adjacent position of this point is larger than that of the pixel at the adjacent position of other points, this point will be taken as the guidewire point P', otherwise, this point will be abandoned. In the experiments, there will be a small number of points with errors, so it is necessary to conduct curve fitting for the obtained guidewire points. Through the adaptive polynomial curve fitting [3] of the discrete guide wire points, the position of the guide wire can be obtained.

2.3   Marker Fetch

According to the prior knowledge, the marker is on the guide wire. Therefore, the marker can be determined from the position of the guidewire. In order to reduce errors, this paper introduces the known position information of adjacent frame markers in the detection process of non-first frame image markers. However, the detection methods of these two kinds of markers are different, and their methods are detailed below.

Marker Detection of First Frame. In an intracavitary imaging instrument, the marker moves along the guidewire and the size of the marker is fixed. Therefore, in coronary angiography images, the marker points fall on the guidewire and show small dark spots, and the size of the imaging changes little. In this section, marker detection is performed on the guide wire. In this paper, a filter of similar size to the marker is designed according to the imaging characteristics of the marker. The filter is filtered along the guide wire to obtain the marker point with the maximum response value. In the method of this paper, the marker points of non-first frame need to refer to the known marker of adjacent frames, so the accuracy of the marker points of first frame is required to be very high. Considering noise points and other influencing factors, the detection algorithm cannot achieve complete accuracy. In order to reduce the error of subsequent algorithms, the first frame marker is accurately detected by means of algorithm and manual confirmation.

Marker Detection of Others. In the experiments, there are generally two markers on the intracavitary imaging instrument, whose shapes are exactly the same and the distance between them remains unchanged. A marker is at the intracavitary imaging site, and it is also the key detection point in this paper. In this method, taking advantage of the invariant distance between the marker points, we will also detect the other marker, and constrain the position the key marker through the point, so as to improve the detection accuracy of the key marker. According to the above characteristics, this paper proposes a method of auxiliary detection marker based on adjacent frames. The formula is as follows:

$$S_{(i,j)} = \alpha(d_i + d_j) + \beta \left| d_{(i,j)} - d \right| + \delta((1/f_i) + (1/f_j)), \qquad (2)$$

$$S_{(i)} = \alpha d_i + \beta l_i + \delta(1/f_i), \qquad (3)$$

where α, β and δ are proportional coefficients. i and j represent candidate points ($i = j = 1 \ldots 10$). The known adjacent frame marker points are projected into the image of the frame, and then the projection points are taken as the center, and the points with large response values are filtered in a certain range through the filter as candidate points (10 candidate points are obtained for each position in this paper). d_i and d_j are the distance between the candidate point and the guide wire. f_i and f_j are the response value of the filter. $d_{(i,j)}$ is the curve distance between candidate points on the guide wire. d is the curve distance of adjacent frame marker points on the guide wire. In this paper, the threshold of relevant step size (the threshold length is 5 pixels) is set, when the minimum distance between all candidate points and the guide wire is greater than the threshold, we know that a mark is out of bounds. Then we calculate the position of the key marker by Formula 2. l_i are the distance between candidate points and projection points. Since the experimental data is 15 fps, this paper sets the pullback speed of two adjacent frames as 10 pixels per frame.

Since the marker is located on the guide wire, it is closer to the guidewire when d_i and $d_i + d_j$ are smaller. Since the distance between the marker points is fixed, the distance closer the mark point is to the fixed value, when $\|d_{i+j} - d\|$ is smaller. Similarly, when the smaller the l_i, the closer it is to the pullback speed.

As the characteristic response value of candidate points is larger, the probability of marking points is higher. At this time, according to the results calculated by Formulas 2 and 3, $\min S_{(i,j)}$ and $\min S_i$ candidate points are obtained as the markers.

3   Experiments

The experimental data are 14 sets of real intraoperative pull-back data, they are respectively from two devices. Ten of the coronary angiography images had a frame rate of 7.5 fps, while the other had a frame rate of 15 fps. All data pull-back time is around 3 s. The total frame number of all coronary angiography is 668, of which the total frame number of pull-back is 332.

In the coronary angiography image, the marker is an $m*n$ matrix $(m, n \leq 6)$, and the marker by the algorithm is a pixel point. Then, this paper will conduct quantitative analysis of the experimental results through an evaluation criteria. The correctness of detection is judged by whether the detected marker falls within the range of real data. If the detection point falls outside the real data, this is a failed detection. If the detection point falls in the real data, the detection of the frame is correct. By counting the detection results on all frames, the Correct Detection rate (CD) and Wrong Detection rate (WD) of marker Detection can be obtained. The specific formula is as follows:

$$CD = \frac{n_a}{n}, WD = \frac{n_b}{n}, \tag{4}$$

where n is the total number of frames per group of data, n_a and n_b are the number of correct detection and error detection.

Based on the above two evaluation criteria, the quantitative analysis results of this method are shown in Table 1. Due to the problems in data collection, some of the experimental data in this paper have frames in which marker points disappear in coronary angiography data. After the analysis and summary of the experimental data, the reasons for the disappearance of the marker in the table. In Table 1, before the disappearance of the marker, the average detection accuracy of the marker is 0.9291, which indicates that the accuracy of this method is better. And in the last three sets of data, the method proposed can obtain better detection results when no marker disappears in the image. However, the average accuracy of the overall results of all the data is only 0.5329.

The method can detect and track the mark points through the auxiliary detection function of adjacent frame images, which enhances its accuracy. Compared with the machine learning method, this method does not need the tedious training stage. At the same time, this method reduces the calculation of unnecessary data and corrects the results of the algorithm through a small amount of manual intervention, thus improving the efficiency and accuracy of the algorithm and making it more practical.

Table 1. The results of the experiment

Number	Total of frames	Effective frame (Before mark disappears)			Result of overall data		The reason of mark point disappears and frame number		
		Frame number	Correct detection	Wrong detection	Correct detection	Wrong detection	Marker out of vessel	Contrast strong	Vessels overlap
1	15	5	1	0	0.3333	0.6667	1	2	
2	32	20	0.9524	0.0476	0.625	0.375		3	7
3	17	14	1	0	0.8235	0.1765		3	
4	17	6	1	0	0.3529	0.6471		11	
5	17	9	0.8889	0.1111	0.4706	0.5294		8	
6	16	9	0.8889	0.1111	0.5	0.5		7	
7	16	8	0.75	0.25	0.375	0.625		3	
8	16	8	1	0	0.5	0.5		8	
9	13	3	1	0	0.2308	0.7692		10	
10	17	7	0.5714	0.4286	0.2353	0.7647		8	
11	17	1	1	0	0.0588	0.9412		6	1
12	47	47	1	0	1	0			
13	45	45	0.9836	0.0164	0.9836	0.0164			
14	47	47	0.9722	0.0278	0.9722	0.0278			
Average	24	16	0.9291	0.0709	0.5329	0.4671			

4   Conclusion

In this paper, we propose a detection and tracking method based on vascular centerline-guidewire-marker. This method is suitable for the detection of markers in coronary angiography images. Firstly, we get the marker of the first frame through a small number of manual interaction methods combined with the algorithm. Then, markers are tracked in the whole sequence by means of adjacent frame assistant detection. Finally, 14 groups of data are verified through the experiment (Table 1). In the case that the marker did not disappear, the accuracy of the results reached 0.929. Future work will solve the problem of marker tracking in the absence of markers mentioned.

References

1. Bauer, C., Bischof, H.: A novel approach for detection of tubular objects and its application to medical image analysis. In: Rigoll, G. (ed.) DAGM 2008. LNCS, vol. 5096, pp. 163–172. Springer, Heidelberg (2008). https://doi.org/10.1007/978-3-540-69321-5_17
2. Bennink, H.E., et al.: A novel 3D multi-scale lineness filter for vessel detection. In: Ayache, N., Ourselin, S., Maeder, A. (eds.) MICCAI 2007. LNCS, vol. 4792, pp. 436–443. Springer, Heidelberg (2007). https://doi.org/10.1007/978-3-540-75759-7_53
3. Brannigan, M.: An adaptive piecewise polynomial curve fitting procedure for data analysis. Commun. Stat. **10**(18), 1823–1848 (2007)
4. Damon, J.: Properties of ridges and cores for two-dimensional images. J. Math. Imaging Vis. **10**(2), 163–174 (1999)

5. Ezra, E., Sharir, M., Efrat, A.: On the ICP algorithm. In: Symposium on Computational Geometry (2006)
6. Fan, Z., Pei, L., Liu, X., Zhou, S.: Vascular centerline extraction of CTA images based on minimal path and Bayesian tracking. In: International Congress on Image & Signal Processing (2018)
7. Frangi, A.F., Niessen, W.J., Vincken, K.L., Viergever, M.A.: Muliscale vessel enhancement filtering. In: Wells, W.M., Colchester, A., Delp, S. (eds.) International Conference on Medical Image Computing & Computer-assisted Intervention, vol. 1496, pp. 130–137. Springer, Heidelberg (1998). https://doi.org/10.1007/BFb0056195
8. Li, Z., Zhang, Y., Liu, G., Shao, H., Li, W., Tang, X.: A robust coronary artery identification and centerline extraction method in angiographies. Biomed. Signal Process. Control **16**, 1–8 (2015)
9. Velho, L., Carvalho, P., Gomes, J., De Figueiredo, L.: Mathematical Optimization in Computer Graphics and Vision. Morgan Kaufmann, Burlington (2011)
10. Wink, O., Niessen, W.J., Viergever, M.A.: Multiscale vessel tracking. IEEE Trans. Med. Imaging **23**(1), 130–133 (2004)
11. Xiao, R., Yang, J., Li, T., Liu, Y.: Ridge-based automatic vascular centerline tracking in X-ray angiographic images. In: Yang, J., Fang, F., Sun, C. (eds.) IScIDE 2012. LNCS, vol. 7751, pp. 793–800. Springer, Heidelberg (2013). https://doi.org/10.1007/978-3-642-36669-7_96

Healthy Vessel Wall Detection Using U-Net in Optical Coherence Tomography

Shengnan Liu[1]([✉]), Denis P. Shamonin[2], Guillaume Zahnd[3],
A. F. W. van der Steen[1], Theo van Walsum[4], and Gijs van Soest[1]

[1] Department of Biomedical Engineering, Erasmus MC,
Dr. Molewaterplein 40, 3015 GD Rotterdam, The Netherlands
s.liu@erasmusmc.nl
[2] Medical Image Processing Department, Leiden University Medical Center,
Leiden, The Netherlands
[3] Computer Aided Medical Procedures, Technische Universität München,
Boltzmannstraße 3, 85748 Garching bei München, Germany
[4] Biomedical Imaging Group Rotterdam,
Department of Medical Informatics and Radiology, Erasmus MC,
Dr. Molewaterplein 40, 3015 GD Rotterdam, The Netherlands

Abstract. Intravascular optical coherence tomography can be applied for high-resolution imaging in the coronary arteries with ischemic heart disease. The differentiation of the healthy and diseased vessel wall can be used to assess the extent and severity of coronary artery disease, and to guide therapeutic interventions. The aim of this study is to develop a recognition framework that can be potentially used for real-time intra-operative application. Structures in an image were labeled into five categories: diseased, healthy, luminal, guide-wire, and others. A U-net was implemented to directly take Cartesian images as input without any additional processing steps. A sigmoid activation and binary cross-entropy loss were applied to perform multi-labeling segmentation. Three transformations were specifically proposed in the polar domain for data augmentation. For evaluation of the proposed framework, 200 images from 20 patients were used and a triple-leave-2-out cross validation was carried out. Performance was evaluated using the average loss in the validation dataset, and the Dice scores were reported as well. Results showed that the proposed framework can perform the segmentation generally with an average performance of 0.88 ± 0.02 in Dice scores. These preliminary results suggest that the proposed framework can be potentially applied for assisting diagnosis in real-time. In the future, we intend to include more data, also take into consideration artifacts such as bad flushing, more deformed lumen, and side-branches.

Keywords: OCT · Tissue recognition · Coronary artery disease

This study is funded by Shenzhen Vivolight Medical Device & Technology Co., Ltd.

© Springer Nature Switzerland AG 2019
H. Liao et al. (Eds.): MLMECH 2019/CVII-STENT 2019, LNCS 11794, pp. 184–192, 2019.
https://doi.org/10.1007/978-3-030-33327-0_22

1   Introduction

Intravascular optical coherence tomography (IVOCT) is an imaging modality relying on near-infrared optical interferometry. It is used during coronary interventions, such as stent implantation in treatment of coronary artery disease. The structures of the arterial wall can be visualized in IVOCT, either in its healthy three-layer form or as affected by atherosclerosis, which leads to the formation of heterogeneous plaques in the inner intima layer. The high-contrast images provide rich detail at a near-histology resolution ($\sim$10 µm) and have substantially contributed to a better understanding of ischemic heart disease. While automatic segmentation of free lumen geometry is now possible, automated differentiation of the healthy and diseased vessel wall is urgently needed for assessing the extent and severity of coronary artery disease and guiding therapeutic interventions. Currently, identification and characterization of healthy and diseased arterial segments still relies primarily on human interpretation of the images. With data sets now routinely exceeding 500 frames per acquisition, this is a labour- and time-consuming task. Here we introduce a deep learning approach for automatic segmentation of healthy and diseased regions, the lumen area, as well as a guiding metal wire used during the interventional procedure.

IVOCT images are acquired by sending near-infrared light signals towards the lumen wall and receiving the back-scattered light as a sequence of magnitudes sampled at consecutive depths. By spinning the laser round, consecutive rays are acquired to cover all the radial directions and are saved in the polar domain (shown in Fig. 1A). The polar image is usually transformed into Cartesian coordinate for the visualization of artery cross-section (shown in Fig. 1B). The catheter is pulled back while spinning during imaging, yielding hundreds of such 2D images, hence the 3D image stack is also referred to as a 'pullback'.

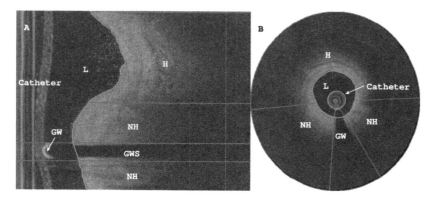

Fig. 1. Labeled IVOCT image shown in polar (A) and Cartesian (B) coordinates. Labels are: H: healthy, NH: non-healthy, GW: guide-wire (structure), GWS: guide-wire shadow, L: lumen.

Due to the fact that neighbouring images are highly similar, data need to be sampled from many patients and labeled manually. The key factor which aggravates the burden for data labeling is the complexity of structures in IVOCT images. The definition of certain types of plaque can be rather ambiguous. Plaques sometimes are differentiated by the amount of lipid content, which appears subtle in IVOCT images [1]. Also the occasional presence various plaque components makes it difficult for data collection and organization. Furthermore, due to a limited penetration depth of light and high attenuation in the tissue, it is quite often that the back border of the structure is invisible. This causes expert analysts being doubting, thus slowing down the labeling. These points limit the potential of clinical application for real-time estimation of plaque distribution.

In the literature, an machine learning tool [2] was applied for healthy wall detection using feature extraction and energy-based dynamic searching. As toolboxes are becoming more and more ready for use, deep learning networks are increasingly introduced to solve problems in the medical imaging field. A recently reported work [3] performed classifications per a 1-D signal by training a fully-connected neural network using 4469 images followed by a conditional random field approach for noise cancellation.

In this work, we explored the potential of using a U-net implementation for multi-label segmentation involving little pre- and post-processing steps. Using 200 images from 20 patients we trained the U-net to perform the segmentation. Cartesian images were directly used as input and neighbouring frames were included as multi-channels to include continuous information. A set of specific transformations in the polar domain are proposed for IVOCT data augmentation. A triple-leave-2-out cross validation was applied to evaluate the performance regarding to the proposed transformations.

2   Method

Figure 1B shows a cross section of the coronary vessel. Images were labeled into five categories: luminal (L), guide-wire (GW+GWS), non-healthy (NH), healthy (H), and others (O). These structures were reported to be observed in IVOCT images with high confidence [1]. The round object at the center is the imaging catheter. The catheter is usually rather soft and needs to be mounted to a stiff metal wire as guiding. Since metal is highly opaque and reflecting for light, this leads the guide-wire to appear as a bright new-moon shape (GW) with a shadow region (GWS) afterward. We assume such a sector structure can be learned and detected as one object. For simplicity, this guide-wire structure will be referred to as GW in the context. The dark region surrounding the catheter is the vessel lumen, containing flush media instead of blood during OCT imaging. The lumen area is determined by the vessel wall boundary, which was first detected using a dynamic searching approach [2], then examined by an expert and manually corrected if necessary. It is noteworthy that, the guide-wire structure and the lumen region were labeled to overlap each other, this is a task of multi-label classification, i.e. one pixel can be assigned with multiple labels.

Healthy regions appear as a three-layer structure with clearly visible boundaries in between (H in Fig. 1B), while unhealthy regions are defined when this structure is not visible anymore (NH in Fig. 1B). Due to a limited penetration depth of light and to the complexity of the tissue components, the back border is quite often invisible. This happens more often in unhealthy regions than healthy regions. As aforementioned, this usually causes difficulties in accurate depth labeling. Therefore, healthy and non-healthy are labeled angle-wise and the backside border is defined with a fixed depth of 700 μm behind the lumen border. The remaining regions are labeled as 'others' (0).

2.1 U-Net Implementation

The U-net architecture [4] is used for segmentation. We follow the original network structure and use the Adam optimizer. Input images were reshaped to 256×256, and two neighbouring images were used, yielding in total three input channels. The ground-truth label was one-hot encoded in a binary image of size $256 \times 256 \times 4$. The sigmoid activation was applied to allow multiple labels for pixels shared by both the lumen and the guide-wire. Let $\{z_{i,j,c}| \, i,j \in \{1,2,\cdots,M\}, \, c \in \{1,2,\cdots,C\}$ be the sigmoid output of the last layer. Here, $M = 256$ is the length/width of the output image and $C = 4$ is the number of classes. Let $\{t_{i,j,c}\}$ denote the ground-truth label. The objective function $\mathcal{L}$ was defined to combine both the binary cross entropy loss and the Dice loss $\mathcal{L} = \lambda \mathcal{L}_{bce} + \mathcal{L}_{Dice}$. Thus here the cross entropy loss is:

$$\mathcal{L}_{bce} = \frac{-1}{C \cdot M^2} \sum_{i,j,c} \left[t_{i,j,c} \cdot log(z_{i,j,c}) + (1 - t_{i,j,c})\left(1 - log(z_{i,j,c})\right) \right] \quad (1)$$

and the Dice loss is:

$$\mathcal{L}_{Dice} = 1 - \frac{\sum_{i,j,c} 2 \cdot z_{i,j,c} \cdot t_{i,j,c} + \epsilon}{\sum_{i,j,c} z_{i,j,c} + t_{i,j,c} + \epsilon} \quad (2)$$

Here, λ is a parameter to balance the magnitudes of two errors. During the training, we observe $\mathcal{L}_{Dice}$ tends to be fourfold over $\mathcal{L}_{bce}$, thus we set $\lambda = 4$. We also set $\epsilon = 1$ to avoid zero division. Using sigmoid activation and binary cross entropy loss, the network is trained to recognize pixels with multiple labels.

2.2 Data Augmentation

Data augmentation was essential, given the limited number of training images available. It is well-known that performance of the U-net can be boosted with proper augmentation. Data augmentation was performed via common transformations including noise addition, rotation, flipping, and shifting. Transformations specific to such tubular IVOCT images were also applied, including central cropping, polar angular deformation and polar radius deformation.

Central Cropping: For a given cropping ratio α, a probability p_{cc} following an uniform distribution $\mathcal{U}(0,\ 1)$, and an input image I_{in} with of size $M \times M$, the cropped image I_{crop} is defined in Eq. 3.

$$I_{crop} = \begin{cases} I_{in} & \text{if } p_{cc} < 0.5, \\ I_{in}[i,\ j],\ \lfloor \frac{(1-\alpha)\times M}{2} \rfloor \le i,\ j \le \lceil \frac{(1+\alpha)\times M}{2} \rceil & \text{otherwise.} \end{cases} \tag{3}$$

Since the image is catheter-centered and there is a large region dominated by noise after a certain depth behind the lumen wall, this transformation is expected to help the network to exclude noisy regions from training and to focus more on the features in the regions of interest.

Polar Deformations: Applying grid deformation usually can improve the performance of the network to tolerate new data. However, normal B-spline deformation will deform the regular round shape of the catheter, which is usually a rare case happening in reality. An angular and radial deformation was applied in the polar domain, while also systematically maintaining a rounded shape for the catheter. Given a probability $p_{pd} \sim \mathcal{U}(0,\ 1)$, the deformed image I_{def} is given as:

$$I_{def} = \begin{cases} I'_{in} & \text{if } p_{pd} < 0.5, \\ I'_{in}\left[\mathcal{F}(\theta_i), \mathcal{G}(\rho_j)\right] & \text{otherwise.} \end{cases} \tag{4}$$

Here, $(\mathcal{F}, \mathcal{G})$ denotes the transformations in the polar domain, defined by piecewise linear interpolations on a set of grid points $\{g_{i,\ j}\}$:

$$\left\{ g_{i,\ j} | (\theta_i,\ \rho_j),\ i \in \{0,\ 1,\ \cdots,\ N_\theta - 1\},\ j \in \{0,\ 1,\ \cdots,\ N_\rho\} \right\} \tag{5}$$

$\{g_{i,\ j}\}$ are defined by $\{\theta_i\}$ separating the angle space into N_θ sectors with an interval of $2\pi/N_\theta$, and $\{\rho_j\}$ defining N_ρ circles center at the catheter. $\mathcal{F}$ is the transformation defined with an angular component:

$$\mathcal{F}(\theta_i \pm 2\pi) = \theta_i + \delta\theta_i, \quad \delta\theta_i \sim \mathcal{U}\left(-\frac{\pi}{N_\theta}, \frac{\pi}{N_\theta}\right) \text{ for } i \in \{0, 1, \cdots, N_\theta\} \tag{6}$$

The continuity of transformations in all directions is guaranteed by the periodic design in $\mathcal{F}$. And $\mathcal{G}$ is the radial transformation:

$$\mathcal{G}(\rho_j) = \rho_j + \delta\rho_j, \quad \delta\rho_j \sim \mathcal{U}\left(-\frac{M}{4N_\rho}, \frac{M}{4N_\rho}\right) \text{ for } j \in \{2, 3, \cdots, N_\rho - 1\} \tag{7}$$

Radii $\{\rho_k | k \in \{1, 2, N_\rho\}\}$ are fixed such that the imaging range and the radius of the catheter undergo a minimal change.

By determining N_θ and N_ρ, the changing range can be modified to define the deformation at different extent. The range of such change for $\delta\theta_i$ and $\delta\rho_j$ was defined using the number of sampling points to avoid the updated grid points from 'folding back'.

3   Experiments

Two hundred OCT 2-D images were selected out of 20 pullbacks which were acquired from 20 patients. Frames from the same patient were chosen with large separations deliberately to avoid similarities between neighboring images. Pullbacks were generated using the C7XR swept-source IVOCT system and C7 Dragonfly Imaging Catheter (St. Jude Medical, Minnesota, USA). Raw polar images were log-compressed, linearly re-scaled to 8-bit, and converted into Cartesian coordinates. In order to maintain a similar resolution, the initial input images are 512×512, and re-sized to 256×256 after central cropping.

3.1   Model Evaluation

The performance was evaluated for the three types of augmentations: polar angular deformation (N_θ), polar radius deformation (N_ρ), and central cropping (α). In order to assess whether using these transformations for data augmentation can improve the performance of the segmentation framework, a triple-leave-2-out cross-validation strategy was used. Eighteen patients were randomly chosen, from which images were used for training the network. Images from the remaining two patients were used for evaluation and comparison. This experiment was repeated three times and the average loss calculated in validation data was reported to evaluate the performance of the trained model. Dice scores are reported to be as a general evaluation of the proposed framework.

To improve the training efficiency, the '*hyperopt*' [5] package was used. Moreover, an 'early stopping' strategy was implemented, such that the training stops when the validation loss cannot be improved within 100 iterations, and the model with the best performance is saved. This dramatically reduced the time for each experiment to <3 h. However, the hyper-parameter selection is still time-consuming. In order to speed up the selection, we first ran 20 experiments, then manually selected the parameters that yields the optimal performance at that moment for comparison. The evaluating parameters (N_θ, N_ρ, α) were then semi-automatically determined to be chosen out of $\{(\text{None}, 13), (\text{None}, 14), (0.6, 1.0)\}$, 'None' indicates no transformation is applied.

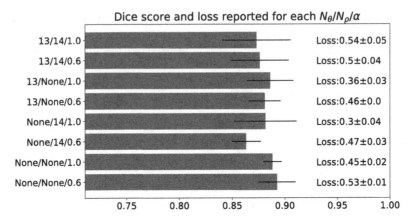

Fig. 2. Bar chart of mean Dice indices and loss reported for each $N_\theta/N_\rho/\alpha$. 'None' indicates that the polar deformation is not applied. The black line in each bar indicates the standard deviation (std) of three evaluations. The respective validation losses are reported in the right panel as Mean ± std.

4   Results and Discussion

In Fig. 2, the performance for all the evaluations were reported as the validation loss and the Dice scores using mean and std values. In general, the proposed framework can train the segmentation network to achieve an average mean of 0.45 and average std of 0.03 in validation losses, and average mean of 0.88 and average std of 0.02 in Dice scores. The low std values show a consistent performance of the proposed approach. Using only central cropping (None/None/0.6) gives the best Dice score. Using no proposed augmentations (None/None/1.0), the validation Dice scores are also relative high (second) with a small std (0.008). Nevertheless, considering the validation loss as a metrics combining both cross entropy and Dice losses, the values are relatively high in both scenarios (0.53 and 0.45).

Using only radius deformation or angular deformation give the lowest loss (0.3 and 0.36), indicating that the proposed transformations may improve the validation performance of the segmentation framework. However, more data should be included for further extensive validations which also need to take into consideration more irregularities such as bad flushing, extremely deformed lumen, and side-branches. Segmentation in one validation image using only radius deformation is demonstrated in Fig. 3. The deformed image during training was also given in Fig. $3B_0$.

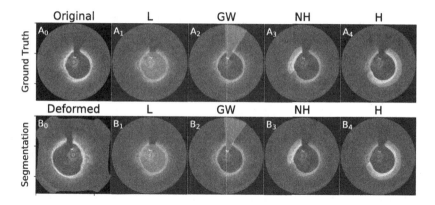

Fig. 3. A_0 is an original image, and A_{1-4} are the ground-truth labels of L, GW, NH, H showed as overlays of A_0. B_0 is the deformed image of A_0, and B_{1-4} are the result labels of the segmentation network where 0.5 was applied as a threshold. In practice, the transformations are not applied to validation data, B_0 is only presented for the visualization of transformations.

To summarize, the contributions of this work include as follows. We developed a framework for the segmentation of structures in IVOCT images. We contribute to implement U-net to perform multi-label robust segmentation. The multi-label design grant the proposed framework to be easily extended for the segmentation of other intravascular structures either by additional labels or by merging the segmenting output. The Cartesian images were directly used as the input of the network and no additional pre- and post-processing is needed. The input image size of the network is also relatively small (256×256). Implemented using parallel computation, segmenting one pullback is expected to be fast. Furthermore, we simplified the label generalization by using a semi-automated way for the delineation of the lumen and guide-wire structures, and using the angle-wise label with a fixed depth as the backside border for labeling the healthy and non-healthy regions. Experiments showed that a relative small training set can achieve a robust and decent performance on new pullbacks. This would largely reduce the burden of expert analysts for label generalization in large clinical studies.

5 Conclusion

To conclude, we developed a framework for the segmentation of structures in IVOCT images. A U-net was implemented to perform multi-label segmentation. No additional pre- and post-processing steps are required and the labeling standard was clarified. Using polar deformations as data augmentation, the network was trained in less than 400 images. Validation experiments showed that the proposed design allows achieving an average Dice score of 0.88 for the segmentation of healthy, diseased, luminal, and guide-wire structures. Results strongly suggest that the proposed framework is promising for real-time clinical applications in the future.

References

1. Tearney, G.J., et al.: Consensus standards for acquisition, measurement, and reporting of intravascular optical coherence tomography studies: a report from the international working group for intravascular optical coherence tomography standardization and validation. J. Am. Coll. Cardiol. **59**, 1058–1072 (2012)
2. Zahnd, G., et al.: Contour segmentation of the intima, media, and adventitia layers in intracoronary OCT images: application to fully automatic detection of healthy wall regions. Int. J. Comput. Assist. Radiol. Surg. **12**(11), 1923–1936 (2017)
3. Kolluru, C., et al.: Deep neural networks for a-line-based plaque classification in coronary intravascular optical coherence tomography images. J. Med. Imaging. **5**, 1 (2018)
4. Ronneberger, O., Fischer, P., Brox, T.: U-Net: convolutional networks for biomedical image segmentation. In: Navab, N., Hornegger, J., Wells, W.M., Frangi, A.F. (eds.) MICCAI 2015. LNCS, vol. 9351, pp. 234–241. Springer, Cham (2015). https://doi.org/10.1007/978-3-319-24574-4_28
5. Bergstra, J., Yamins, D., Cox, D. D.: Making a science of model search: hyperparameter optimization in hundreds of dimensions for vision architectures. In: Proceedings of the 30th International Conference on Machine Learning (ICML 2013) (2013)

Advanced Multi-objective Design Analysis to Identify Ideal Stent Design

Ramtin Gharleghi[1], Heidi Wright[1], Somesh Khullar[1], Jinbo Liu[1], Tapabrata Ray[2], and Susann Beier[1(✉)]

[1] UNSW Syndey, Sydney 2023, Australia
s.beier@unsw.edu.au
[2] UNSW Canberra, Canberra 2023, Australia

Abstract. Coronary stents are the preferred option for treating diseased coronary arteries. When implanted, the stent is deployed at the lesion to restore the lumen area by scaffolding the vessel open. However, stents still have a relatively high failure rate of 2–8%, with many patients requiring further interventions due to restenosis and stent thrombosis. It is known that blood flow disruption caused by the presence of a stent can trigger signalling pathways that accelerate restenosis or trigger thrombus formation. This work aims to find design variable values that minimize these adverse flow conditions using Multi-Objective optimisation.

Keywords: Stent design · Multi-objective design analysis · Hemodynamics

1 Introduction

Despite significant advances in stent design and materials, in-stent restenosis remains a serious problem and up to 8% [1] of patients experience complications after stent implant. Improvements in material biocompatibility and progress on drug eluting stents has reduced direct adverse reactions to the stents over the years [2]; however failures due to cellular responses triggered by alterations in blood flow are little accounted for. The primary determinant of hemodynamic changes induced by the stent is the stent geometry. Several hemodynamic measures have been linked to restenosis and thrombosis [3] and minimizing these adverse hemodynamic conditions can lower associated risks.

Many design variables share a complex relationship and have been connected to adverse hemodynamic outcomes. Whilst considering these design variables piece-wise is useful in developing the initial understanding of contribution of each design feature to altered flow, more global design improvements can be made upon this knowledge. As multiple hemodynamic objectives need to be

This project was undertaken with the assistance of resources and services from the National Computational Infrastructure (NCI), which is supported by the Australian Government.

H. Liao et al. (Eds.): MLMECH 2019/CVII-STENT 2019, LNCS 11794, pp. 193–200, 2019.
https://doi.org/10.1007/978-3-030-33327-0_23

optimized, this can be characterised as a multi-objective optimisation problem [4] (MOOP). Except in trivial cases, it is not possible to find a single best solution to such problems. The goal in MOOP is to characterize possible trade-offs between objectives studied by finding Pareto efficient solutions. A Pareto efficient (also called non-dominated solution) is one where no objective can be improved without sacrificing another objective.

The primary hemodynamic objective studied in previous experiments has been minimising areas with low wall shear stress (WSS). Many studies have shown that WSS values less than 0.5 Pa promote growth factor expression and neointimal thickening [5], predisposing these areas to atherosclerotic plaque formation [3,6]. Time averaged wall shear stress (TAWSS, averaged over one cardiac cycle) has a similar effect, with levels <0.5 PA associated with atherogenesis [7]. High WSS (>2.5 Pa) areas are associated with adverse vessel remodelling [8].

Previous studies attempting to optimize hemodynamic impact of stents have several limitations. Many consider only three or four design variables [9,10], which limits the conclusions that can be drawn from the study as important factors are not considered. In some cases crucial variables such as strut thickness and spacing were left out due to the difficulty of constraining them such that designs remain physically feasible [11]. Most studies used a Newtonian model for blood flow, which introduces significant error compared to the use of non-Newtonian models which accurately account for the shear thinning behaviour exhibited by blood [12]. Although most studies report thicker struts result in worse hemodynamic performance, a few have found better performance with thicker struts [13]. This might be due to other factors that were not accounted for in the study.

Pant et al. [14] analysed the effect of three design variables (length of stent ring, strut width, connector height) on six objectives representing a variety of hemodynamic, mechanical and drug diffusion effects. However, the hemodynamic aspects of the analysis were quite simplified, and did not consider high or time averaged WSS and utilized a Newtonian fluid model.

Here, we aim to identify optimal values for a wider selection of stent design characteristics to minimize multiple adverse hemodynamic metrics. The design variables are subject to several constraints to keep the design feasible and maintain structural integrity of designs generated.

2   Methods

2.1   Stent Design

Variable Selection. Strut width and thickness is frequently studied due to its effect on hemodynamic conditions and structural strength of the stent. We have analysed strut width and thickness between 60 μm and 120 μm, as well as rectangular and circular cross section struts (note that for circular cross section struts only one dimension, the diameter, is used). Strut angle was allowed to vary between 25° and 50° to ensure that the stent is physically valid. The cell height (CH, distance between strut rings) was varied between 0.86 mm and 2 mm based on the work of Beier et al. [15]. Two strut alignments were considered, 0° and 180° alignment based on common stent design. Three different shapes of connectors were tested (see Fig. 1), along with three arrangements of connectors between strut rings, as shown in Fig. 2. Selected design variables were parametrised in a CAD model to automatically generate new stent designs. All stents were designed for 50% luminal protrusion in an idealized cylindrical vessel with radius of 1.5 mm. Latin Hypercube Sampling [16] was used to generate 30 initial designs with six peaks to explore the design variable space.

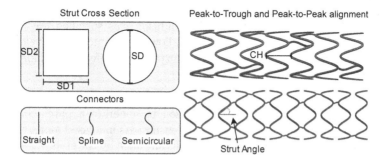

Fig. 1. Design variables used for this study.

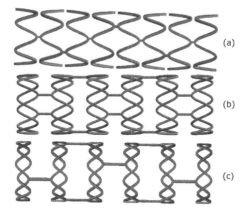

Fig. 2. Connector arrangements (a) one connector per strut ring, alternating location between rings; (b) two connectors per strut placed 180° apart, alternating between rings; (c) Alternating 1-2-1 number of connectors per strut ring.

2.2   Computational Modelling

Boundary Conditions. Previous studies have suggested the velocity profile in coronary arteries is blunted due to pulsatile flow conditions [17], although it should be noted that with the presence of flow extensions to allow the flow to fully develop the choice of inlet velocity profile has little effect on WSS values [18]. For this work a blunt profile of the following form was specified:

$$V(r) = V_{max} \cdot \left(1 - \frac{r}{R_{max}}\right)^{0.143} \tag{1}$$

A physiological flow rate versus time of 0–102 ml/min was applied at the inlet, adapted from Nichols et al. [19], assuming 75 beats/min. A constant static pressure was specified at the outlet. No-slip condition was specified for the vessel wall. The inlet and outlet were extended to allow the flow to fully develop before reaching the stent and avoid downstream disturbance affecting hemodynamics in the stent region.

Mesh Generation. ANSYS 19.1 was used to generate a patch-conforming unstructured tetrahedral mesh. The mesh density was increased along the stent, to allow better modelling of hemodynamic disturbance by the stent. A boundary layer consisting of prismatic elements was added to better resolve flow near the walls, as accurate wall shear stress measurement is crucial for this experiment. Independence of the solutions from mesh size was tested using one of the stent designs.

Simulation. ANSYS CFX 19.1 (Second order backward Euler) was used to solve the transient simulation. Shear thinning behaviour of blood was accounted for by using the Carreu-Yasuda model [20]. Four cardiac cycles were simulated, with only the results of the fourth cycle used to avoid any start-up effects. The simulation was performed with 10^{-4} RMS residual target and a timestep of 0.008s. We considered the percentage of area vessel exposed to low and high WSS and low time-averaged WSS, with adverse thresholds of <0.5 Pa, >2.5 Pa and <0.5 Pa respectively. Low and high WSS are measured during peak flow timestep. These three objective functions will need to be minimized to improve patient outcomes.

2.3   Multi-objective Design Optimisation

The Pareto trade-off curve is the boundary formed by plotting the non-dominated solutions found. This curve can be used to find the optimal design criteria depending on the desired trade-offs between the multiple objective functions studied. One approach is to create a single objective function incorporating all objective functions considered [21]; however it is difficult to account for non-convex objective functions and non-continuous design variables. Response surface models (RSM) are often used to model the relationship between the input space (design variables) and output (objectives). These act as an estimator of the real response, with sufficient refinement the RSM can be quite accurate. Gaussian process regression (kriging) is a very commonly used RSM. After construction of RSMs for the variables being studied, new data points are generated and their performance is tested to refine the predictions of the model. Non-dominated genetic sorting algorithm (NGSA II) is a viable approach for multiple objective RSM optimization [14]. Expected hypervolume improvement (EHVI) is also commonly used to optimize Krigs [9]. In this work, five updates were made to the original thirty stents generated, each update adding two stents. One stent candidate was selected by NGSA while the other was selected using EHVI.

3   Results

Using the simulations, we obtain the wall shear stress characteristics of each stented artery. The average computational time for each stent was 3 h and 16 min using 32 cores, excluding meshing and pre- and post- processing. The objective functions are calculated during post-processing, and the Pareto efficient stents are identified. We study three objective functions: (1) percentage of area exposed to low WSS during peak flow, (2) percentage of area exposed to high WSS during peak flow, (3) percentage of area exposed to low time averaged WSS. Figure 3 shows the Pareto trade-off curve calculated based on this data.

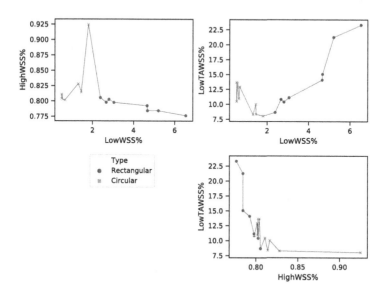

Fig. 3. Pareto trade-off curves for pairs of objectives studied. The strut cross section type is shown for each step.

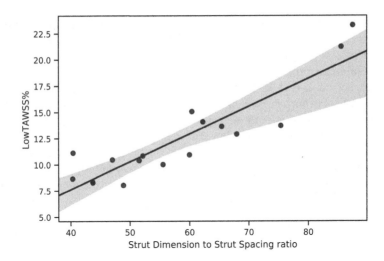

Fig. 4. Ratio of strut dimension to strut spacing is a good predictor of LowTAWSS. Coloured band shows 95% confidence interval.

4 Discussion

Using this methodology, trade-off curves between the different hemodynamic objectives can be constructed. An optimal stent design can then be picked based on the importance of each objective and the need to balance these adverse flow conditions. From Fig. 3 it is clear that trying to optimize a single objective often results in large increases in other objective functions, so it might be wise to pick stent solutions from the central regions of the Pareto curves.

An interesting feature of the Pareto curves (Fig. 3) is that different vessel cross sections seem to favour optimizing different objectives. This implies an inherent trade-off where a circular cross section reduces Low WSS and TAWSS areas whereas rectangular cross section reduce high WSS areas. As each cross section forms distinct parts of the Pareto curve, it is advisable that future studies utilize both cross section types.

Figure 4 shows the relation between LowTAWSS area and the ratio of strut thickness to cell height (Note that for rectangular vessels, average of the two dimensions is used). This ratio seems to be a good predictor of LowTAWSS ($r^2 = 0.86$, p = 0.002), however it has little effect on LowWSS and HighWSS (p > 0.15). This was suggested as an important factor in Beier et al. [15] albeit without statistical analysis. This allows for more customization where strut thickness or cell height can be adjusted without much effect on the overall hemodynamics provided that the other quantity is also adjusted to compensate. Of course, excessively low values of this ratio can compromise structural integrity of the stent, so it is important to incorporate mechanical properties as additional objectives or ensure the constraints placed on design variables will guarantee a structurally sound stent.

In the future, these methods can be expanded to a variety of objective functions in order to ensure that mechanical and chemical characteristics of the stent are also taken into account. This can lead to developments of better stent designs and a decrease in the restenosis rate currently seen in patients.

5 Conclusion

This study shows that this is an effective methodology to investigate influence of a large number of design variables on hemodynamic measures. Updates performed using NGSA and expected hypervolume improvement are able to explore points close to the Pareto curve, although more updates are required to improve the accuracy of current predictions. This has the potential to result in novel stent designs which take flow disruption caused by the stent and its potential adverse effects into account.

References

1. Moses, J.W., et al.: Sirolimus-eluting stents versus standard stents in patients with stenosis in a native coronary artery. New Engl. J. Med. **349**(14), 1315–1323 (2003). 05261
2. Alfonso, F., et al.: A prospective randomized trial of drug-eluting balloons versus everolimus-eluting stents in patients with in-stent restenosis of drug-eluting stents: the RIBS IV randomized clinical trial. J. Am. Coll. Cardiol. **66**(1), 23–33 (2015). 00157
3. Malek, A.M.: Hemodynamic shear stress and its role in atherosclerosis. JAMA **282**(21), 2035 (1999). https://doi.org/10.1001/jama.282.21.2035
4. Deb, K.: Multi-objective optimisation using evolutionary algorithms: an introduction. In: Wang, L., Ng, A., Deb, K. (eds.) Multi-objective Evolutionary Optimisation for Product Design and Manufacturing, pp. 3–34. Springer, London (2011). https://doi.org/10.1007/978-0-85729-652-8_1. 00294
5. Kraiss, L.W., Geary, R.L., Mattsson, E.J., Vergel, S., Au, Y.T., Clowes, A.W.: Acute reductions in blood flow and shear stress induce platelet-derived growth factor-A expression in baboon prosthetic grafts. Circul. Res. **79**(1), 45–53 (1996)
6. Morbiducci, U., Kok, A.M., Kwak, B.R., Stone, P.H., Steinman, D.A., Wentzel, J.J.: Atherosclerosis at arterial bifurcations: evidence for the role of haemodynamics and geometry. J. Thromb. Haemost. **115**(3), 484–92 (2016). https://doi.org/10.1160/TH15-07-0597. 00051
7. Wentzel, J.J., et al.: Relationship between neointimal thickness and shear stress after wallstent implantation in human coronary arteries. Circulation **103**(13), 1740–1745 (2001). https://doi.org/10.1161/01.CIR.103.13.1740
8. Dolan, J.M., Kolega, J., Meng, H.: High wall shear stress and spatial gradients in vascular pathology: a review. Ann. Biomed. Eng. **41**(7), 1411–27 (2013). https://doi.org/10.1007/s10439-012-0695-0
9. Putra, N.K., Palar, P.S., Anzai, H., Shimoyama, K., Ohta, M.: Multiobjective design optimization of stent geometry with wall deformation for triangular and rectangular struts. Med. Biol. Eng. Comput. **57**(1), 15–26 (2019). 00001
10. Tammareddi, S., Sun, G., Li, Q.: Multiobjective robust optimization of coronary stents. Mater. Design **90**, 682–692 (2016). 00025

11. Gundert, T.J., Marsden, A.L., Yang, W., LaDisa, J.F.: Optimization of cardiovascular stent design using computational fluid dynamics. J. Biomech. Eng. **134**(1), 011002 (2012). https://doi.org/10.1115/1.4005542. 00070

12. Johnston, B.M., Johnston, P.R., Corney, S., Kilpatrick, D.: Non-newtonian blood flow in human right coronary arteries: transient simulations. J. Biomech. **39**(6), 1116–1128 (2006). https://doi.org/10.1016/j.jbiomech.2005.01.034

13. Balossino, R., Gervaso, F., Migliavacca, F., Dubini, G.: Effects of different stent designs on local hemodynamics in stented arteries. J. Biomech. **41**(5), 1053–1061 (2008). https://doi.org/10.1016/j.jbiomech.2007.12.005. 00165

14. Pant, S., Limbert, G., Curzen, N.P., Bressloff, N.W.: Multiobjective design optimisation of coronary stents. Biomaterials **32**(31), 7755–7773 (2011). https://doi.org/10.1016/j.biomaterials.2011.07.059. 00082

15. Beier, S., et al.: Hemodynamics in idealized stented coronary arteries: important stent design considerations. Ann. Biomed. Eng. **44**(2), 315–329 (2016). https://doi.org/10.1007/s10439-015-1387-3. 00026

16. Stein, M.: Large sample properties of simulations using Latin hypercube sampling. Technometrics **29**(2), 143–151 (1987). 01410

17. Tang, T.D., Giddens, D.P., Zarins, C.K., Glagov, S.: Velocity profile and wall shear measurements in a model human coronary artery. In: ASME Winter Annual Meeting Proceedings, Atlanta. ASME, New York (1991). 00010

18. Myers, J.G., Moore, J.A., Ojha, M., Johnston, K.W., Ethier, C.R.: Factors influencing blood flow patterns in the human right coronary artery. Ann. Biomed. Eng. **29**(2), 109–120 (2001). https://doi.org/10.1114/1.1349703. 00327

19. O'Rourke, M.F., Nichols, W.W.: McDonald's Blood Flow in Arteries: Theoretical, Experimental and Clinical Principles. Hodder Arnold, London (2005). 04949

20. Razavi, A., Shirani, E., Sadeghi, M.: Numerical simulation of blood pulsatile flow in a stenosed carotid artery using different rheological models. J. Biomech. **44**(11), 2021–2030 (2011). https://doi.org/10.1016/j.jbiomech.2011.04.023

21. Amirjani, A., Yousefi, M., Cheshmaroo, M.: Parametrical optimization of stent design; a numerical-based approach. Comput. Mater. Science **90**, 210–220 (2014). https://doi.org/10.1016/j.commatsci.2014.04.002. 00012

Simultaneous Intracranial Artery Tracing and Segmentation from Magnetic Resonance Angiography by Joint Optimization from Multiplanar Reformation

Li Chen[1], Gaoang Wang[1], Niranjan Balu[1], Mahmud Mossa-Basha[1],
Xihai Zhao[2], Rui Li[2], Le He[2], Thomas S. Hatsukami[1],
Jenq-Neng Hwang[1], and Chun Yuan[1(✉)]

[1] University of Washington, Seattle, WA, USA
cyuan@uw.edu
[2] Tsinghua University, Beijing, China

Abstract. Time-of-flight (TOF) Magnetic Resonance Angiography (MRA) is a useful imaging technique which reflects blood flow and vasculature information. However, due to the low signal and contrast of arteries in TOF MRA, it is challenging to extract vascular features such as length, volume and tortuosity, through segmentation and tracing. Hence, in this paper, a simultaneous artery tracing and segmentation method is proposed to a generate quantitative intracranial vasculature map from TOF MRA. Instead of using original images, segmentation from a neural network model is used to initiate tracing, avoiding the low signal or contrast for small arteries. A tracing method is proposed based on cross-sectional best matching, followed by an optimization scheme from the multiplanar reformatted view. Centerline positions, lumen radii and centerline deviations are jointly optimized for robust tracing within artery regions. Finally, the refined artery traces are used for better artery segmentation. The method is validated on eight TOF MRAs of both healthy subjects and patients with cerebrovascular disease, showing good agreements with human supervised tracing and segmentation results for representative features such as artery length (<4% mean absolute difference), volume (>0.80 Dice), and tortuosity (<3% mean absolute difference). Our method out-performs three other popular tracing and segmentation methods by a large margin.

Keywords: Artery tracing · Artery segmentation · Magnetic Resonance Angiography · Optimization · Multiplanar reformation

1 Introduction

Magnetic Resonance Angiography (MRA) methods, like Time-of-flight (TOF) allow visualization of intracranial arteries without radiation dose or contrast agents. Beyond the clinical use of MRA for stenosis identification, a whole brain vasculature map can

---

Electronic supplementary material The online version of this chapter (https://doi.org/10.1007/978-3-030-33327-0_24) contains supplementary material, which is available to authorized users.

H. Liao et al. (Eds.): MLMECH 2019/CVII-STENT 2019, LNCS 11794, pp. 201–209, 2019.
https://doi.org/10.1007/978-3-030-33327-0_24

be generated through digital reconstruction of intracranial arteries, such as artery tracing and segmentation. The vascular features extracted from the vasculature map include artery length, volume and tortuosity, which provides quantitative measurements for pathological or blood flow conditions [1, 2]. However, due to the complex network structure of human intracranial arteries, and the low signal intensity and low image contrast for distal branches from TOF MRA, it is challenging for automated quantifications of the vasculature map, especially for patients with compromised cerebral blood flow due to cardiovascular diseases.

Artery segmentation and tracing from MRA are two methods used for digital reconstruction of intracranial arteries in order to measure the vascular features.

Artery segmentation which classifies every voxel into artery or non-artery, allows better visualization of artery structures and facilitates identification of stenoses and aneurysms [3]. Existing automated MRA segmentation approaches include region growing [4], active contours [3], and convolutional neural network [5]. However, artery segmentation alone cannot determine the layout and inter-connected relation of intracranial arteries, which limits the information in the vasculature map.

One solution is 3D artery tracing, which converts artery voxels into interconnected tree structures with radius varying cylinders. The criteria for connecting neighboring points is critical, for which local Hessian-based estimation [6], and Kalman filtering [7] have been attempted. But the performance of the methods by tracing directly from the original image may suffer due to the low artery signal or contrast, which is commonly seen in TOF MRAs. To ensure robust tracing, refinement of the artery centerline by re-centering is usually followed by tracing. Adjusting centerline positions by applying intensity features [6] or segmentation results [8] from re-sliced 2D cross-sectional planes is usually used, but the neighboring slice information is not considered. The multiplanar reformation (MPR) of arteries, considered as straightening the artery along its centerline (example in Fig. 4(c)), has been used in clinical reading and reported to be beneficial for coronary and renal artery stenoses detection [9, 10]. MPR view incorporates neighboring information and therefore is better suited for a global centerline refinement on the whole artery and correction of errors in artery tracing.

This paper introduces a novel method by simultaneously performing artery tracing and segmentation with the help of robust artery refinement in MPR views. Tracing and segmentation use results from each other to improve their individual performances. Instead of tracing directly from original images, artery segmentation from a deep neural network model is used to enhance the contrast of small arteries and constrain artery tracing in a restricted region. The artery refinement from MPR ensures trace smoothness, radius fitness, and avoids centerline deviation. The refined traces can then be used to further improve the artery segmentation results, so that both centerline features (length, tortuosity) and voxel features (volume) of arteries are accurately extracted.

2 Method

The method has four steps: artery rudimentary segmentation, tracing from segmentation, MPR refinement and segmentation from tracing. Flow chart is shown in Fig. 1.

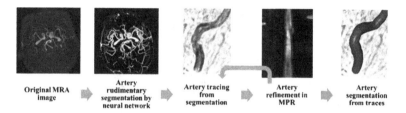

Original MRA image   Artery rudimentary segmentation by neural network   Artery tracing from segmentation   Artery refinement in MPR   Artery segmentation from traces

Fig. 1. Flow chart for the proposed method

2.1 Rudimentary Segmentation

Original images are normalized using the Nyul method [11], and rudimentarily segmented using a neural network model [5]. Trained from the semi-automatedly segmented arteries from more than 163 subjects [2], the model can segment small arteries with low contrast to the background. Centers of each 3D connected region in the segmentation image are considered as seed points to initiate tracing one at a time.

2.2 Tracing from Segmentation

From each position, a cross-sectional plane can be generated from each of the evenly distributed positions around the half sphere towards the tracing direction with 30° increments in each axis (in total 37 possible directions). Arteries are traced by iteratively finding the best matching cross-sectional planes based on the matching criteria. Direction selection during one iteration as an example is shown in Fig. 2.

Matching Criteria. Three metrics are used to select the best matching cross-sectional planes: circular similarity, neighboring similarity and signal change rate.

Based on the assumption that the cross-sectional plane along the centerline of an artery is a circle [12], the circular similarity is calculated as the Dice similarity coefficient (DSC) [13] of the segmented region in the cross-sectional plane with a perfect circle of the same area. The circular similarity is 1 for perfect circle.

A smooth trace should be continuous between neighboring cross-sectional slices both in geometry and intensity. The DSC for neighboring segmented regions, and the relative signal difference in their center pixels from the original image are used for evaluating neighboring relations.

Matching score is defined as weighted sum of circular and neighboring similarities (weights of 0.8 and 0.2 used in this study) minus signal change rate. The highest score is used for selecting the best match. As an example, in Fig. 2, the yellow direction has higher score than the red one, so it is selected as the stretching direction.

Tracing Procedure. Initiated from a seed point in the artery region as a starting point $p_0 = (x_p, y_p, z_p)$, circular similarity is used to find the best matching trace direction n_i from the cross-sectional plane $C_i(u, v)$. Neighboring similarity is not combined, as there are no neighbor slices available in the first iteration. The positions of $p_{-1} = p - n_i$ and $p_1 = p + n_i$ are added to the trace with the radius $r_{0,1,-1}$ calculated from the masked region in $C_i(u, v)$.

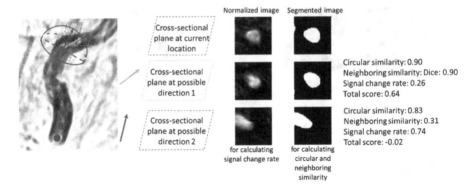

Normalized image   Segmented image

Cross-sectional plane at current location

Cross-sectional plane at possible direction 1

Circular similarity: 0.90
Neighboring similarity: Dice: 0.90
Signal change rate: 0.26
Total score: 0.64

Cross-sectional plane at possible direction 2

Circular similarity: 0.83
Neighboring similarity: 0.31
Signal change rate: 0.74
Total score: -0.02

for calculating signal change rate

for calculating circular and neighboring similarity

Fig. 2. Direction selection in one iteration of tracing. For illustration, the red and yellow directions are selected from the 37 directions on the half sphere in the tracing direction. Three metrics are calculated from the cross-sectional slices for deciding the best tracing direction. (Color figure online)

Starting from the second iteration, the trace is stretched at both sides in each iteration until each reaches the ending criteria. Taking positive tracing side at iteration j as an example, search space for next trace position is updated with $t_j = p_{j-1} - p_{j-2}$ and the normal direction along the tracing direction n'_i yielding the highest metric from the rotated cross-sectional plane $C'_i(u, v)$ is used for stretching the traces to the new position $p_j = p_{j-1} + n'_i r_{j-1}$. Radius of the target position r_j is roughly estimated from the masked area and used as the stride for the next iteration. Traced region in the segmentation image is painted with zeros and the seeds inside the region are removed to avoid repeat tracing.

The iteration on each side of stretching is ended when p_j is out of image boundary, or the maximum combined similarity from all $C'_i(u, v)$ is below a certain threshold (0.1 in this study).

2.3   Artery Refinement from Multiplanar Reformation

The position and radius of the centerline based on cross-sectional plane matching does not incorporate global information, therefore the refinement step applies MPR to overcome centerline deviation and abrupt radius change along the centerline. A three-stage optimization scheme is used for the artery refinement, i.e., trace position refinement, trace radius refinement, and trace deviation correction.

Trace Position Refinement. The 3D position of points in the trace is refined using the optimization function considering losses for trace smoothness and their intensity.

$$L_1(p) = \sum_i L_1(p_i) = \sum_i \left\{ w_{dist} \left(||d_i||^{(1)} + \gamma ||d_i||^{(2)} + \gamma \left(d_{x,i}^{(2)} + d_{y,i}^{(2)} + d_{z,i}^{(2)} \right) \right) - w_{int}[I_n(p_i) + I_s(p_i)] \right\}$$

(1)

where $d_i = (p_i - p_{i-1}) = (d_{x,i}, d_{y,i}, d_{z,i})$, $I_n(p)$ and $I_s(p)$ are intensity values of normalized (M_n) and segmented (M_s) MPR images at position of $p_i = (x_i, y_i, z_i)$. (1) and (2) represent 1st and 2nd order of derivative. γ is the parameter to control the first and second order weights. w_{dist} and w_{int} are weights for controlling the smoothness and intensity loss.

Trace Radius Refinement. After the trace position refinement, centerline positions are fixed, and the radius of each point is refined using the following equation.

$$L_2(r) = \sum_i L_2(u_{l,i}, u_{r,i}, v_i) = \sum_i L_2(l(v_i), r(v_i), v_i)$$
$$= \sum_i w_{smooth}\left[l^{(1)}(v_i) + r^{(1)}(v_i) + \gamma l^{(2)}(v_i) + \gamma r^{(2)}(v_i)\right]$$
$$- w_{grad}\left[M_u(l(v_i), v_i) + M_u(r(v_i), v_i)\right] \tag{2}$$

where $l(v)$ and $r(v)$ are the left and right boundary for artery radius in MPR image M_n. M_u is the derivative of M_n in its horizontal direction.

Trace Deviation Correction. Ideally, the mean location of the left and right radius boundaries $\frac{l(u,v) + r(u,v)}{2}$ in the MPR image should always be in the vertical center of the MPR image $(v = v_m)$. Any deviation away from the vertical center in u direction $o = \frac{l(v) + r(v)}{2} - v_m$ needs to be re-centered.

Iterative Refinement from Different Angles. MPR images M_{deg} are reconstructed using rotation angles from {0, 90, 45, 135} by repeating *Rep* times (3 in this study). Arteries are iteratively refined every 25 iterations of tracing and at the end of tracing.
     Nelder-Mead algorithm [14] is used for optimization in this study.

2.4   Segmentation from Tracing

From the refined traces, regions inside the tubes are filled to be the refined segmentation results. As the trace is represented by a cylinder model, if a more detailed artery area information is needed, cross-sectional planes can be generated along the centerline and the artery region can be segmented based on refined radius boundary.

3   Evaluations

3.1   Accuracy for Quantification of Vascular Features

Four images each from a healthy community study [15] and a group of patients with intracranial atherosclerosis [16] are used for evaluation. The data collections followed local institutional review board guidelines. Three-dimensional TOF images were scanned on 3.0T MR scanners with: repetition time/echo time = 25/3.5 ms, flip angle = 20°, in-plane resolution = 0.35 mm × 0.35 mm, slice thickness = 1.4 mm.
     Considering the unrealistic work load for manually labeling voxels for all regions of intracranial arteries in 3D images, a semi-automated tool [17] is used for tracing artery regions with manual corrections. The centerlines are considered as ground truth

for the evaluation. As the completeness of artery detection is not our focus, only two major clinically important arteries (from the distal internal carotid artery (ICA), M1 segment of middle cerebral artery, until the most distally clearly visualized segment) per case are used for validation. Excessive traces are removed, and traces might be reconnected at bifurcations to allow same branches being compared with the ground truth.

Table 1. Extracted vascular features compared with ground truth.

Methods	Subject groups	Mean absolute length difference	Mean volume DSC	Mean absolute tortuosity difference
Tracing with refinement	Healthy group	1.86%	0.85	2.75%
	Disease group	3.64%	0.80	2.94%
Tracing without refinement	Healthy group	40.72%	0.53	20.94%
	Disease group	16.87%	0.55	15.16%

Vascular features of artery length and tortuosity (length divided by the Euclidean distance between the first and last point) are used to evaluate the tracing performance, assessed by the mean percentage of absolute difference with the ground truth. DSC is used to evaluate the segmentation performance (artery volume difference).

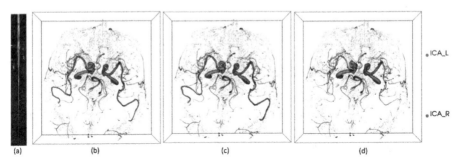

Fig. 3. (a) MPR view for ICA (b) Tracing results generated from the proposed method (ICA_L: green and R: red). (c) Ground truth for the traced arteries. (d) Tracing results without artery refinement in the ablation test (Color figure online)

From Table 1, the mean absolute length and tortuosity difference is within 4 percent, and the mean Dice similarity score of volume is more than 0.8, indicating excellent agreement [18]. Performance in the disease group is slightly worse than the healthy group. An example of 3D rendered artery traces with ground truth is shown in Fig. 3. All the 3D renderings of arteries are in the supplementary materials.

The performance of this method is compared with other three artery segmentation and tracing methods (colliding fronts, fast marching, iso-surface) implemented in open-source Vascular Modeling Toolkit (VMTK, www.vmtk.org). The comparison results for left side arteries from healthy subjects are shown in Table 2. All three comparison methods suffer from weak signals in distal arteries, so that the tracing is stopped earlier. Right side arteries are not processed due to the processing time. VMTK methods fail for the diseased group. One visualization figure is in supplementary materials.

Table 2. Performance comparison with other segmentation and tracing methods.

Methods	Mean absolute length difference	Mean volume DSC	Mean absolute tortuosity difference
Our method	**2.33%**	**0.86**	**2.36%**
Colliding fronts	14.27%	0.69	7.91%
Fast marching	33.55%	0.43	10.32%
Iso-surface	27.28%	0.73	11.62%

3.2   Continuity of Tracing

To evaluate the tracing continuity, a semi-automated snake based method [19] is used to trace the ICA. Due to the tortuous ICA structure and flow artifacts reducing luminal contrast, the snake method needs an average of 4.9 manually given seeds (including the seed used in our tracing method) to trace the whole artery segment, but all arteries traced by our method need only one seed, showing better performance.

The ablation test of artery tracing without refinement showed worse performance in Table 1, and the tracing iterations are aborted earlier for 4 of the arteries.

3.3   Improvement for Segmentation

Confined in regions within traces, artery segmentation is further improved, especially when multiple arteries are close to each other. An example is shown in Fig. 4.

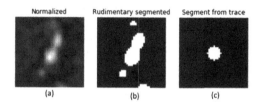

Fig. 4. Improved segmentation from tracing when two arteries are close. Cross-sectional slice for normalized image (a), rudimentary segmentation (b) and improved segmentation (c)

4 Limitations

Several limitations exist in this method. A selected set of major arteries from each subject is assessed. A small sample size (N = 8) is used for validation. Parameter tunings are also expected to further improve the performance.

5 Conclusion

In this paper, a simultaneous artery tracing and segmentation method with artery refinement from MPR view is proposed. The use of segmentation results to trace arteries allows tracing continuity and trace accuracy. The use of tracing allows centerline features quantified from a specific artery. The use of MPR view for artery refinement improves robustness by correcting mistakes in artery tracing.

References

1. Choi, C.G., et al.: Detection of intracranial atherosclerotic steno-occlusive disease with 3D time-of-flight magnetic resonance angiography with sensitivity encoding at 3T. Am. J. Neuroradiol. **28**(3), 439–446 (2007)
2. Chen, L., et al.: Quantitative assessment of the intracranial vasculature in an older adult population using iCafe (intraCranial artery feature extraction). Neurobiol. Aging **79**, 59–65 (2019)
3. Bogunović, H., et al.: Automated segmentation of cerebral vasculature with aneurysms in 3DRA and TOF-MRA using geodesic active regions: an evaluation study. Med. Phys. **38**(1), 210–222 (2010)
4. Yi, J., Ra, J.B.: A locally adaptive region growing algorithm for vascular segmentation. Int. J. Imaging Syst. Technol. **13**(4), 208–214 (2003)
5. Chen, L., et al.: 3D intracranial artery segmentation using a convolutional autoencoder. In: Proceedings - 2017 IEEE International Conference on Bioinformatics and Biomedicine, BIBM 2017, pp. 714–717 (2017)
6. Aylward, S.R., Bullitt, E.: Initialization, noise, singularities, and scale in height ridge traversal for tubular object centerline extraction. IEEE Trans. Med. Imaging **21**(2), 61–75 (2002)
7. Lee, S.H., Lee, S.: Adaptive Kalman snake for semi-autonomous 3D vessel tracking. Comput. Methods Programs Biomed. **122**(1), 56–75 (2015)
8. Lee, J., Beighley, P., Ritman, E., Smith, N.: Automatic segmentation of 3D micro-CT coronary vascular images. Med. Image Anal. **11**(6), 630–647 (2007)
9. Ropers, D., et al.: Detection of coronary artery stenoses with thin-slice multi-detector row spiral computed tomography and multiplanar reconstruction. Circulation **107**(5), 664–666 (2003)
10. Berg, M.H., Manninen, H.I., Vanninen, R.L., Vainio, P.A., Soimakallio, S.: Assessment of renal artery stenosis with CT angiography: usefulness of multiplanar reformation, quantitative stenosis measurements, and densitometric analysis of renal parenchymal enhancement as adjuncts to MIP film reading. J. Comput. Assist. Tomogr. **22**(4), 533–540 (1998)

11. Nyul, L.G., Udupa, J.K., Zhang, X.: New variants of a method of MRI scale standardization. IEEE Trans. Med. Imaging **19**(2), 143–150 (2000)
12. Kang, J., Heo, S., Hyung, W.J., Lim, J.S., Lee, S.: 3D active vessel tracking using an elliptical prior. IEEE Trans. Image Process. **27**(12), 5933–5946 (2018)
13. Dice, L.R.: Measures of the amount of ecologic association between species. Ecology **26**(3), 297–302 (1945)
14. Gao, F., Han, L.: Implementing the nelder-mead simplex algorithm with adaptive parameters. Comput. Optim. Appl. **51**(1), 259–277 (2012)
15. Jiang, L., et al.: Associations of arterial distensibility between carotid arteries and abdominal aorta by MR. J. Magn. Reson. Imaging **41**(4), 1138–1142 (2015)
16. Mossa-Basha, M., et al.: Inter-rater and scan–rescan reproducibility of the detection of intracranial atherosclerosis on contrast-enhanced 3D vessel wall MRI. Br. J. Radiol. **92**, 20180973 (2019)
17. Chen, L., et al.: Development of a quantitative intracranial vascular features extraction tool on 3D MRA using semiautomated open-curve active contour vessel tracing. Magn. Reson. Med. **79**(6), 3229–3238 (2018)
18. Bartko, J.J.: Measurement and reliability: statistical thinking considerations. Schizophr. Bull. **17**(3), 483–489 (1991)
19. Wang, Y., Narayanaswamy, A., Tsai, C.L., Roysam, B.: A broadly applicable 3-D neuron tracing method based on open-curve snake. Neuroinformatics **9**(2–3), 193–217 (2011)

Author Index

Printed in the United States
By Bookmasters